AF796906

Thank you for helping us make 2000 a great success.

Happy Holidays
Christopherson Travel

U T A H

Picture Research by
P. Bradford Westwood

American Historical Press
Sun Valley, California

U T A H

Unusual Beginning to Unique Present

Wayne K. Hinton

Frontispiece: *Despite the rigorous demands of pioneer life, cultural and recreational activites were surprisingly common in early Utah. Pioneer artist Dan Weggeland captured this frolicking scene of ice-skaters of all ages enjoying a clear winter's afternoon. Courtesy, LDS Church Museum of History and Art*

Pages six and seven: *The spectacle of Utah's Fiery Furnace in Arches National Park is as breathtaking as it is unique. Photo by Mark E. Gibson*

Published 2000
Printed in the United States of America

Library of Congress Catalogue Card Number: 00-108463
ISBN: 1-892724-10-3

Bibliography: p. 212
Includes Index

Contents

For Carolyn
and my children,
whose interest
and support
have assured me
that I shall always
have readers

UTAH
UNION FOR EVER

Acknowledgments

I should like to acknowledge the Utah State Historical Society for its support of research and publication of Utah history since 1928 and for the help of its library staff and its director in support of this project.

A debt of gratitude has also been incurred to Brad Westwood for his work in assembling many of the photographs. Lynn Campos did an outstanding job of typing the manuscript. I must also thank my wife, Carolyn, for reading the manuscript, for making suggestions and for supplying some of the photographs.

The administration of Southern Utah University—President Steven D. Bennion, Provost Ray Reutzel and Dean Rodney D. Decker—deserve a heartfelt thank you for their encouragement of this project. I also thank the staffs of the Gerald R. Sherratt Library at Southern Utah University, the Utah State Historical Society, the LDS Church Archives, Brigham Young University, the University of Utah and Utah State University for their assistance in providing materials used in preparation of *Utah: Unusual Beginnings to Unique Present*.

Most of all, I owe a special debt to all the great teachers and colleagues who went before to break the ground in researching and writing Utah's history. It was their work that stimulated my own interest and that I have drawn upon heavily in the preparation of this work. Some such as Leonard J. Arrington, Juanita Brooks, Eugene Campbell, S. George Ellsworth, LeRoy Hafen, Richard Poll, and Andrew Karl Larson, have passed on, but their works are their legacies. Others, including Thomas G. Alexander, James B. Allen, Everett Cooley, Brigham Madsen, Dean May, Helen Papanikolas, Charles Peterson and Ted J. Warner, are still an inspiration. I also acknowledge the encouragement and wise counsel of many of my colleagues in the Social Science Department at Southern Utah University.

Finally, I am greatly indebted to Carolyn Martin at American Historical Press for her editing of this work. Thank you Carolyn. You were always encouraging, helpful and pleasant. No one could ask for better editorial support.

Wayne K. Hinton
Cedar City, Utah
August 31, 2000

Utah's 50-year struggle for statehood became a reality only after the practice of polygamy was officially abandoned by the Mormon Church. When statehood was granted in 1896, Utah was fervently patriotic and firmly associated with the rest of the nation. The name of this unofficial statehood queen is uncertain, but her turn-of-the century message makes it clear that Utahns wanted statehood. Photo by George Edward Anderson. Courtesy, Heritage Prints-Rell Francis

Harsh Lands

Throughout the length and breadth of the 84,990-square-mile geographical area that is known today as Utah, the elements of the physical landscape—the landforms, climate, vegetation, soils, and other elements used by man—can be described as harsh yet complexly beautiful. The land is harsh in that an enormous effort was required to settle it successfully. It exacted a major effort of muscle, skill, and will to turn vegetation from sagebrush to agricultural productivity.

Some of the desert areas of Utah that are of the harshest nature have been widely regarded as desolate and so godforsaken as to be compared to the red sand of the Sahara. The lack of precipitation in many localities is compounded by the absence of reliable rivers. Settlement sites were chosen on the best available lands, but even then the resource base for an agrarian economy was restricted by heat, drought, lack of trees, infertile soil, limited level land, and, most important, water shortage. It is little wonder that where only sage and greasewood could be seen, the land seemed rather forbidding to farmers. George A. Smith, an early Mormon colonization leader in southern Utah, suggested that "... if the Lord got up all the rough, rocky, and broken fragments of the earth in one, he might have dropped it here." Utah, consequently, is today a vast area of open spaces with sparse population, except for the Wasatch Front. At times, less appreciative observers have regarded this land as nothing more than a remote obstacle to travel.

Bryce Canyon National Park, named after Ebenezer Bryce, a Mormon farmer who was the first modern-day settler in the region, is just one of Utah's dramatic and rugged scenic wonders. Pictured here is Bryce Point. Photo by Frank Tiller

Above: *Unusual red sandstone formations in Goblin Valley in south Emery County, approximately 30 miles west of the Green River, make for an almost lunar landscape. Photo by Josef Muench, courtesy, Utah State Historical Society*

Below: *In 1890 H.H. Nichols of the United States Geological Survey recorded a fault scarp at the base of the mountains near Farmington north of Salt Lake City, which was produced by a fracture on the earth's crust. From Grove Karl Gilbert,* Department of Interior Monographs of the U.S. Geological Survey, *Vol. 1*

Yet Utah is an extraordinary land of many contrasts. It is a place of desert plains and mountain peaks. The summers are hot in the deserts, but the 15 percent of the Utah landscape that rises to elevations of more than 7,500 feet provides a soothing coolness. At 9,500 feet winter is never far away, and above 10,000 feet snow clings to some peaks year round. By nature these mountains are not only cooler but also are moister than valleys. The mountains act as a barrier to eastflowing moist air from the Pacific. Air forced to rise in passing over the mountains is expanded and cooled, and clouds are formed. If the clouds contain sufficient moisture, precipitation occurs as rain or snow. Because of the low evaporation rates in the mountains, the fallen moisture lingers, nurturing alpine forests. These provide timber resources, hunting, skiing and other forms of recreation, grazing, and—most crucial of all—watersheds.

The varied landscape affords the beauty and contrast of high mountain lakes and low-lying sand dunes, cactus and mountain flowers, Gila monsters and the moose and elk. Recreational pursuits are just as varied as the countryside and the flora and fauna. One may scale sheer rock faces or go sailing. The fly fisherman may test his skills and the hunter his abilities. Some ski, some backpack and camp, others bike

Above: *Red Rock Pass is where Lake Bonneville spilled over and drained into the Snake River and then on to the Pacific Ocean. Professor Grove Karl Gilbert, who surveyed the Great Salt Lake for the Department of Interior in 1890, first proposed Red Rock as the outlet for the great body of water in the* American Journal of Science *in 1878. From* Lake Bonneville, *United States Geological Survey, 1890, courtesy, Utah State Historical Society*

or rock-hunt, and there certainly is enough vitality to the Utah landscape to fulfill the creative desires of nature photographers.

The form of the land is the sum of past geological activities. Utah lies between 37 degrees and 42 degrees north latitude in the western region of North America that is a part of the earth's crust known as the North American Plate. This section is slowly sliding along over the Pacific Plate and a smaller area called the Gorda Plate. The slipping of the North American Plate has caused wrinkles or folds in the earth's surface. In addition to folding, over the past several million years Utah has been impacted by the earth's heaving, buckling, cracking, faulting, and bending. Faulting is simply breaks in rock strata at weak spots in the earth's crust.

The Wasatch Fault runs along the west side of the Wasatch Mountains in the northern part of Utah, and the Hurricane Fault runs through the southern half of the state. Earthquake activity is a constant reminder that the fault lines are a potential threat to landforms, property, and life and limb. Each year many small earthquakes are recorded in Utah. Fortunately for the human inhabitants, most are along the Wasatch Mountains or the High Plateaus.

Wind, rain, snow, streams, and, in some places, ice have

Above: *Manti-La Sal National Forest is one of the many natural wonders that attracted settlers to the Utah area. Photo by Justine Hill*

Right: *Blue skies and billowing clouds contrast with the sharp, scraggy peaks of Zion Canyon National Park. Photo by Harry Fockler*

Above: *This lone farmhouse was built by Christian Otteson of Huntington in Emery County. Many farmers who lived outside of the Wasatch Front chose to live on their farms instead of in small communities as most settlers had. Using irrigation, farmers such as Otteson could create a living landscape from the arid land. Photo by George Edward Anderson, courtesy, Brigham Young University Photo Archives*

Facing page: *The San Juan River Gooseneck was created by water progressively cutting deeper through layers of limestone, shale, and sandstone throughout millions of years. Photo by Philip W. Tompkins for the Utah Writers Project, courtesy, Utah State Historical Society*

also constantly worn away at the earth's surface, scarring and shaping it. Over time some areas have been lowered and taken over by shallow inland seas, and some have even become swamps. There have also been, over the aeons, periods of dry weather when vast areas of sand dunes developed as layer after layer of sand, gravel, clay, and sediment was laid down, buried, and then uplifted. Scattered throughout the state there have been volcanic activities spreading cinder cones, lava, and other materials over the face of the earth. Under the surface, masses of molten materials have pushed up to bulge overlying rock strata and then slowly cooled into crystalline rock, which is exposed only as overlying strata are eroded.

Three major physiographic or landform provinces meet in Utah. Two, the Basin and Range Province, or the Great Basin as it is popularly known, and the Colorado Plateaus dominate; but the third, the Rocky Mountain Province, consisting of the Wasatch and Uinta ranges, is beautiful as well as ecologically and strategically important.

During the Ice Age, when an ice cap covered much of North America but did not extend as far south as Utah, a giant lake 145 miles wide at some points and 346 miles long, covering an area of 19,750 square miles, spread over much of the interior of the self-contained Great Basin. Ancient Lake Bonneville, named for the soldier, erstwhile explorer, and would-be fur trapper Captain B.L.E. Bonneville, washed up against the foothills and spread through canyons and through mountain valleys such as Cache, Ogden, Morgan, and Heber. Lake Bonneville's waves washed the shore, creating benches, or terraces, along the shoreline that can still be seen along the western foothills of the Wasatch Mountains.

With a warming climate glaciers and snow melted, and the level of Lake Bonneville rose. At the northern end of the lake, at a site known today as Red Rock Pass, the water broke out and flowed into the Snake River valley and on to the Pacific Ocean. As the level of the lake fell, the mountain streams cut through the benches in many places, seven in the Salt Lake Valley alone, on their way to the lake. Where these streams emptied into the lake, deltas and alluvial fans were created. Today these almost-level benchlands along the Wasatch Front are the preferred locations for fruit orchards and residential developments. Here the soils are well drained and free of frost from early in the spring. Even when some of the main surface streams cease to flow in late summer, wells can be sunk to tap underground water flowing through the loose materials of the fans. It is here on the 5 percent of the state land surface bordering the eastern fringe of the Great Basin and the western front of the Wasatch Mountains, from

Brigham City on the north to Payson on the south, that 80 percent of Utah's population resides.

Most of western Utah is a part of the Basin and Range Province. This vast region stretches beyond Utah to the Sierra Nevada on the border of Nevada and California and eastward to the western slope of the Wasatch Range. This province was recognized as being self-contained, having no outlet to the Pacific, by John C. Fremont. Because of its major characteristic, a succession of undrained depressions divided by dozens of small ranges and mountains, Fremont called the region the Great Basin. Actually, the Great Basin is not a single gigantic basin but more than 150 desert basins, mostly closed, which are separated from one another by more than 150 discontinuous, subparallel mountain ranges tending roughly to run northeast-southwest. Within the basin, erosion and sedimentation have been more rapid than the faulting process. As a result, the mountains have been lowered and the basins have heen filled, forming almost level alluvial plains. The alluvial fill materials have been washed down from the slopes.

Many of the basins of the Great Basin have distinct lake beds or playas in their lowest sections, where waters flowing in during periods of heavy precipitation form shallow ponds or lakes that soon evaporate in the desert heat, leaving behind alkali or salt flats. Many of these playas are so impregnated with salt that no vegetation grows. The largest and most spectacular occurrence of this phenomenon is the Bonneville Salt Flats.

Where sufficient inflow of water still exists along the east side of the Great Basin, the remnant lakes such as Great Salt Lake and Utah Lake remain prominent features of the Utah Great Basin landscape. Utah Lake, a freshwater lake, is connected to the Great Salt Lake by the Jordan River. At 1,500 square miles the Great Salt Lake is the largest inland body of salt water in the Western Hemisphere. Its water is one-fourth salt, but in recent years the high run-off to the lake has diluted the salt content to 14 to 19 percent. These lakes provide recreation in the form of fishing, boating, and waterfowl hunting. The Great Salt Lake is also the source of minerals with an estimated value of more than four billion dollars.

The Great Basin has no great river or drainage system. Its rivers and streams run nowhere: they drain into the basin. Much of it is noted for its aridity. Despite this fact, the eastern edge of the Great Basin, known as the Wasatch Front, is the site of the state's best-watered valleys. Mountain streams, such as the Weber, Provo, and Bear rivers, all begin in the western end of the Uinta Range within a short distance of one another; and each cuts directly through the Wasatch, running into the Great Basin to provide water for the state's major population centers adjacent to these streams.

Rising above the valleys and basins with their playas are the mountains of the Basin and Range Province. These ranges vary from low hills a few miles long to impressive peaks such as the Deep Creek and Stansbury mountains, which rise to more than 12,000 feet. Thus it is that some say the Great Basin has two timber lines. One marks the lower-elevation deserts where no timber is found; the other, the higher elevations above which no timber grows.

A high degree of mineralization has occurred in these ranges, and both old and new mining districts are scattered through the region. Most of the minerals are metallic, such as gold, silver, platinum, lead, zinc, and copper, and some clays and other nonmetals are produced also. At one time the huge Bingham open-pit copper mine was said to be the largest mining operation in the world. Here Kennecott Copper Corporation excavates ore from the exposed upper sections of a massive intrusion that is about forty miles square. Bingham is a huge curiosity, a giant man-made scar in the earth in the Oquirrh Range west of the Salt Lake Valley.

To the east, rising above the Great Basin, is the Rocky Mountain Province, represented in Utah by two very impressive but dissimilar mountain ranges, the Wasatch and the Uinta. The Wasatch Range extends some 200 miles south from the Soda Springs, Idaho, area to Mount Nebo, at 11,877 feet the highest peak in the range, near Nephi in central Utah. Geologists consider the Wasatch Range to be extremely complex, with a wide variation of rock types. Its west face, with exposed rock, is considered to date to the earliest geological ages, the Early Cambrian Pioche Formation (560 million years ago). The many sharp ridges set the Wasatch Mountains apart from nearby mountain systems. The east slope of the Wasatch tilts to the Uinta Mountains on the north and the Colorado Plateau on the south.

The Uintas, the highest range in Utah, run 150 miles east from the Wasatch to the border of Colorado. Unlike the complexity of the Wasatch, the Uintas consist of a core of quartzites flanked by upturned sedimentary beds. Many peaks in this range are more than 12,000 feet in elevation and some exceed 13,000, including Kings Peak, the highest point in the state at 13,498 feet. The general east-west orientation of the Uintas is unusual for mountain ranges in North America. As Utah historian Charles Peterson observed, it puts the Uintas "... out of kilter in a land of north-south ranges."

Taken together, the Wasatch and Uinta mountains form a long spur of the Rocky Mountains. Ice Age glacial remains are prominent in the high Uintas, and thousands of glacial lakes dot the landscape. The Wasatch Mountains also contain glaciated areas that give rise to a landscape noted for its scenery as well as its magnificent ski slopes, upon which falls the "greatest snow on earth," Utahns claim.

To the south and east of the Rocky Mountain Province lies the vast, unique area of the Colorado Plateau. Of Utah's thirteen national parks and monuments, all but three are on the Colorado Plateau, and all achieved their designations for reasons of distinctive scenery and geology. The Colorado Plateau, with its immensity, aridity, and ruggedness, dominates the Utah landscape. It appears to have been created out of odds and ends, and as it occupies about two-thirds of the state's land surface, the plateau has served to prohibit agricultural expansion. On the other hand, this rugged area is the home of national parks, recreational areas, and vast reserves of coal, oil, natural gas, and oil shale.

There are three major sections of the Colorado Plateau—

Photographer George Edward Anderson photographed all that captured his sense of history, drama, and the picturesque while traveling though Central and Southern Utah. Anderson directed his lense across Monroe Canyon, southeast of Monroe in Sevier County for this striking image. Courtesy, Heritage Prints—Rell Francis

the High Plateaus, the Uinta Basin, and Canyonlands. Though there are dissimilarities from region to region, the unifying characteristic of the Colorado Plateau is that the layers of underlying sedimentary rocks are essentially horizontal. Unlike the Great Basin, the Plateau drains outward to the Gulf of California and the Pacific through one of the nation's great drainage systems, the Colorado River system, running through the deep canyons of the Plateau. Despite the presence of the Colorado system, this is an and section generally without water.

The High Plateaus section extends southward from Mount Nebo through southern Utah into Arizona. Viewed from the valley floor, the western edge of the High Plateaus seems to be a continuation of the Wasatch Range. Viewed from the air, the Plateaus show areas of rolling surface quite in contrast to the sharp ridges of the Wasatch. The High Plateaus run about 200 miles in length and vary in width from 25 to 80 miles, but for most of their length the width is roughly 40 miles. The summit areas of the High Plateaus rise to elevations of more than 11,000 feet; large areas of gently rolling forestlands in the Dixie and Fishlake national forests exist at the 10,000-foot level and beyond. To the south the High Plateaus stand out as multicolored steep cliffs, of which the Pink Cliffs are the highest. There are also the White Cliffs, Vermillion Cliffs, and Chocolate Cliffs, all named for their unique coloration.

Toward its southern extremities, the High Plateaus are made up of three belts of plateaus with valleys intervening. The valleys are drained by branches of the Sevier River and its tributaries to the Great Basin. The Sevier flows from the Plateaus northward, cutting through the center of the High Plateaus in the Sevier River Valley. The various streams of the Sevier system occupy a graben, a structural valley caused by faulting rather than stream erosion. Besides dividing the region into a series of eastern and western plateau blocks, the Sevier River system provides a source of water and a relatively flat fertile valley for irrigated agriculture.

The Uinta Basin is just that: a basin that would be a vast, shallow lake bed were it not for the Green River, which cuts through the upturned beds of the Roan Plateau. The basin is about 170 miles in length and about 100 miles in width. Despite its desolate look and light rainfall, two major streams cut across it to empty into the Colorado River. The Duchesne and Green rivers provide not only recreation and scenic beauty but also opportunities for irrigated agriculture on the rich soils south of the Uinta Mountains.

One of the more interesting geological features of the basin is the Morrison Formation, containing the world's most com plete dinosaur skeleton plus 23 nearly complete and about 300 partially complete dinosaur remains. These petrified bones range from 6 to 84 feet in length. The dinosaur quarry has been designated the Dinosaur National Monument. There are also other fossils of significance at the ClevelandLloyd Dinosaur Quarry in Emery County. During the Mesozoic Era, when dinosaurs walked the earth, late Jurassic and Cretaceous periods, (160 to 66 million years ago), much of eastern Utah was a swampland, a favorite haunt of these large mammals. It is speculated that the dinosaurs were trapped in sandbars and died there, and their bones became buried.

The Canyonlands region includes beds of sandstone and limestone dipping gently to the south. This entire region has been uplifted, with few disturbances of the almost-horizontal beds, and the streams crossing the surface have eroded deeply, creating steep-sided canyons that follow the meandering pattern established when streams flowed nearer sea level and cut sideways rather than downward. This phenomenon has provided spectacular scenery but has proven difficult for travelers and settlers. The horizontal beds and somewhat even surfaces are broken by uplifted areas and by volcanic ranges, all adding to the variety of the scenery. The laccolithic peaks of the Henrys, the Abajos, and the dome-shaped La Sal Mountains, the second-highest range in Utah, are considered among the youngest mountains in the world, dating to the Oligocene age (23 million years ago). The rolling plateaus; narrow, deep canyons; mountains rising suddenly from nowhere; bare, rocky surfaces; spires; eroded sandstone cathedrals and towers; natural bridges; and multitudinous colors of the canyonlands provide a uniquely beautiful scenic attraction.

The great beauty of Utah is one of its choicest natural resources. The varied landscape is one of the great wonders of nature. Despite its harshness, the land has been good to the people. Enough fertile valleys edged by desert exist to provide for minimal agricultural needs. The midlatitude climate is invigorating with its great seasonal variations. Utah streams are generally small in volume, short in length, and variable in flow, but they are so well conserved and used that they meet most existing needs. Even though much of the soil is not rich and, overall, Utah is devoid of rich farming belts, the valleys where land and water meet have become the sites of thriving settlements. The three provinces of Utah have a multitude of minerals and oil and gas resources. The high mountains contain forests and streams. This harsh land has been a challenge to settlers over the years, but its advantages outweigh liabilities. In the modern era of rapid travel, leisure time, and affluence, the harshness, the wildness, and the variety of the landscape may be the greatest natural resource of all.

Ancient Peoples

Although the first Utahns have long since left the scene, their legacy is rich, interesting, and useful. Over the past 13,000 years several tides of ancient peoples swept across the face of the land that is now Utah, settling down for short or long periods of time and then moving on. Although these various ancient peoples had little technology, they enjoyed, from all that we can determine, a contented tenure.

Understanding these ancient peoples can be useful in helping us gain a fuller understanding of ourselves. Their stories provide us a sense of perspective relative to our own place in the totality of human experience. Alert, sensitive, creative people came here, settled down-in some instances for thousands of years—and then disappeared almost from human knowledge or memory. We know them today only from what they could not take with them or what they discarded along the way: their artifacts. They would not have imagined that their trinkets, tools, houses, moccasins, food, and even their very bones would one day provide the stuff of romantic legend and folklore.

The first explorers of Utah were prehistoric Indians. These earliest people did not read or write. All we know of them

---

When the Anglo-Americans arrived in Utah, the Utes were divided into bands including the Timpanogas around Utah Lake, the Pahvants around Fillmore, and the Uintahs in eastern Utah, among dozens of other small bands. This Ute warrior and his bride were photographed by John K. *Hillars sometime* in 1873 *in the Unitah Valley. Photo by John K. Hillars. Courtesy, Smithsonian Institute*

Above: *Crafted by some of Utah's oldest inhabitants, this small split-twig figurine is just inches long and made from one unbroken twig length. These figurines have been dated at approximately 3,500 B.C. From* Cowboy Cave, *University of Utah Anthropological Papers, #104, 1980*

Facing page, top: *These are the simple wickiups that served as shelter for the Paiute Indians who lived near St. George on the Rio Virgin River. The Paiute roamed the desert in bands, hunting small game and foraging for vegetation. Their huts were only six to 10 feet in circumference and served as little more than windbreaks. Photo by John K. Hillers. Courtesy, Smithsonian Institute*

Facing page, bottom: *Walters and Cowboy caves, located at the base of these canyon cliffs, contained the dung of horses, camels, sloths, bison, and mammoths. Two small mammoth tusks were found in the excavation of Cowboy Cave. Courtesy, University of Utah Anthropological Papers, #104, 1980*

is what anthropologists and archaeologists can infer from their artifacts. Ingeniously, they have pieced together a sketch of Utah's prehistoric societies. As we still have only vague notions of how people lived here at various periods in prehistoric time, it should be noted that enormous gaps remain.

The sequence of adaptive strategies of prehistoric peoples in Utah includes three categories:

1. Paleo-Indians, who focused on hunting large mammals known as megafauna, possibly to the exclusion of other food resources. These big-game hunters appear to have occupied Utah from about 12,000 years ago to possibly as late as 9,000 years ago.

2. Archaic, those who utilized a "total" exploitation of an unaltered environment. These hunters and gatherers may not have utilized every possible food item, but remains from Archaic sites indicate they must have utilized an extremely wide spectrum of resources. The Archaic peoples of the so-called Desert Culture occupied Utah from about 8,000 years ago to near the beginning of the Christian era.

3. Formative, which is characterized by the propagation of domestic plants and, in many cases, the development of ceramic technology. Formative societies would include the Anasazi from just before the birth of Christ to A.D. 1300, the Fremont Culture from about A.D. 200 to 1300, and the Numic period of the Shoshonean-speaking peoples of the Gosiutes, Utes, and Southern Paiutes during the years A.D. 1300 to 1776.

People who do not live in constructed shelters and have no means of cutting large trees have no interest in forests. Pasturage was of no direct use to these people who had no domesticated animals. Since farming was unknown to them, they did not concern themselves with level land or stream flow. The Paleo-Indians were hunters. The game they sought were giant mammoths, giant sloths, and, later, giant bison. The ancients hunted them with thrusting spears tipped by beautifully crafted fluted points.

Paleo-Indian sites are characterized by easily recognized chipped-stone projectile points from which large flakes have been removed along the point's midline. These large flake scars are referred to as flutes and the points as fluted points. There are two primary varieties: the earlier type, the Clovis point, and the later, more elaborate type, the Folsom point. In North America the Clovis point is usually associated with hunting mammoths and North American camels, while the Folsom point is usually associated with the hunting of a large, now extinct, form of the bison.

In Utah only a single excavated site, Danger Cave, dates

to the early Paleo-Indian period. It is located just off Interstate 80 near Wendover, and although it remains undeveloped, it has been designated as Danger Cave State Park. This site contains layer after layer of material laid down sequentially from about 11,500 years ago to a much more recent time. The cave contains a variety of material and information from later periods, but unfortunately the earliest occupants, the Paleo-Indians, left little beyond a few hearths, some flaking debris, and a bifacially worked blade/knife. However, we do know from Danger Cave and from a similar site of the same time period just across the state line in east-central Nevada that mountain sheep and camels were a part of the diet. Cowboy Cave in eastern Wayne County, usually identified with the Archaic period, does contain some evidence that the bones of large mammals found there below cultural deposits may also have been worked by the hands of Paleo-Indians.

Most fluted-point discoveries in Utah have been on open sites throughout the state. The large majority of the finds have not been associated with other contextual material. Finds have been made on the Colorado Plateau in a variety of environmental settings. By far, the majority of points have been found in the Sevier and Escalante Desert areas of west-central Utah.

Both mammoths and camels that date to the fluted-point period have been confirmed in Utah. What appear to be elephant-like figures have been identified on rock-art panels in the state, and they may be the handiwork of Paleo-Indians. However, rock art is difficult to interpret, since bizarre, imaginary animal forms abound, and it is too easy to read something into rock art that is not there. But taken together with other available evidence, the rock art suggests the impor-

tance of mammoths to Paleo-Indians in Utah.

The next prehistorical cultural adaptation which began about 8,000 years ago is know as Archaic. The major sites for the shelters of Archaic peoples were caves and rock shelters. Two Archaic sites, the Cowboy Cave in Wayne County and the Sudden Shelter on the north bank of Ivie Creek in Sevier County, have been excavated in southern Utah. To the north some time prior to 6000 B.C., a band of Archaic Indians took up residence in a cave west of the Great Salt Lake, which is today called the Hogup Cave. Perhaps with some vacant periods, Hogup Cave was occupied for the next several thousand years.

Fortunately, the people who occupied these Archaic sites

were not very tidy. They dropped table scraps, broken baskets, worn shoes, and so forth onto the dirt floors and left them there. The resulting layers of artifacts deposited tell anthropologists and archaeologists much about these ancient peoples. For one thing, they reveal that life was not all hunting and gathering. The Archaics made gaming sticks and depicted split-twig animals in pictographs.

Although the Archaic peoples were hunters, there were by this time no giant animals or megafauna. The Archaics netted animals, made rabbit snares, and hunted ducks. A staple in their diet was salt-tolerant vegetation including cattails, pickleweed, burrowweed, and sedge. Red meat was something of a luxury for them.

Their fortunes were largely determined by climatic changes and conditions. For a rather long period, perhaps from 6000 to 3500 B.C., they lived a rather settled life, and their population increased as the receding waters of the Sevier and Great Salt lakes exposed more lake-edge resources. Eventually the waters dropped too low, and waters feeding the marshes dried up. Now the people had to live off such upland resources as Indian ricegrass, mountain sheep, deer, and rabbits. This new life-style necessitated seasonal migrations that probably retained the lake edges as their home base. About 1500 B.C. the fickle lake waters began to rise again, as they are wont to do today, reaching levels not known to the Archaic peoples. As the water rose to cover even Hogup Cave, it was too high for the marsh and lake-edge subsistence pattern. The population declined. After more than 6,000 years of continuous habitation, the Archaic desert peoples left the lands to a later people who perhaps arrived on the scene as early as the beginning of the Christian era.

In the realm of artifacts, the hallmarks of the Archaic peoples of the Desert Culture were the milling stone and basketry. The basketry of the Desert Archaic was initially twined; coiled techniques were introduced later. They also wove other textiles such as mats and bags. Additional artifact items include lanceolate or triangular stemmed and notched projectile points, netting fur cloth, fiber sandals, hide moccasins, dart shafts, digging sticks, clubs, bone awls, and scapula saws.

The formative adaptive strategy for prehistoric Indians in Utah is represented first by the Anasazi. Anasazi peoples were those who built the large, attractive villages dotting southeastern Utah, including the impressive sites at Hovenweep National Monument. The name Anasazi comes from a Navajo word meaning "the ancient ones." They lived near the same time as the Fremont, but while the Fremont had a patch of corn, beans, and squash here and there, the Anasazi became highly dependent upon agriculture, building impressive systems of dams and canals to water their fields.

The Anasazi did not move much—their domain in Utah was limited mostly to a very narrow range in the southeastern part of the state, especially the canyons along the San Juan River drainage. However, at Boulder, Utah, in Garfield County, an Anasazi site dating from around A.D. 1200 has been excavated and a state park established to interpret the native artifacts and to explain village life. There is also within Utah the Virgin Branch of the Kayenta or Western Anasazi, with sites in Kane and Washington counties in the southern and western parts of the state. This is the most westerly variant of the Anasazi pattern. Whereas the cultural development of the Anasazi in Colorado, New Mexico, and southeastern Utah has been carefully studied to the point where we know more about these people than about any other prehistoric Southwestern people, we still know comparatively little of the Virgin Branch of the Kayenta Anasazi.

Several developmental stages have been identified and dated for the Anasazi, covering their 1,300 years of growth from a basket-making people, barely distinguishable from the Archaic Desert peoples, to their mastery of farming and masonry from about A.D 1200 to 1300. About the time of Christ, the Anasazi began growing maize and squash. They continued to gather and hunt, but these newly acquired domesticated crops were now the largest part of their diet. From A.D. 1 to 700 the Anasazi developed the beginnings of pottery making, agriculture, and house building. This period is often divided into the Basket Maker I period to A.D. 500 and the Modified Basket Maker period, A.D. 500 to 700. In the latter period, the Anasazi began growing an improved kind of corn, plus beans, an important protein source. With the improved diet, the Anasazi lived longer and healthier lives.

The years between A.D. 700 and 1050 are sometimes referred to as the Developmental Pueblo period. With the growth of population the Basket Makers moved out of their caves and onto mesas near their crops, where they constructed villages called pueblos. After A.D. 750 the Anasazi developed rapidly, especially in the art of building homes and villages. This achievement had only modest beginnings, as the first pueblos were only groups of adobe and poles, later adobe and stone, and finally cut-stone houses arranged in an "L," a semicircle, or a rectangle. Usually, houses were constructed in a configuration that left an open court in the cen-

Above: *This corrugated jug was made by the Fremont Indians in about 1100 A.D. and found at the Five Finger Ridge archeological site in Clear Creek Canyon. Courtesy, Brigham Young University, Museum of Peoples and Cultures*

Facing page, left: *The later Anasazi Indians constructed sturdy houses, fortifications, and other structures on steep canyon cliffs and mesas in the Southwest. This masonry structure is located in the Hovenweep National Monument area in southeastern Utah. The Anasazi Indians grew crops using complex irrigation systems. Sometime during the last part of the fourteenth century, the Anasazi withdrew from Utah. Photo by Philip W. Tompkins. Courtesy, Utah State Historical Society*

Facing page, right: *These Paiute Indians near their wickiups in Washington County on the Rio Virgin River were photographed by John K Hillars. Courtesy, Smithsonian Institute*

ter. Here pithouses were built. Over time, they came to be used not so much for storage as for ceremonial rooms called kivas. The men of the village conducted religious ceremonies in the kivas, and public religious observances and dances were held in the open court. In Utah a common structural feature of the Developmental Pueblo period was the jacal wall, made by setting a row of posts or logs upright in the ground close to one another and filling the spaces between them with adobe. This resulted in a solid wall about six inches thick.

Beginning about A.D. 1050 and running to 1300 was the Great Pueblo period, which marked the greatest growth in Anasazi Culture. During the period, large villages were built, often nestled under protective sandstone cliffs. Often these large villages contained hundreds of rooms consisting of walls with finely executed masonry. The interiors were sometimes plastered with adobe and decorated with red, yellow, and black designs.

The great investment of time and effort in these structures was justifiable only if the builders intended to stay. Agricultural developments made this sedentary dwelling style possible. The Anasazi now raised not only corn, beans, and squash but also cotton, which they spun, dyed, and wove into decorative patterns. They also succeeded in domesticating the turkey, and thereby acquired a dependable meat supply to add to their regular vegetable diet.

Religious ritual became more elaborate; decorative arts advanced with turquoise necklaces, leather robes, and flint knives, and the pottery was now nothing short of exquisite, having great variety of form and carefully decorated in black-on-white geometrical patterns. Other artifacts include clay cooking and storage pots, ladles, mugs, and bowls.

About A.D. 1300, at the height of their progress, the Anasazi disappeared from Utah, leaving their massive pueblos to the ravages of weather, time, and, worst of all, vandals. It is still not known exactly why, after more than a thousand years of cultural development, the Anasazi packed and left. Tree rings show a severe drought struck in A.D. 1276 that lasted most of the rest of the thirteenth century. Perhaps the Anasazi were simply starved out. Maybe, bit by bit, in order to compensate for poor farming years, they moved into a foraging pattern to survive. Some have thought that perhaps migrations of aggressive Navajo and Apache peoples might have overrun and decimated the essentially gentle Anasazi. At any rate, it is clear that they and the Fremont disappeared from Utah about A.D. 1300, to be succeeded by nomadic desert wanderers whose descendants remained in Utah until historic times.

About A.D. 200 the people who painted so many of the

Above: *Relatively peaceful, the Paiutes often fell victim to marauding Utes who would capture Paiute children such as these and sell them to the Spanish settlers to the south. Photo by John K. Hillars, courtesy, Smithsonian Institute*

Facing page: *The Northern Shoshoni were nomadic hunters and traders who lived in what is now Wyoming, Idaho, and northern Utah. Comparatively small in number, the Shoshoni, which means valley dwellers, were ultimately pushed north into mountainous lands by hostile tribes. Photo by Charles R. Savage, courtesy, LDS Church Archives*

Photographer C.R. Savage posed many Utah Indians in his studio. Like many other photographers of his day, Savage sometimes staged his models to fit the prevailing American images of the American Indian, be it the noble yet warlike savage, or the poor and degraded heathen. Nevertheless, these three portraits of Ute and Shoshoni Indians are revealing. Courtesy, LDS Church Archives

haunting, heroic-size pictographs, such as those at Parowan Gap, began to spread over much of Utah. They are commonly called the Fremont peoples. This culture was first identified along the Fremont River and takes its name from that fact. The Fremont Culture included a very large geographical area and a great diversity of life-styles. Because their habits and customs were not identical throughout Utah, Nevada and Western Colorado, distinct groups have been identified, including the Uinta Fremont, the Great Salt Lake Fremont, the San Rafael Fremont, the Sevier Fremont, and the Parowan Fremont. Some scholars have preferred to designate those who lived in the Great Basin as simply Sevier peoples. In some ways, the life-styles of the Fremont peoples were so similar to those of the Archaic peoples that some students of the Fremont Culture have been tempted to wonder whether they were descendants who picked up enough new habits and tools through contact with others to make them appear to be a wholly different race.

The Fremont continued—like the Archaic peoples—to concentrate their numbers in the narrow strips of the Basin and Range and Colorado Plateau valleys where water meets land. However, new technologies seemed enough in the judgment of many scholars to make the Fremont an entirely different people, whatever their habitat or ancestry. Their major technological innovation was the bow and arrow. With this weapon they could shoot an arrow farther, harder, and more accurately than the Archaic peoples could launch a projectile with their atlatl, a notched stick used to gain leverage in throwing a spear. This obviously enhanced the Fremont people's hunting skills and thus their diet.

The caves of the Archaic peoples may have provided them with convenient homes requiring a minimum capital investment. A cave served as instant home-sweet-home. But caves were awkward in that they were not always comfortable or ideally suited. A major advance the Fremont made over the Archaic peoples was that from somewhere they learned to build shelters. Their shelters were typically underground, with poles and dirt forming a roof. Access was gained through a hole in the roof. These shelters were much easier to heat and much cozier in scale than the caves of the Archaic peoples, and they were built wherever food and water existed. Fremont Indians also erected rectangular granaries above ground that were made entirely of adobe or unmortared stone. Often two or three homes and granaries were built close together to form tiny villages.

Somewhere the Fremont had picked up the art of growing maize and, later, beans and squash. The corn they raised was a variety of dented corn that was particularly drought resistant and required a relatively short growing season to mature, making it particularly well suited to the Great Basin environment. Though the Fremont may not have farmed as extensively as the Anasazi, there is no doubt that they did supplement their diet with home-grown vegetables.

The Fremont peoples also made and left among their other artifacts a simple, gray, coiled pottery, adaptable to many uses, including the boiling of food, a cooking technique unknown to the Archaic peoples, whose only vessels were woven baskets. Even though the simple gray pottery predominated, the Fremont also made painted and corrugated ceramics.

Today we know little of the Fremont cultural and religious

life. Numerous pictographs of a distinctive type, with horned, triangular-shaped human figures, often wearing elaborate necklaces and loincloths, give some clues. The human figures are often surrounded by stylized deer, sheep, or other animals. The Fremont also left charming clay figurines that were carefully molded of unified clay and painted ochre, buff, and green. No one seems to know with certainty what the figurines or the pictographs meant to the Fremont peoples, but some think that since both are apparently associated with game and harvest, they may well be magical charms invoking successful hunting and harvesting. There are also Fremont decorative arts extant in necklaces, wristlets, and pottery designs pressed into wet clay and, at a later period, painted.

At one time scholars surmised that the Fremont may have been relatively isolated and provincial. Now, however, it appears that their range of commerce and contact with other peoples must have been considerable. In their family groupings or clan societies there must have been significant exchanges. The Fremont Culture is now seen by scholars as an amalgam of the cultural influences of surrounding peoples. They were eclectic, drawing from all directions for survival skills developed by others in their endeavor to cope with the harsh environs they inhabited.

Nevertheless, their skills were not enough to sustain them from the vagaries of nature, or assimilation, or invasion, or whatever caused their abandonment of Utah. Sometime around A.D. 1300 the Fremont peoples passed from the scene, leaving us with their haunting images and artifacts, which cause us to continue to speculate.

After more than a thousand years of continuous habitation, the prehistoric Fremont and Anasazi either left or were driven from Utah, or their cultural adaptation became unrecognizable. Perhaps before they left, maybe even causing them to leave or possibly absorbing them, there was a transplantation of another people into the area. These new Utahns, who spoke languages of a common origin that we call Shoshonean, proceeded to settle in about A.D. 1300 and to practice a hunting and gathering life-style somewhere between that of the Fremont and the earlier Archaic peoples.

The lives of these early Numic Indians, as nearly as we can tell, were very stable. Traditional clothing, tools, foodstuffs, and housing could continue hundreds of years without significant change or interruption. For these desert people, the most reliable staple in their diet was the pinyon nut. They also caught fish and small animals for food and raised some rare patches of corn.

The main groups of Shoshonean language peoples settling

Famous western surveyor Major John Wesley Powell leans on his horse and inquires as to the location of a water pocket in northern Arizona not far from the Utah border. Photo by John K. Hillars, courtesy, Smithsonian Institute

in Utah included the Western Shoshones in the northwest, the Northern Shoshones in the northeast, the Gosiutes in the west-central, the Utes in the central and east-central areas, and the Southern Paiutes in the southern part of Utah. These peoples had the bow and arrow, made good baskets, and did a little potting. Commonly, they did not inhabit the pithouses of the Fremont, preferring to reside in temporary brush shelters or wickiups. There was little or no tribal organization originally; people tended to live in small family bands, and little conflict occurred between groups.

The Shoshonean peoples had been in place a few hundred years when a race entirely alien brought changes that were more swift and devastating than any these people had known or dreamed of. The newcomers were pale, armored, mounted intruders from Spain who had moved northward from their established bases in northern Mexico provinces to arrive finally in Utah in the latter half of the eighteenth century.

The Spanish first encountered and described the Utes—the most powerful and widespread of the Numic peoples in Utah. Contact with the Spanish dramatically changed the Utes from the peoples their great-great-grandfathers had been. Of all the changes the Spanish brought, the most important and powerful came through the Ute adoption and use of the horse. Successful adaptation to the equine culture meant that the range of the normal migration of the Utes was significantly increased. This made it desirable for the Utes to organize into groups larger than the small clan or family, and chieftains now presided over the affairs of the larger group.

The horse gave the Ute warriors a great psychological and logistical advantage in warfare with nonmounted tribes. Some Ute bands took advantage of their access to horses to become a warlike people, making raids on neighboring bands and tribes to plunder goods and kidnap children. Children thus taken were transported to the nearest Spanish settlements to be sold as slaves for work in domestic service or mines. In this way the Utes had come to plague their unmounted Utah relatives, the Gosiutes in the north and Paiutes in the south, pushing them back onto marginal lands and occupying the more desirable parts of Utah for themselves. Some Utes spurned the new life and continued in quite sedentary lives, fishing from mountain lakes, raising a little corn, and making crude pottery. As a group, however, the Utes were widely feared and respected when fur traders, explorers, and then settlers arrived.

North of the Utes were the Gosiutes, the Utah tribe that was the least touched by Spanish influence. Living in small family groups much as when they arrived in Utah 400 years earlier, they followed seasonal migrations in search of pinyon nuts, rabbits, berries, roots, and even crickets, which they dried and ground into a meal and baked. The white explorers of Utah began calling the Gosiutes the "Diggers," and tended to think of them as the most impoverished and pitiful of Indians. On the contrary, however, the Gosiutes may well have been the most ingenious in extracting a living from the sparse environment to which they had been relegated. Some of their implements may have been crude, but they were quite serviceable. They were skilled in the making of trapping nets and in the use of the bow and arrow. But since they were a peaceful group, they were almost totally devoid of defensive skills for self-protection.

To the south were the Paiutes, whose life-style was much like that of the Gosiutes. Their habitats were even warmer and more arid but did afford more opportunity for irrigated agriculture. Along the Virgin and Santa Clara rivers, on the Kaibab Plateau, and in the Moapa and Las Vegas valleys of southern Nevada, the Paiute led a more sedentary life than the Gosiutes. They planted corn and gourds, later adding melons and other items that they watered from nearby streams. They were excellent basket makers, using intricate techniques to fashion vessels of all sizes and shapes—even making protective hats for the women. They, like the other Shoshonean-speaking peoples, had the bow and arrow. Flint knives and clubs were also used for hunting, but the Paiutes were a peaceful and gentle people. Largely because of their proximity to the Spanish, they suffered considerably from raids by both Spanish and Ute slave hunters.

When Fathers Dominguez and Escalante visited Utah in 1776, they gave us the first written descriptions of the Utah Indians. Prior to this the Utah inhabitants were known as prehistoric. The Spanish, with their descriptions, transformed the Shoshonean peoples residing in Utah from prehistoric to historic. It was, of course, these historic Indians with whom later explorers, fur traders, and settlers came to deal. However, if history begins when people live in a locality, Utah history began with the ancient peoples who lived in the region for thousands of years. The Paleo-Indians, Archaic, Anasazi, Fremont, and Shoshonean-speaking tribes were the first to know the land we now call Utah as their home and the first to make a living from the land. They knew where to harvest and where to hunt. They excelled in making full use of nature's gifts through acquiring necessary skills and living as much at peace with nature as is humanly possible. From afar we can only learn of, admire, and appreciate the values and accomplishments of these ancient peoples, the true Utah natives.

Pre-settlement Explorations

Within fifty years of Columbus' landing in America, the quest for gold, God, and glory led Spanish explorers northward from Mexico toward the unusual land of Utah. As part of the Coronado expedition of 1540, Don Garcia Lopez de Cardenas, in charge of a small scouting party, marched northwest for twenty days through a desert country until he was halted by the Grand Canyon of the Colorado at Grand View on the South Rim. Within a short journey of Utah's southern border, this party, having been thoroughly intimidated by a thoroughly intimidating landscape, retreated quickly to its base camp at the Zuni pueblos in New Mexico. Coronado, upon his return to Mexico City, issued a report so pessimistic as to slow the Spanish push into the north country. Nevertheless, within an interval of 55 years, colonists were sent to settle New Mexico. But for the next 170 years New Mexico continued to be a precarious frontier outpost of New Spain, and Utah remained unexplored by its Spanish claimants.

It took international rivalries for empire to provoke the Spanish to push north once again. In order to retain a hold

The Spanish voraciously explored the New World with visions of great wealth, traversing much of Central America in the 40 years following Columbus' landing in America. When Francisco Coronado, seen here in Gerold Cassidy's painting, traveled north in search of treasure in 1540, he found only humble Indian communities and difficult terrain. Coronado's report of his explorations was so grim that active exploration by the Spanish turned away from the north to South America. Painting by Gerold Cassidy, courtesy, Museum of New Mexico

Above: *Fathers Dominguez and Escalante traveled into Utah Valley via the Spanish Fork River in September 1776. Utah Lake was teeming with several kinds of fish and the valley floor was a blanket of grasses with plentiful game. Drawing by Paul Salisbury, courtesy, Utah State Historical Society*

Below: *Dan Bernardo Miera y Pacheco, who accompanied the Dominguez-Escalante expedition, made a number of maps that marked not only the general topography of the area, but also many of the major campsites of the expedition. Courtesy, Utah State Historical Society*

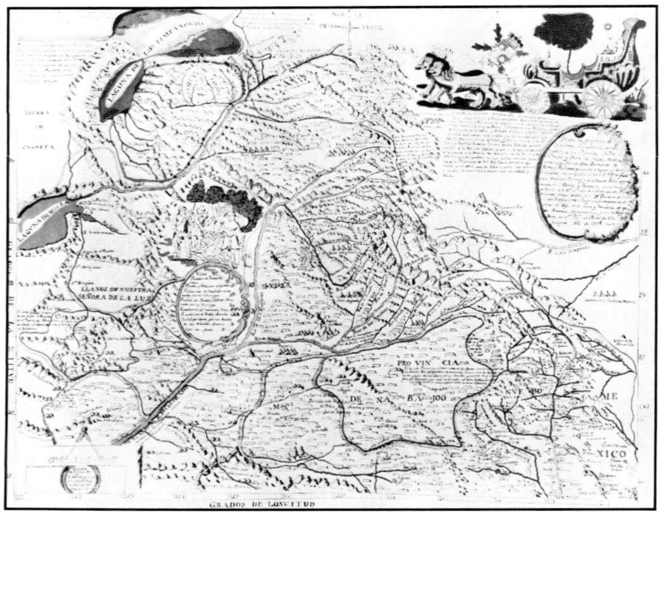

on upper California, settlement was necessary. In 1769 San Diego was founded, and the next year Monterey was established. Both outposts were weak, vulnerable, and far from other Spanish settlements. They would need regular contact and a steady source of supplies from older, better-established frontier outposts. Efforts to open a feasible land route to California were initially thwarted by rugged terrain and by hostile Indian tribes situated astride more direct routes. The Spanish speculated that perhaps a less hazardous road could be found more to the north.

Prior to this Spanish interest in a circuitous route from Santa Fe north and then west to Monterey, there may well have been several unofficial and unauthorized approaches out of New Mexico into Utah. Today we can with certitude substantiate the route led by Juan Maia Antonia Rivera that progressed northwest out of Santa Fe in 1765 in search of silver mines. This party entered Utah in October northeast of Monticello, passing the La Sal Mountains to go down Spanish Valley to Moab on the Colorado River. It was not until 1776, however, that another well-documented Spanish excursion into Utah occurred.

Father Francisco Atanasio Dominguez was appointed to organize a party commissioned to discover a feasible route from Santa Fe to Monterey. The Franciscan Father chose as his first lieutenant and party diarist a young Franciscan priest, 24-year-old Fray Silvestre Velez de Escalante, known to history as Father Escalante. Because of Escalante's journal and a map made by another of the 12 explorers in the company, Don Bernardo Miera y Pacheco, this expedition was first to open Utah to European awareness.

The over 1700 mile trek began from the Palace of Governors at Santa Fe on July 29, 1776. Well outfitted with extra riding and pack horses, the company was also encumbered with a herd of cattle driven ahead for fresh meat. Through August and early September the explorers meandered their way north and slightly westward from New Mexico through Colorado, emerging into Utah on September 11 at Jensen on the Green River.

As they progressed, the diarist recorded trail data, resources, the nature and disposition of Indians encountered, and prospects for future mission activity. With two Laguna guides, Silvestre and an 11-year-old boy called Joaquin, whom they had met en route, they proceeded from the Green River south and west to the Spanish Fork Canyon, which they followed until they arrived in Utah Valley on September 23.

During their three-day stay near Utah Lake, the Spanish were impressed by the land and the Ute Indians—so much so that they made a well-intended promise (never kept) to return to settle among and baptize the Indians. Intent on reaching California and hoping to keep ahead of winter's cold, the Fathers took their leave of Utah Valley on September 25 and hurried southward.

A few days later their provisions began to run low. On October 5 their new Ute guide, Jose Maria, whom they employed in Utah Valley, deserted them. To complicate matters further, on October 8 they were snowbound, cold, and virtually out of provisions, so the Fathers decided to abandon the quest for Monterey. Rather, they would continue south, cross the Colorado, and return to Santa Fe by way of the Havasupai, Hopi, and Zuni pueblos. This decision was unpopular with three members of the party, who protested and demanded that they press on to Monterey, where hoped-for glory and reward awaited them. To placate the dissidents, it was agreed to put the matter in God's hands by drawing lots. On October 11 at a spot near Minersville about halfway between Milford and Cedar City, the lot indicating a return to Santa Fe was drawn.

Their southerly course then took them past present-day Kannaraville, Hurricane, and Kanab and on to the seemingly impossible canyon of the Colorado. For two weeks they wandered over extremely difficult terrain, seeking a river ford. When a spot was located, it proved necessary to carve steps into the stone of the cliff wall for about eight feet in order to get the horses to the riverbank. On November 7 they crossed at the Crossing of the Fathers, which is now under 550 feet of water on the Utah side of Lake Powell at a spot in Glen Canyon Powell, known today as Padre Bay.

Having negotiated a river crossing, they hurried on and returned to Santa Fe on January 2, 1777. Although their five months' journey had failed to find a land route to Monterey, the explorers were able to present to the governor the Escalante journal, containing a truly remarkable account of the trail, a detailed description of the Indian peoples encountered, and some estimate of the natural setting and resources of Utah; Miera's map, the first such rendering of Utah by a firsthand observer; and the 11-year-old Indian boy, Joaquin. The Miera map portrayed rather accurately some large segments of Utah, but it confused Utah geography for years by mistakenly showing a river flowing westward out of the Great Salt Lake, a Green and Sevier rivers connected as a composite Rio Buenaventura, flowing westward to the Pacific. These mistakes perpetuated geographical myths that took years to die. Following the Dominguez-Escalante expedition, there seems to have been almost continuous contact with Utah Indians by Spanish traders from New Mexico. Although the Spanish Fathers had failed to open a trail to Monterey, the Padres had opened a portion of the traders' trail (later known as the Old Spanish Trail), and they had made the Great Basin accessible to Spanish commerce out of New Mexico.

Within another half century events brought white men to Utah in larger numbers, perhaps as many as 300-500 trappers and traders a year. Out of a heated competition for beaver pelts and international rivalry for lands, mountain men arrived on the scene to further challenge the solitude of the Shoshones, the Gosiutes, Utes, Paiutes, and Navajos to crisscross the trails and streams, and to build forts and winter shelters.

For Utah the fur-trade epoch was initiated in earnest in 1824, when adventurous trappers and traders arrived from three directions, representing three diverse interests. From the southwest, out of New Mexico, came French-Canadian-American trappers, who were generally independents. This intrusion is best represented by such notables as Etienne Provost, Antoine Robidoux, and Christopher "Kit" Carson. From the north and northwest came British trappers of the great Hudson's Bay Company, led by Peter Skene Ogden with his Snake River Brigade. Americans employed by the William H. Ashley-Andrew Henry Company, formed at St. Louis, arrived from the east.

Beginning in 1822, Ashley and Henry had sought to enlist adventurous men for a projected fur expedition into the

Rocky Mountains. Among the recruits were some of the most famous of mountain men, including Jedediah S. Smith, John H. Weber, James Bridger, James Clyman, David E. Jackson, Thomas Fitzpatrick, Moses "Black" Harris, William L. Sublette, Daniel T. Potts, Jim Beckwourth, Hugh Glass, Milton G. Sublette, and many others. They were to work on salary, their expenses paid by and profits accruing to the company.

Two detachments of Ashley-Henry men, led by Jedediah Smith, headed west, following a route that took them south of the established trading paths on the upper Missouri. In the early spring of 1824 they arrived on the upper Sweetwater. Here they sought to cross the Continental Divide into the Pacific watershed. Twelve years earlier the returning Astorians of John Jacob Astor's trading company had traversed the South Pass from west to east, but their achievement had been neglected and lost to subsequent Rocky Mountain travelers. In 1824 Ashley's men "rediscovered" the famed South Pass, which afforded a gentle ascent through a level saddle in the Rockies. Even wagon traffic could cross the Continental Divide without great difficulty. A major highway to the Far West was opened. It was to be followed by fur trappers, missionaries, farmers, gold-rushers, and Mormons. South Pass opened Utah more effectively to the exploitation of Ashley's men. Here was a reliable route to virgin trapping grounds, inhabited by relatively friendly Indians. Quick profits and high adventure ensued.

Thomas Fitzpatrick led a small party back to company headquarters at St. Louis for supplies and also made known the existence of South Pass. The remaining company employees split into two groups. Jedediah Smith headed up one small party, which eventually made its way to the Hudson's Bay Company's Flathead Post at Eddy, Montana; and John H. Weber led the main trapper contingent into Cache Valley, where they wintered on the Bear River.

Smith and his six companions arrived on November 26 at the Flathead Post, where Peter Skene Ogden was making preparations for his campaign into the Snake River country against the Americans. As Ogden's brigade moved out on December 20, 1824, he and his party of 131 were dogged every step of the way by the "sly cunning Yankee," Jedediah Smith.

Ogden's advance into northern Utah was not the first incursion by British fur trappers. In 1819 Michael Bourdeau led a North West Company expedition to the Bear River, which Bourdeau named for the great number of bears on its borders. They followed the Bear River to Bear Lake and then to Willow Valley, now Cache Valley, where Bourdeau gave his own

Jim Bridger was enticed into trapping for the Ashley-Henry Fur Company by a want ad printed in the Missouri Republican. *The 1822 ad was titled "To Enterprising Young Men." Courtesy, Special Collections and Manuscripts, Utah State University*

name to a stream that is known today as Blacksmith Fork. Ogden, knowing of Bourdeau's previous journey, hoped to trap in the Bear River country. However, he discovered that the Americans had beaten him there. John H. Weber and his men had wintered on the Bear during the four months it had taken Ogden to make the trek from the Flathead Post to Utah. Having reaped the best of the beaver crop, Weber headed southward for a rendezvous with Jedediah Smith. As Ogden approached Utah, in the vicinity of Bear River, Smith also headed south to rendezvous with Weber's corps.

Meanwhile, Ogden and his chief clerk, William Kittson, both kept careful accounts of their expedition. These journals provide the earliest eyewitness descriptions of northern Utah. After entering into present-day Utah on May 5, 1825, Ogden's brigade proceeded through Cache Valley to the Ogden Valley. This valley, which was described as a hole because of surrounding mountains, was named for the brigade leader, as was the river that also bears Ogden's name.

The British fur trappers soon learned that the Americans not only had trapped nearly every stream along the Wasatch Front but also were paying more for furs and charging less for supplies than the British. Here then was a competitive opportunity. Soon an unruly band of American trappers under Johnson Gardner rode up Weber Canyon and camped within yards of Ogden's camp. On May 23, 1825, Gardner proclaimed that the British were on United States soil and had better leave or suffer the indignity of being driven off. This was adding ignorance to insult, for the site near Mountain Green on the Weber River was on Mexican soil. Faced with a challenge and near mutiny among his own men, Ogden discreetly withdrew, leaving the Wasatch Mountains and drainage to the Americans. However, during the tense two days before he left, 23 of Odgen's men took their beaver pelts and deserted to the Americans. Thus it was that Kittson labeled the site Deserter Point.

The British fur trappers abandoned northern Utah with Ogden's retreat. They stayed north of the Portneuf River, and the Americans remained to dominate the fur traffic, turning northern Utah into the center of the Rocky Mountain fur trade. Ogden did return in 1828-1829 on the expedition that discovered the Humboldt River after passing through Cache Valley and the desolate area north of the Great Salt Lake, but he never again trapped the Utah streams. Even though Mexico owned the territory, Utah began to become Americanized with the dominance of American trappers. Insofar as beaver trade was concerned, the event at Deserter Point seemed to define the land south of the forty-second parallel as American.

Upon the discovery of South Pass, Thomas Fitzpatrick had taken word of its existence to Ashley-Henry headquarters in St. Louis. Recognizing the importance of this find, the company acted immediately to outfit a train of new trappers and provisions, which William H. Ashley accompanied west. Trapping in the Great Basin-where no rivers had yet been found draining to the outside-compounded the problem of getting fur to market and supplies to the field. South Pass would partially solve this problem. Beginning with the rendezvous ("rendavoze," Ashley called it) of the summer of 1825, the character of fur marketing in the American West underwent an ingenious change. Ashley arranged for supplies to be taken to a designated spot. Through a serious oversight, he failed to bring any liquor to the first rendezvous, but he corrected this negligence thereafter. At an appointed date, usually in July, the company trappers and the independents who wished to trade with the company would hereafter rendezvous for a hectic couple of weeks of cavorting and transacting business.

Since myth, perhaps stemming from the Miera map of 1776, held that rivers drained westward from the intermountain region that is now known as Utah, and since adventure and discovery of virgin fur-yielding rivers were their own rewards, the fur trappers carried out many other important explorations.

In 1824 John H. Weber led the 50 or so men of his Ashley-Henry contingent west from the Green River, where they struck the Bear River, which they followed to Willow or Cache Valley in present-day northern Utah. During the fall, the men made bets as to where the Bear River eventually ended, and young Jim Bridger was chosen to find out. With at least one other companion, he followed the river on horseback to the Bear River narrows, which connects the Cache and Bear River valleys. Here Bridger and his small party became the first white men to see the Great Salt Lake. They followed the river to the lake, where Bridger tasted the water and, because of its great saltiness, pronounced it an arm of the Pacific Ocean.

Etienne Provost is a contender to Bridger's claim of having discovered the Great Salt Lake. Also during 1824 Provost and others had worked their way from New Mexico into Utah. He was one of the earliest of many trappers who came to work Utah from a base in the Southwest following the more liberal policies toward American traders that came with the Mexican Revolution of 1821. In the fall of 1824 Provost moved westward from the Uinta Basin. He pushed up the Strawberry River and crossed the Wasatch Mountains to the Provo River, which was named for him. He followed the river to the valley

of the Utah Lake and then moved northward along the Jordan River. A Snake Indian chief, Bad Gocha, seeking revenge for injuries perpetrated by other whites, conceived an elaborate plot against Provost and his party. He invited Provost's men to smoke the peace pipe. Bad Gocha argued that it was bad medicine to have anything metal nearby during the smoking ceremony. The trapper party put their weapons aside and joined the circle. At a prearranged signal, the Indians attacked with knives they had concealed. Seven of Provost's men were killed, but Provost and three others survived to escape eastward over the mountains. If this attack took place on the upper Jordan River, as some believe, it is likely that Provost saw the Great Salt Lake from the south in the fall of 1824 at nearly the same time that Bridger saw it from the north.

In 1825 Provost returned to the Great Basin with about 30 trappers from the Taos area. They met Peter Skene Ogden on the Weber River on May 22, 1825, and witnessed, but were not a party to, the Ogden-Gardner episode at Deserter Point. Two weeks later he met William Ashley with his trade goods at the Duchesne River, and he accepted a role as guide to conduct Ashley's party via the upper Provo and Weber rivers to the first rendezvous, on Henry's Fork of the Green River. On the route to the first rendezvous, and after it as well, Ashley carried out adventurous first explorations of much of the Green River and the Uinta Basin.

The partnership of Ashley-Henry was passed to William H. Ashley alone and then to a partnership with Jedediah Smith in 1825. The next year Smith, David E. Jackson, and William L. Sublette became owning partners, and four years later the company was sold to the Rocky Mountain Fur Company, of which Jim Bridger is the best-known partner. The Bridger group sold out in 1834 to the American Fur Company. By then the fur era was ending, but before its close the American trappers had explored and trapped all of Utah's major streams and extensively explored the Great Salt Lake country.

During the spring of 1826 Jim Clyman and three others, including Moses Harris and possibly Louis Vasquez and Henry G. Fraeb, spent three weeks paddling around the Great Salt Lake in skin boats, looking for an outlet or beaver streams flowing into the lake. They found the land around the lake was desolate, and there were no outlets. Soon the mountain men began to use the descriptive term "Salt Lake." At the second mountain rendezvous, held at the southern end of the Cache Valley—near Hyrum—Clyman reported his experiences and his disappointment in the Great Salt Lake.

As the 1826 rendezvous broke up, Jedediah Smith headed out in search of unexploited trapping grounds. Smith, who was known as the Knight in Buckskin because of his piety, prayers, and Bible reading, was searching for beaver streams and a navigable river to the Pacific. His search took him past the Great Salt Lake into the southern Utah region that is known today as Dixie. On the way to the Utah Lake area, Smith and his party traveled in familiar surroundings. Southward beyond Utah Lake they were in country that had been little explored by white men since 1776. The party hit the Virgin River in southern Utah, followed it to the Colorado, and then struck out across the deserts to the Mojave. Eventually they made their way to the San Gabriel Mission near Los Angeles, where they were ordered by the Mexican governor to leave by the same route they had come. Evading the order, they headed north into the San Joaquin Valley. Smith left his crew at the Stanislaus River and with two companions (Robert Evans and Silas Gobel) crossed the Sierra Nevada and the basins and ranges of present-day Nevada on the return to Utah. After suffering great privation, they finally came upon the familiar waters of the Great Salt Lake.

They hurried on to the 1827 rendezvous, held on the shores of Bear Lake near Laketown, where they were greeted with considerable joy by the other mountain men, who assumed they had died in the deserts or fallen prey to Indians. As the rendezvous ended, Smith left again for California, taking 18 men and following the same route as the previous year. The

Facing page: *Etienne Provost, a trapper, may have been the first European to discover the Great Salt Lake, although there is no definite proof of this. Traveling down the Provo River to Utah Lake and north through the Jordan River in the fall of 1824, Provost may have seen the Great Salt Lake from the south. Courtesy, Utah State Historical Society*

Right: *The Green River Rendezvous was mostly a business event where company trappers, Indians, and mountain men could gather to sell furs and purchase supplies. The social incentives of such a rendezvous also boosted attendance. Shooting matches, athletic competitions, and drinking bouts were among the various activities enjoyed. Photo by Alfred Jacob Miller, courtesy, Special Collections and Archives, Utah State University*

Below: *Deep in discussion, these trappers smoke their pipes by the firelight. Around them are snowshoes, rifles, and ammunition. Their beaver traps, not to be seen, have probably been set out for retrieval the following morning. Courtesy, Special Collections and Archives, Utah State University*

second southern expedition was plagued with mishaps and calamity. Attacked by Indians on the Mojave, several of the party were killed, and Smith barely escaped with his life. From California, Smith decided to travel into Oregon before returning to Utah. Near the Umpqua River the party was attacked by Indians; only Smith and three others escaped.

Having thus conducted two of the most heroic expeditions of the American West, Smith sold out in 1830 and went to St. Louis, where he planned to retire. In May of 1831 at the age of 32, he was attacked by Comanches while conducting a trading expedition to Santa Fe and was killed. Smith, who had called the valley of the Great Salt Lake his second home, had a great impact on Utah by his rediscovery of South Pass and by his two southwest expeditions, which established him as the first man to travel the length and breadth of Utah and the first to cross the length and breadth of the Great Basin.

Smith and his partners had sold their company to the Rocky Mountain Fur Company. The notable partners of this company included Jim Bridger, Thomas Fitzpatrick, and Milton G. Sublette. The representatives of this company and such independents as Osburne Russell, Thomas L. (Pegleg) Smith, and Joseph R. Walker, who worked for Benjamin L.E. Bonneville, continued to crisscross Utah, trapping and exploring. The continuity of occupancy they provided assured that the influence of the mountain men in place names and travel routes would remain until settled life was established.

There remained enough activity to encourage the establishment of trading posts to fill the void left by the end of the rendezvous era. Even though few facts are available concerning the Utah trading posts, the three best-known were in the Uinta Basin, where they served overland traffic through Colorado or southward to Santa Fe. Kit Carson established the first at the junction of the Green and White rivers in 1833. Philip Thompson and William Craig established Fort Davy Crockett in 1837—naming it for that hero of the Alamo, who had died in the battle—in Brown's Hole on the north bank of the Green River near the Utah-Colorado border. In 1837 Antoine Robidoux, a trapper working into Utah out of New Mexico, located a post at the Whiterocks Fork of the Uinta, which continued to operate until it was destroyed by rival traders in 1844.

The proprietors of these posts and the mountain men trappers were important in the opening and eventual settlement of Utah. They helped to clear up confusion and uncertainty about the terrain and waterways. Encouraged by the pathfinding of the fur trappers, Americans would shortly be flocking by the thousands westward to Oregon and California. The mountain men and traders had opened the West

Above: *Mountain man Thomas Fitspatrick led the Bartleson-Bidwell wagon train party in 1841. Fitspatrick led the group as far as Soda Springs, Idaho. At that time, the company leaders wanted to change their route from Oregon to California via the Bear River and through the Great Basin, in hopes of finding the mythical Buena Ventura River that they believed could be found on the west side of the Great Salt Lake. Fitspatrick refused to leave the established trail, and the party split. Courtesy, Special Collections and Archives, Utah State University*

Page 42: *This view of the north end of Cache Valley was taken by the U.S. Geological Survey in 1877. Although it was more than 50 years later, the scene must have looked very much the same as when Peter Skene Ogden found it in 1825. Courtesy, Special Collections and Archives, Utah State University*

to America—and Utah to the possibility of future immigrations. The Utah landscape had been projected into popular consciousness by the men who came, named the mountains and valleys, found the feasible routes, and left little physical evidence of their passage.

During the years from the end of the fur-trade era until the coming of the Mormons, several companies of California-bound immigrants and two major explorations of Utah by John C. Fremont helped to transform the trader trails into emigrant roads. Thereby major highways were opened into and through the Salt Lake Valley.

Mass emigrant travel to the American West did not begin until the 1840s and remained insignificant until 1843, when 1,100 people traveled the Western roads to Oregon and California. Given the perils of mountain and desert travel, it is not surprising that early roads usually avoided Utah even if it meant a longer route. Among the earliest-known emigrant groups to pass through present-day Utah was the Bartleson-Bidwell Company of 1841. It was probably through ignorance that this party chose a trail over land so forbidding that no one ever again traversed this exact route. Beginning in 1840, John Bidwell organized a party of 69 men, women, and children who were willing to move west to Oregon or California. Since John Bartleson was chosen as train captain, the party became known as the Bartleson-Bidwell Company. Knowing only that California lay to the west, the party was lucky to have Thomas Fitzpatrick and other mountain men guide them as far as Soda Springs, Idaho.

Here the trappers and half the immigrants went north to Fort Hall; thirty-four of the company turned southwest toward what seemed to them the shortest route to California. In this group were Benjamin Kelsey's 19-year-old wife, Nancy, and infant daughter, Ann, who were the first known white females to cross Utah. They skirted the desolate western edge of the Great Salt Lake Desert, their wagons mired so badly into the Salt Flats that two were abandoned before they reached the freshwater springs at the east base of Pilot Peak on September 13. Traveling south to Silver Zone Pass and to Johnson's Springs and finding no river on which they might float rafts they hoped to make from their wagons, they loaded what they could on their livestock and gave the surplus to an either delighted or bewildered Indian. Striking south and then west, they hit the Humboldt and finally arrived at John Marsh's ranch in the San Joaquin Valley on November 4. The first major immigrant party had made its way to California and in the process had brought the first wagons across the Salt Flats. No other immigrant train was to come through Utah until five years later.

The next trailblazers to enter Utah did so for an entirely different purpose than did the Bartleson-Bidwell party. The second and third Western expeditions of John C. Fremont explored Utah, measuring, mapping, and describing the land. Through his marriage to Jessie Benton, Fremont was a son-in-law of Missouri's expansionist senator, Thomas Hart Benton, who was able to use his influence to help secure congressional funding for Fremont's explorations.

Fremont's second expedition, consisting of 39 men, left St. Louis in May 1843 to explore routes to Oregon. When at Soda Springs Fremont's curiosity about the Great Salt Lake country deflected him south of his initial objective, suddenly the expedition took on enormous importance for Utah history. His hope was to solve the myths and mysteries of the Great Salt Lake. Unable to approach the lake directly from the north, his party, reduced temporarily to 13 men for the diversion, climbed out onto the uplands along the edge of the Wasatch Mountains, where, from the top of Little Mountain, they gained a panoramic view of the Great Salt Lake.

Fremont, with five others, including Kit Carson, set out on September 9, 1843, in an 18-foot rubber raft to explore the lake. Due to an air leak, the men had to pump furiously to keep the boat afloat until they could reach the nearest island. Here they were disappointed to find no water or timber. Fremont called it Disappointment Island, but Captain Howard Stansbury renamed it Fremont Island in 1850. From a summit 800 feet above the lake's 4,200-foot level, which Fremont had accurately calculated earlier, they surveyed the lake and prepared a reasonably accurate map of it and its various islands. Before leaving the island, Fremont filled a container with five gallons of lake water, which he subsequently boiled down to fourteen pints of fine-grained salt.

Having mapped and analyzed the lake, the party left, going north to Fort Hall to rejoin the other members of the expedition before going on to Fort Vancouver. From there they moved south into western Nevada, looking for the Rio Buenaventura, the legendary westward-flowing river, which Fremont determined once and for all was indeed a myth. The following May he moved east from California to enter Utah a second time, but now by way of the Old Spanish Trail. He went north through Utah as far as Utah Lake, noting the agricultural potential as he went. The expedition left Utah by way of the Dominguez-Escalante route to the Uinta Basin, to Colorado, and then on to St. Louis.

The detailed notes of the exploration were prepared and published in 1845, describing Fremont's adventures in circling and naming the Great Basin. This volume was widely circulated. Perhaps its major importance for the future of

Utah was that Brigham Young and other Mormon leaders carefully studied copies before they left Nauvoo, Illinois.

Congress almost immediately funded another Fremont trip to the American West. This time his party came to Utah by the route they had used in leaving the year before. During the month of October in 1845, the party explored the Utah Valley, determining the relationship of Utah Lake to the Great Salt Lake and exploring the valley of the Great Salt Lake. They also visited Antelope Island, where they killed several of the animals for which they named the island.

The party then turned its interest to scouting a route to California from the Salt Lake Valley. From the southwestern edge of the Great Salt Lake, they sought the best route to the Humboldt. Kit Carson, fixing his gaze upon a mountain that was a considerable but unknown distance across the desert, headed an advance party. Using the peak as a landmark, they set out in the hope of finding grass and water. In this quest a primary concern was for the livestock, which, when denied food or water for a day or so, would become uncontrollable, either refusing to move, faltering from weakness, or simply wandering off in search of sustenance.

Carson was to light a signal fire if an adequate water and foraging place were found. Fremont impatiently led the main party onto the Salt Flats the next afternoon, even though no word had been received from the advance party. That night they met one of Carson's messengers, who reported that a stopping place with wood, grass, and water had been located. By afternoon they arrived at the base of the mountain, which Fremont named Pilot Peak.

Having made the first track across the center of the Great Salt Lake Desert (Jedediah Smith had crossed the southern edge and Joseph R. Walker had traversed the northern edge), the Fremont party proceeded on to explore large areas of Nevada before arriving at Sutter's Fort in early December. In this crossing Fremont blazed a portion of what was to become Hastings Cutoff.

Langsford W. Hastings, who had gone to Oregon in 1842 and then had arrived in the Sacramento Valley, had ample opportunity to discuss potential immigrant routes to California with John C. Fremont during the winter of 1845-1846 at Sutter's Fort. Hastings had become one of the most avid boosters of California. Even though the United States had a partial claim to Oregon through joint occupation with Great Britain and had no claim to California, Hastings extolled the virtues of California in the hopes of furthering his own and America's interest in that fabled land.

Prior to 1846 Oregon had always attracted from three to ten times California's annual immigration. In 1846 this began to change as 1,500 immigrants arrived in California and 1,200 overland travelers chose Oregon. A significant factor in this turn of events was Hastings' *Emigrant's Guide to Oregon and California,* published in 1845, offering instructions to immigrants on how to make their way west. He held that the trip to California, already 10 to 20 days shorter than the journey to Oregon, could be further shortened by going directly west across the Salt Lake Valley, rather than following the California road northward to Fort Hall. Without ever having been over the route himself, Hastings suggested that from the Salt Lake Valley one could continue with little difficulty to San Francisco Bay.

Conversations with Fremont confirmed Hastings' belief that wagons could be taken over the Salt Flats. He rode east in the spring of 1846 to personally convince immigrants to divert to his proposed cutoff. As he traveled east on horseback, he picked up Fremont's trail and followed it with the aid of his mountain-man guide, Jim Clyman, across the salt desert, up Parley's Canyon, north to Echo Canyon, and to Fort Bridger, built by Jim Bridger in 1843.

Hastings and his friend James M. Hudspeth headed east along the Oregon Trail to convince immigrants to take his proposed route. Just east of South Pass he recruited Wales B. Bonney, who was returning to the states, to carry a letter urging those bound for California to take the new route via the south end of the Great Salt Lake. The magical news that Fremont had pioneered the route and that Hastings would personally guide the immigrants convinced a number of parties to pull away from the mainstream of traffic and head southwest to Echo Canyon.

They soon found that the Hastings route was more than they had bargained for. The great guide had not yet worked out the best route from Fort Bridger to Echo Canyon, and he also assumed that Weber Canyon would provide the easiest access to the Salt Lake Valley. Although it was broad at its beginning, it became extremely narrow and hazardous at its mouth. Those who were pressured into trying it by an overly enthusiastic promoter generally regretted their decision. Devils Gate proved steep and rocky. Wagons rammed into the heels of the draft animals and slipped unnervingly sideways. Double and triple teaming and tying of log drags proved necessary, and even then wagons were lost.

The first group to try the route was the Bryant-Russell party, made up of nine men on muleback. They found the lower Weber Canyon route harrowing, as they frequently passed under and scaled what Edwin Bryant described as "... immense overhanging masses and projections of rock."

Nevertheless, they made their way out of the canyon to the south end of the Great Salt Lake and to Skull Valley. On August 3, as they looked across from the north end of the Cedar Mountains to Pilot Peak, which was closer to 80 miles than the 40 miles Hudspeth and Hastings assumed, they were told, "Now boys, put spurs to your mules and ride like hell!" By doing so, they made it to Pilot Peak and on to California in good condition.

The next group, the Harlan-Young party, led by George W. Harlan and Samuel C. Young, was much larger than the Bryant-Russell Company. Their 40 wagons were the first to transform major portions of the cutoff route into an actual wagon road. Led by Hastings, they followed roughly the same route as the Bryant-Russell Company. At Echo Canyon Hastings left the party to seek a more direct route. The lower Weber Canyon, meanwhile, provided a tremendous obstacle, necessitating backbreaking labor and causing the loss of a wagon and team that crashed at Devils Gate. These difficulties convinced Hastings also to seek another route out of the mountains.

After emerging from the Wasatch, the terrible Salt Flats crossing awaited. Large numbers of livestock and some wagons were lost to the desert mud. Although for miles the Salt Flats appear to be flat and firm, they are deceptive. The top crust is easily broken, and beneath is a desert of mud of a seemingly bottomless ooze. Despite their terrible difficulties, the Harlan-Young party pushed on to their California destination.

Another company, led by Heinrich Lienhard, was almost immediately behind the Harlan-Young party. By the time they arrived at Weber Canyon, Hastings had found a better route and attempted to persuade them to return to Henefer and strike south. Since the Harlan-Young party had gotten wagons through Devils Gate, they decided they could too, and so they disregarded Hastings' advice. Upon reaching the Humboldt on September 8, Lienhard noted in his journal that Hastings Cutoff should be called "Hastings Longtrip." Wagons that had left Fort Bridger two weeks after the Lienhard party, following the Fort Hall route, had already beaten him to the Humboldt junction.

The last party of 1846 to follow the ill-advised Hastings Cutoff was led by George and Jacob Donner and George Reed. Following the well-marked route, they found near Henefer a note in a stick from Hastings advising them to send a messenger after him so that he could point out a better wagon route into the Salt Lake Valley than that through Devils Gate. John Reed was sent ahead, and he found Hastings near the western edge of the Oquirrh Mountains. Hastings rode east with Reed to the summit of Big Mountain, where he pointed out the route the wagons should take. By the time Reed returned, the Donner party had been waiting in camp for four days.

From Henefer the party turned up Main Canyon, cutting a road along Dixie Hollow and up East Canyon Creek until they could pass west over Big Mountain. Here they took a jagged route up Little Mountain and down into Emigration Canyon. Finding the mouth of the canyon blocked with rocks and boulders, they double-teamed their wagons over Donner Hill rather than clear the trail. It took them eleven days to negotiate the road that the Mormon Pioneer Company traversed in three days the next year.

The desert mud of the Salt Flats exacted more than its usual toll on the livestock, people, and wagons of the party. So spent were they from the desert crossing that when they reached the Ruby Mountains they chose to skirt them on the southern end rather than on the much shorter but steeper northern end. Trouble continued. On October 4, as they reached the Humboldt, John Reed killed John Snyder in a fight resulting from Reed's infuriation at an attack upon his wife. The next day Reed was banished from the party.

In late October they reached Truckee Lake, which is now known as Donner Lake. Here disaster struck. Early snows trapped the company beside the lake, and before help could be summoned, 39 of the original 87 members of the group perished.

The migrations of 1846 ended with the tragedy of the Donner Party. During the summer of 1846, many immigrants and perhaps 80 wagons had made their way through the Great Salt Lake Valley to the Salt Flats and beyond to California. Hastings Cutoff had been a trial to all and a disaster to the Donner Party. But nevertheless the route to the valley of the Great Salt Lake had proved practical. The path was marked and laid out the whole way by those who had risked life and property to cross Utah at the prompting of Langsford W. Hastings. The chance they took did not hasten their journey, but it proved most beneficial to the Mormons who followed up the establishment of the practical trail by colonizing the Great Salt Lake Valley in 1847.

The Mormon Kingdom

In order to understand much of Utah history, it is essential to gain insight into the background and the migration of Mormons to Utah because they were the first permanent white settlers. It was a farm boy born a continent away from Utah who embarked on a search for religious insights that transformed Utah's history.

Joseph Smith, Jr., the founder of Mormonism, was the son of an itinerant laborer and farmer who had arrived in Palmyra, New York, in 1816, having migrated from Vermont following a succession of economic misfortunes. The Smith family at first seemed much like hundreds of other Yankee farm families that had made their way from New England to upper New York State in the early 1800s.

Although religiously inclined, the Smiths did not formally associate with organized denominations until a wave of revivalistic enthusiasm swept into western New York in 1819 and 1820. The family matriarch, two brothers, and a sister joined the Presbyterians, while the father remained aloof from affiliation. Joseph Smith, Jr., who was not yet 15 years old, felt a massive confusion from all the conflicting claims and doctrines of the many earnest revivalists. He maintained that he sought insight by praying in a grove near his father's farm.

According to his account, God the Father and Jesus Christ

Photographer James H. Crockwell photographed Mormon pioneer William Carter's reenactment of his historic first plowing in the Salt Lake Valley. Photo by James H. Crockwell, courtesy, LDS Church Archives

Above: *Hill Cumorah near Manchester, New York, was where Joseph Smith was told he could find the golden plates, the basis for the* Book of Mormon. *From* History of the Mormons, *1852*

Facing page: *When the Mormon pioneers arrived in the Salt Lake Valley, they found life difficult, but much of what was needed to sustain existence was readily found. Firsthand accounts describe the valley as having fertile soil for crops, abundant water for irrigation, and tall grasses for livestock. By 1953, when the English convert Fredrick Piercy faithfully sketched the valley, Salt Lake City was a bustling community. Courtesy, LDS Church Archives*

Above: *After Joseph Smith began to translate the* Book of Mormon *from what he called "reformed Egyptian" to English, he felt he needed witnesses who would testify that the book did in fact exist and that it was from God. Courtesy, LDS Church Archives*

appeared to him and informed him that he should join no organized religious group. This experience in the spring of 1820 set him on a course that led to subsequent visions and religious experiences, which included being guided to plates containing the record of ancient inhabitants of America. He was commanded to translate the ancient Egyptian writing on the plates and to publish the translated version.

After much difficulty, Smith was able to employ E.B. Grandin to publish his *Book of Mormon* in February of 1830. (According to Mormon tradition, in ancient times Mormon was the one who compiled the plates that Smith found and translated.) Although Joseph Smith at first called his church, which was formally founded on April 6, 1830, the Church of Christ, the name was changed in 1838 to the Church of Jesus Christ of Latter-day Saints. However, because of the *Book of Mormon,* upon which the new faith was based, the many critics of the new religion began calling Smith's followers Mormons—and the name stuck.

From its organization in a cabin at Fayette, New York, with but six members, Mormonism grew and was soon transplanted westward. In the fall of 1830 four Mormon missionaries were sent among the Western Indians. As they journeyed through northern Ohio, they converted many of minister Alexander Campbell's followers. With Mormons in New York facing increasing hostility from their neighbors and with the new Campbellite converts now constituting more Mormons in Ohio than in New York, the New York Mormons left. They journeyed west to settle a newly opened area just east of what is today Cleveland. By the time of the New York exodus, Mormonism was not just another sect. It represented the establishment of a new religion. The *Book of Mormon* made unprecedented claims as to content and origin. Smith and his close associates held that God's priesthood authority had been restored to them by heavenly messengers, and that all faithful male members should have the priesthood offered to them. This was a compromise between the high-church notion of an ordained elite clergy and the evangelical Protestants' universal priesthood of believers. Finally, Smith had introduced the notion of "revelations" that were the expressed will of God to his followers. The introduction of continuing, current, and immediate revelation provided the element of flexibility of doctrine and gave to church policies the authority of Holy Writ.

In the spring of 1831, Kirtland, Ohio, became the second administrative center for Mormonism. For seven years Kirtland and environs on the southern edge of Lake Erie would remain an important Mormon administrative and gathering center and a staging site for the migration of many Mormons westward into Missouri. In fact, the Ohio and Missouri phases of Mormon settlement were contemporaneous.

In the summer of 1831, just four months after the location of the church administrative center at Kirtland, Joseph Smith visited Mormons in western Missouri, where Mormon missionaries had found converts at Independence. During his visit, in July of 1831, Joseph Smith received a revelation designating Jackson County, Missouri, as the gathering point of the Latter-day Saints and the place for the city of Zion.

A major doctrine, now repeatedly stressed and emphasized, was the gathering. Mormons in response moved to western Missouri, but a broad interpretation of the gathering was the requirement to relocate in a Mormon community. The gathering doctrine asked converts to relocate out of such

cities as Boston and New York and to gather with the Saints in Jackson County or Kirtland. The gathering would assemble the faithful in Mormon communities beyond non-Mormon influences that were considered corrupting; it would create an orderly, close-knit Mormon community out of disparate converts and facilitate implementation of a communal economic innovation termed the Law of Consecration and Stewardship.

Some of the Ohio Saints converted by Sidney Rigdon, a minister who had embraced Mormonism himself, were living a communal economic system before Joseph Smith arrived in Ohio. The Law of Consecration and Stewardship was given in revelation in February 1831 in response to Joseph Smith's inquiry into the communal order already in existence. The new order pulled back from any ideas of total equality of property. Even though one was allowed to enjoy the fruits of one's labors "according to circumstances ... wants and needs," everyone was to "consecrate" all worldly assets beyond the basics to the church each year to provide for the needs of the poor and to meet the requirements of general church finances. Although the law of supply and demand would still operate to some extent in allocating goods and services, the Saints were expected, under this religious and economic law, to sacrifice to further community projects, such as the building of the Kirtland Temple, and to provide for the needy. When the temple was dedicated in March of 1836, it stood as a symbol of the individual Mormon sacrifices for community needs. Ever since, even though the Law of Consecration was dropped, Mormonism has been recognized as a faith that exacts a high level of commitment and loyalty.

For about a year after Joseph Smith's designation of Independence as the site of the New Jerusalem, the number of Mormons increased steadily in Missouri. Little or no overt hostility was evident among the established settlers, but soon fears developed over Mormon potential political influence and distrust of Mormon attitudes relative to slavery in the slave state of Missouri. Conflict ensued.

In July of 1833 Missourians organized open resistance against the Mormons. Prominent church leaders were tarred and feathered, and the Mormon press, a store, and a blacksmith shop were destroyed. At gunpoint, church leaders were forced to sign a written agreement to leave Jackson County by the next April. When the Missourians became convinced that the Mormons were not planning to leave, they organized again and expelled the Mormons in November of 1833.

Upon hearing of the expulsion, the prophet, as Smith had come to be known, led a company of Kirtland Saints to Missouri to help restore property to Jackson County Mormons. In the meantime, the expelled Saints had crossed the Missouri River northward into Clay County, where they were kindly received by county residents, who provided them food and temporary shelter. The Smith expedition, known as Zion's Camp, failed to restore Mormon property, but it did provide the Mormon leaders valuable experience in group migration that could be drawn upon at a later date.

Even though they tried every legal means at hand for redress, the Mormons were not allowed to return to Jackson County. Suddenly Clay County residents became concerned about the growing number of Mormons in their midst. Lists of grievances were drawn up, and the Mormons were presented with petitions for their withdrawal from Clay County.

Eventually a gentlemen's agreement was reached wherein an area to be known as Caldwell County would be created out of sparsely settled lands to the northeast that would be reserved primarily for Mormons. The Mormons, for their part, agreed not to settle in other counties without permission of previous settlers. Soon Far West was established as the largest of several thriving Mormon communities in Caldwell County and vicinity. Mormons also settled in neighboring Carroll and Daviess Counties.

Meanwhile, problems developed in Ohio over the inability of Mormons to make distinctions between secular and religious affairs. Leaders of the new faith became involved in politics and economics and in the process alienated non-Mormons and disaffected some Mormons. When a bank sponsored by Joseph Smith without state approval failed in 1837, threats against his life became so ominous as to cause him to flee and head for Far West. Shortly after Smith's departure, about 500 other Ohio Mormons set out in wagons headed for Missouri. By the early 1840s all Ohio Mormons had either left or joined other religious groups, and the Ohio era of Mormonism was closed.

Joseph Smith arrived at Far West in March 1838 to find conditions there also very unsettled. Mormon successes in Caldwell County were causing anxiety among residents of neighboring counties. In October conditions deteriorated to the point that open violence broke out, whereupon Governor Lilburn W. Boggs issued an order that the Mormons must leave the state or be exterminated. Subsequent conflict led to several deaths, including the killing of 18 Mormons huddled for protection in a blacksmith shop at Hauns Mill.

After the jailing of Joseph Smith on false charges of treason and murder at Liberty, Missouri, the Mormon Saints were forced to move once again, this time eastward across the Mississippi to Quincy, Illinois. Since the move was undertaken in the dead of winter, it was most fortunate that the Quincy residents welcomed and cared for the Mormons with much compassion. From that time on, Mormons told and retold the stories of mob violence and their forced flight. The theme of

Above: *Joseph Smith stands with his brother, Hyrum, in the late 1830s. To date no photograph has been found of the brothers who died only years after photography became widely available. From* History of the Mormons, *1852*

Facing page: *Here on the Susquehanna River on May 15, 1829, Joseph Smith recounted that John the Baptist had ordained to them the Aaronic Priesthood of God. The concept of a divinely given authority, to administer in God's name on earth, would be one of the underpinning doctrines of this evolving new American religion. Photo by George Edward Andersen, courtesy, LDS Church Archives*

unjust persecution became indelibly stamped on their consciousness.

The refugee camp at Quincy was but a temporary respite. Joseph Smith escaped from jail in Missouri to rejoin his flock, and then, in April 1839, he began the purchase of lands in large tracts on both sides of the Mississippi River. Again the Mormons were to gain painful experience in pioneering a new settlement. But soon a flourishing new community in Illinois on a broad bend of the Mississippi River, known as Nauvoo, was established.

Under liberal charter from the Illinois legislature, a town militia, the Nauvoo Legion, was organized and a university was chartered. However, the most dramatic developments were doctrinal innovations. New ceremonies were taught by Joseph Smith that were to be implemented in the temple the Saints were laboring to build. Plural marriage—the taking of more than one wife—was taught through a revelation received by Joseph Smith in July 1843.

Rumors of polygamy caused an uproar in and about Nauvoo. Charges and denials were repeated. Garbled versions of the practice were published. To compound the controversy, Joseph Smith became immersed in political controversy with the announcement of his candidacy for president of the United States. The Saints were increasingly brought under attack from those residing in neighboring towns such as Warsaw and Carthage. When a group of apostates set up an anti-Mormon newspaper in June of 1844, which discussed plural marriage openly, Smith and the town council at Nauvoo ordered the press of the *Nauvoo Expositer* destroyed.

Suppression of this press brought an immediate response, which included the jailing of Joseph Smith at Carthage. On June 27, 1844, an armed mob broke into the jail and shot and killed Joseph Smith and his brother Hyrum, then fled out of fear of a possible Mormon reprisal. Sorrowfully and secretly, the Mormons buried their martyred leaders.

By August the 12 apostles who had been on missions to various locations were finally gathered to Nauvoo, and heated discussions ensued as to who should be chosen to lead the church. Leadership was conveyed to the Quorum of Twelve Apostles, with Brigham Young as its president. It was not until December of 1847 that the first presidency was reorganized and Brigham Young was officially installed as church president.

Smith's death appeased the enemies of the church only temporarily. By September 1845 mobs began burning Mormons' homes in outlying areas. Brigham Young warned his followers not to return the attacks and to withdraw to Nauvoo for greater safety. State officials, after an investigation, ad-

Above: *On a spring night in 1832, a band of 40 men rushed into Joseph Smith's room and took him outside where they stripped, beat, and tarred and feathered him. From* The Mormons

Facing page, top: *On July 20, 1833, a mob of Missourians destroyed a printing press and other Mormon property, threatening more physical harm if they stayed in Jackson County. This painting is attributed to Mormon artist, C.C.A. Christensen. Courtesy, LDS Church Archives*

Facing page, bottom left: *In October 1838 nearly 30 Mormon families had created a settlement on the Hauns Mill site. Many were living in tents and wagons, having iust recently arrived. Non-Mormon settlers were angered by the steady stream of Mormons that were settling in the area and attempted to scare them away. On October 30, this anger, turned to violence as about 240 men rode into the camp and attacked—leaving 18 men and boys dead or dying and another 15 severely wounded. From* History of the Mormons, *1852*

Facing page, bottom right: *This drawing depicts the death of Joseph Smith. The last minutes of Joseph Smith's life has been a matter of myth, supposition, and confusing testimony. From* The Mormons

Page 53. *This portrait of Brigham Young was taken one year before the great colonizer's death in 1877. Photo by Charles R. Savage, Courtesy, Utah State Historical Society*

mitted they could not guarantee protection and advised the Mormons to emigrate again.

Even though Church leaders announced that they planned to leave in the spring, mob pressures increased; and so, on February 4, 1846, wagons started to leave the city, headed westward across the Mississippi. Thus was begun an exodus of major importance for Utah's future. Surely there were no people better prepared than the Mormons to settle a remote, harsh, and distant land. They had the previous experience of building new settlements on several occasions. Their subculture, with its sense of community, respect for the authority of their leaders, unity, and orderliness, made them ideal pioneers for settling the Great Basin. It was now the Mormons' hope to find a remote, untouched wilderness so that they might be left alone to build their unique society.

The premature departure from Nauvoo caused unusual suffering and difficulties. The trek across Iowa was a near disaster, due to inadequate provisions for some families who had left unprepared and with insufficient organization. Cold weather and spring thaws further compounded the problems.

Halfway across Iowa a supply station was established at Garden Grove, and 25 miles farther west Mount Pisgah was founded. Shelters were built and crops planted, and then the Mormons pushed on, knowing that others would follow who would harvest. Even though by mid-June the advance company led by Brigham Young had reached the Missouri River, the generally slow progress across Iowa caused the Mormon leaders to reconsider their plan to continue to the Great Basin in 1846. Instead, they established settlements at Kanesville (now Council Bluffs, Iowa) on the east side of the Missouri River and Winter Quarters west of the river in present Nebraska. By April of 1847, when the pioneer company was ready to begin the trek to Utah, more than 10,000 Mormons were residing in temporary dugouts and log cabins in Iowa and Nebraska.

In the meantime Mormons in the Eastern states prepared to go to California by sea. Coincidentally, on February 4, 1846, the same day the first company of Saints left Nauvoo, the *Brooklyn,* with 238 Mormons aboard, set sail from New York for San Francisco. Samuel Brannan, the leader of Eastern Mormons, saw his charges safely to California and detailed a company to begin an agricultural colony near present-day Modesto. He then rode east to meet Brigham Young to prevail upon him to bring the main Mormon companies on to California. When Brigham Young refused, Brannan left Utah and subsequently became California's first millionaire. He never returned to Utah, and only a few of his group in California ever went to Utah to help build the Mormon Kingdom in the Great Basin.

When war with Mexico erupted in May 1846, President James K. Polk saw an opportunity to respond to several requests from Mormon representatives for aid in their westward migration. He negotiated with Mormon envoy Jesse C. Little to recruit Mormon soldiers to serve in the war. Prospective volunteers in the Mormon Battalion were to be given arms, equipment, and military pay. Captain James W. Allen, under orders from Colonel Stephen W. Kearney, arrived in the Mormon camp at Mount Pisgah and offered to recruit able-bodied men between the ages of 18 and 45 to serve for 12 months.

The loss of so many able-bodied men would definitely make an advance party in 1846 unfeasible and would impose burdens on the families of the recruits who might remain behind. When Brigham Young's non-Mormon friend Thomas L. Kane gave assurances that the federal government had no ulterior motives, that the hard cash paid to the men would be beneficial to the desperately poor migrants, and that they would have government permission to continue to camp on Indian lands, the Mormons decided to participate in the recruitment of 549 men who became the Mormon Battalion.

In addition to the soldiers some families set out with the battalion, traveling south to Fort Leavenworth, where the men were equipped and organized for a march to Santa Fe and then to San Diego. Most of the women and children and about 150 of the men, who had been slowed by sickness, were separated from the battalion—some before and some after reaching Santa Fe—and then were sent in three "sick detachments" to the site of Pueblo, Colorado, to winter. There they found a contingent of 43 Mississippi Mormons, who wintered with the sick detachment and with whom they made their way to the Salt Lake Valley in July of 1847.

The remaining men of the battalion, and five women who had stayed on as laundresses, left Santa Fe on October 19, marching to the Colorado River and to southern California. They arrived in late January 1847, not having fired a shot at a hostile soldier. Their only "dangerous" engagement had been with a herd of ferocious wild bulls west of El Paso.

After serving as troops of occupation, the battalion members were discharged July 16, 1847. About 85 reenlisted for another eight months, and the others planned to go to the Great Basin. However, after meeting with Sam Brannan, about half of the discharged veterans sought winter employment in California, including the six who participated in the gold discovery at Coloma on January 24, 1848. Some of the veterans arrived in Salt Lake in October and November of 1847, and others came to the valley in 1848.

In the meantime, the majority of the exiled Mormons spent the winter of 1846-1847 at Winter Quarters and other sites near the Missouri River. There they faced hunger, exposure, and even death; but active preparations were finalized for sending a pioneer company to choose a definite site for settlement and for the movement of the main body of Mormons. As early as January, Brigham Young announced the basic organizational structure of the migration: companies were divided into groups of tens, fifties, and hundreds, each presided over by a captain. The companies were to be divided so that the poor and the families of the battalion members would be evenly distributed and no group would bear an undue burden. Instructions concerning appropriate ethical and moral behavior were also given. The march to a new home was to be a cooperative and brotherly undertaking.

Along with their commitment to a Christian brotherly exodus "led by God," the Mormons made practical and wise preparations. They gathered scientific instruments that would be useful, such as sextants, barometers, thermometers, and telescopes. Maps based on John C. Fremont's map of 1843, which was published in 1845, were prepared for the companies. Men skilled in needed crafts and trades and the tools of their trades—plows, saws, and other essential equipment—were assembled. During the winter, lectures were given on methods of irrigation should it prove necessary in the arid climate beyond the Rocky Mountains.

In early April the 144 men who were to comprise the select Pioneer Company to mark the trail and choose the settlement site were ready. When one of the men became ill, the Pioneer Company underwent changes, and as it moved out on April 16, 1847, it consisted of 143 men, 3 women, and 2 children.

The Mormon Pioneer Company and the subsequent migration companies of 1847 were noted for the relative ease and efficiency with which they accomplished the trip from Winter Quarters to the Great Basin. Brigham Young personally presided over the Pioneer Company, overseeing virtually every detail and offering continuous advice. In order to reduce contact with the many other immigrants on the Oregon Trail in 1847, the Mormons avoided the main Oregon Trail and traveled on the north side of the Platte River.

After South Pass, along the Big Sandy and Little Sandy rivers, they had occasion to meet and interview several of the mountain men who were personally acquainted with the Great Basin country. Moses Harris, Jim Bridger, and Miles Goodyear were interviewed with great interest and concern. They all voiced some reservations about resources or the growing season in the basin, but generally the information was positive enough to confirm Brigham Young's notion of settling in the vicinity of the Great Salt Lake.

At Fort Bridger the company left the Oregon Trail to take Hastings Cutoff. Near Echo Canyon the immigrant train spread out into smaller sections, due to outbreaks of a disease they believed to be mountain fever. On July 19 a scouting party under Orson Pratt sent to scout the Donner trail of 1846 glimpsed the Salt Lake Valley from Big Mountain. On July 22 the first wagons rolled into the valley. The next day they began plowing and planting, and they dedicated the land to God as a home for the Saints. On the afternoon of July 24 Brigham Young, who was recovering from a severe bout of mountain fever, had his driver stop his carriage so that he might gaze upon the valley from a spot near the present "This is the Place" monument. Wilford Woodruff later recalled that Brigham Young, after a few moments, said, "It is enough. This is the right place, drive on."

Having found an isolated site for their settlement, the Mormons immediately began a cooperative effort to develop the country so that it might blossom like a rose. Crews were appointed to plow, plant, survey, build fences, saw timber, build a public shelter called the "bowery," and explore. They recognized that they were settling a new land where it would be possible to shape society and to root out all that was undesirable. Their wish to build a better world made the isolation of the Great Basin an attraction to them. The Mormons had moved beyond the line of settlement to a remote land hun-

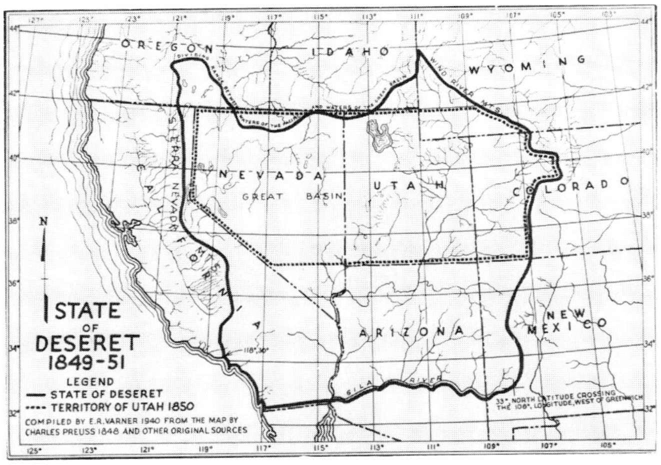

Above: *Brigham Young's original boundaries for the state of Deseret included parts of every Western state except Washington. The other border represents the 1850 territorial boundaries. Photo by E.R. Varner, courtesy, Utah State Historical Society*

Top: *This dramatic scene depicts the final expulsion of the Mormons from Nauvoo in September 1846. Interestingly, copies of this illustration were offered for sale in the 1880s, when the Mormons were once again persecuted, this time for the practice of polygamy. Photo by Charles W. Canter, courtesy, LDS Church Archives*

dreds of miles in any direction from the nearest settled site. It was their wish to be left alone. Their cooperative group characteristic and the experiences they had gained over the previous 17 years made them ideal pioneers for this harsh land. They would move in the directions urged by their leaders.

On July 25 Brigham Young enunciated the principles that were to be followed in the Mormon utilization of this new land. These were in sharp contrast to the highly individualistic approach that characterized most other frontier settlements. No one was to buy or sell land. Everyone was to have land measured to him for a city lot and for farming purposes. Everyone was to be industrious and take care of what he was given. There was to be no private ownership of essential resources such as streams and timber, and only dead timber would be used for fuel.

Once the initial work was well under way, Brigham Young turned over the reins of government to a High Council of 12 men, who oversaw the wards in Salt Lake City. He returned to Winter Quarters, from which word was sent to the Mormons scattered throughout the world that a settlement place had been found and that they should gather at the first opportunity to the "valley," or the land they would call Deseret, at the first from a *Book of Mormon* word meaning "beehive."

The founding of Utah did not represent the completion of

the Mormon Kingdom. More than 100,000 Mormons were organized and brought to Utah from the Eastern states, Europe, and the Pacific islands in the years before Utah achieved statehood. Many of these immigrants were assisted by unique Mormon enterprises such as the Perpetual Emigrating Fund Company and the experiment of the Handcart Companies.

Thousands of Mormon refugees remained in Iowa awaiting evacuation. To facilitate their gathering to the valley, Brigham Young proposed the establishment of a revolving fund that would raise money and volunteer teams to take the poor to the Mormon commonwealth of Deseret. Loans would be made to immigrants, to be paid back and the money used again for others; thus it was a perpetual emigrating fund, or P.E.F.

It was essential, if homes were to be found for all those Young expected to gather to his Kingdom, that the net of Mormon influence be cast wide. Sensing the need to establish the borders of the empire as broadly as possible, Brigham Young set the initial boundaries of the provisional State of Deseret, organized in 1849, to encompass a vast territory.

Almost as soon as the Pioneer Company arrived in Salt Lake Valley, Brigham Young sent out exploring parties to identify potential settlement sites and to claim them for Mormon occupancy. Included in Deseret was most of present-day Utah, Nevada, and Arizona, and large parts of Wyoming, Idaho, Oregon, Colorado, New Mexico, and California. These ambitious boundaries were cut back substantially in the Compromise of 1850, which created Utah Territory. Other reductions occurred until 1868, when Utah was reduced to its present boundaries. Nevertheless, Mormon colonies were established in virtually all of these areas as well as in Mexico and Canada. No wonder Brigham Young is widely regarded as the greatest colonizer of the American West.

Immigration swelled the population of the Utah Territory to 11,380 by 1850. In 1852 the evacuation of Saints from Iowa was completed. Converts in the British Isles now awaited eagerly their turn to embark on chartered ships for America. Until 1855 these converts were sent to New Orleans, up the Mississippi River, and then overland. For health reasons entry into the United States was changed to Philadelphia, New York, or Boston. The immigrants then traveled by rail westward to the Mississippi and later to the railhead as it advanced farther west.

The great financial strain from such immigration activity made it impossible for the P.E.F. to continue to finance the enormous numbers of overland wagon trains needed. Brigham Young therefore suggested a unique plan for handcart travel to Utah. Implemented in 1856, the plan called for equipping immigrants with handcarts at the railhead in Iowa City. These carts would be pushed or pulled to Utah with all of the needed worldly possessions of the Mormon poor. In 1856 five handcart companies with 1,891 immigrants crossed from Iowa City to Salt Lake City. The last two of these, the Willie and Martin companies, left Liverpool late, arrived at Iowa City late, and were further delayed awaiting the construction of handcarts. Their impatience overcame prudence, and they left Iowa City late in July. Early snows trapped them in the mountains, and before relief parties from Utah could accomplish a total rescue, more than 200 members of the Willie and Martin companies had died and many of the survivors had suffered severe frostbite. With Brigham Young warning that any other Mormons so foolish as to leave so late would be cut off from the Church, the experiment continued through the 1860 immigrant season. More than 3,000 Mormons walked from the rail terminus to Salt Lake City, pulling or pushing a handcart.

From Iowa City the Mormon outfitting post went west to Florence, Nebraska, in 1857, and then, as the railroad crept westward, outfitting posts moved to the new railheads farther west. A new plan was for Church teams to pick up freight and passengers at the railhead and bring them to Utah. These teams went out annually in April to meet the arriving immigrants. With the completion of the railroad to Ogden in 1869, immigrants for the first time rode the train all the way to Utah. The first arrivals by rail in June of 1869 closed the Church team operation. Nevertheless, the P.E.F. continued to bring immigrants to Utah until 1887, when the Edmunds-Tucker law, designed to end polygamy and Mormon domination of Utah, disincorporated the company. Between 1850 and 1887 the P.E.F. had aided directly or indirectly more than 100,000 Mormon immigrants to Utah.

The Mormon leaders had overseen the evacuation of Nauvoo, established temporary communities in Iowa and Nebraska, sent soldiers to aid in the conquest of the Mexican Cession Territory, crossed the plains to the Great Basin where they made a permanent settlement, and designated the region as a refuge and domicile for their people. They had then set about with energy and commitment to reclaim Utah's harsh lands with an expanded immigration and colonization program. When one takes into account the origins of Mormonism; the history of persecutions of this people; their unusual beliefs, practices, and society; and their immigration and colonization of a land chosen because it was uninhabited and not regarded as a paradise, then indeed the origin of Utah constitutes a unique story in the settlement of the American West.

Territorial Utah

The first permanent white settlers of Utah, the Mormons, were confronted with the secular goals of growth and survival in their quest to dominate the new homeland they had begun to settle. When they left Winter Quarters in April 1847, they were headed for a land owned by Mexico; but that claim was being challenged by the United States in the Mexican War, which broke out in May of 1846. In February 1848, ownership of the Mexican Cession Territory, was transferred to the United States. The Mormons were once again subject to the laws, policies, and politics of the United States. Regardless of this, the Mormon Church continued to dominate political, social, and economic life in Utah.

Soon the Mormons were to find that their sought-for isolation was a mixed blessing. No one would immediately challenge their ways, but there was no nearby manufacturing or supply center, and the unknown land was yet to prove that it could support large numbers of people. Nevertheless, City Creek was dammed to divert water onto the land to soften it in preparation for plowing and planting. Time and effort

When Johnston's army passed through Salt Lake City, the citizenry had moved south into Utah Valley. All that remained in the deserted city were men ready to set the city ablaze if the army did not peacefully pass through its boundaries.

Above: *In January 1851, Jedediah M. Grant was appointed mayor of Salt Lake City by Brigham Young, and was formally elected by popular vote in April of that same year. The tall and lanky Grant, a close friend of Young, was a commanding figure who presided over the new city with a strong hand. Courtesy, LDS Church Archives*

Above right: *John Smith, an uncle to the prophet Joseph Smith, was called by Brigham Young in the late summer of 1847 to preside over the Salt Lake Valley as president, to govern, along with 12 appointed high councilors, the newly arriving Mormon emigrants.*

Facing page, top: *Originally settled as part of the so-called Mormon corridor to the Pacific, Fillmore was established in part as a stopover for emigrants who were expected to come to Utah from the Pacific. Fillmore was once located in the center of the territory of Deseret and was considered the appropriate location for the territorial capitol. From* A Journey to Salt Lake, *Remy, 1861*

Facing page, bottom: *President Brigham Young would periodically tour the settlements to give council and encouragement. This photograph of Young and his party on the Colorado Plateau in Arizona was taken by pioneer photographer Charles R. Savage in 1870. Courtesy, LDS Church Archives*

demonstrated that irrigation was vital to successful agriculture. For farming purposes, the choice of the Salt Lake Valley as an initial settlement site was most fortunate. This valley was crossed by seven small streams flowing from the Wasatch Mountains on the east, which were fed by melting snows. Canals of short duration, two to three miles, were constructed, and small brush diversion dams were put into place to conduct water to the canals and onto the land. These initial irrigation tasks were accomplished with minimal capital expenditure and effort. This was very fortunate, as the summer was nearly spent and the land needed to be put under immediate cultivation. With little capital to invest and no time to waste, there was perhaps no place in the American West where irrigated agriculture could be initiated as readily as in the Salt Lake Valley.

It was essential that much work be accomplished as quickly as possible before winter set in. Right behind the Pioneer Company were the sick detachments of the battalion and the Mississippi Saints who had wintered in 1846 at Pueblo, Colorado. Behind them came four companies of immigrants from Winter Quarters, numbering about 1,500 people.

Due to several factors the first two years were lived on the edge of poverty and starvation. The crops expected from the July 1847 planting did not materialize. With no vegetables and little flour, it was resourcefulness that saved lives. Indians taught the settlers to dig roots, particularly the bulb of the sego lily, which, in recognition of its lifesaving role, was later designated Utah's state flower.

During the mild weather of the first winter much outdoor work was accomplished, and spring planting was begun as early as March. By May lettuce and radishes were being harvested. The bright prospect for a bountiful harvest was soon blighted, however, as late frost and black-cricket attacks caused considerable damage. Just as many settlers were despairing of harvesting anything more than the early spring vegetables, flocks of California gulls arrived from the Great Salt Lake to devour the swarms of crickets. In gratitude to the gulls for salvaging much of the wheat crop and enough green peas that people became tired of eating them, the gull was named the Utah state bird, and monuments have been built in commemoration.

Having survived the first year, the settlers had high hopes for a better second season in the valley. However, incoming immigrants without adequate food supplies, a harsh, cold second winter, and another cricket invasion imposed a continuing scarcity on Utah's pioneers.

Because of an expected continuing influx of immigrants, no sooner had the Pioneer Company arrived in the valley than Brigham Young dispatched exploring parties to identify and claim further oases for Mormon occupancy. The number of hospitable oases in the Great Basin was indeed limited. Even today less than 4 percent of the state's land is utilized for farming. Brigham Young quickly discovered that the Utah lands that were best and easiest to water were often too cold for anything but limited agriculture. Those areas that were warm enough were often too dry, so farming oases were

sought where streams large enough for irrigation flowed during the heat of the summer months. Not many existed.

An additional consideration in the expansion of the Mormon domain was the drive for self-sufficiency. Natural resources essential for manufacturing were sought. Areas that might support the raising of semitropical crops such as cotton, grapes, sugar cane, madder, mulberries for a hoped-for silk industry, and indigo were sought to complement the row crops and grain crops finally being reliably produced in the north. Since South Pass and the Sierra Nevada were closed five to six months a year by snow, Brigham Young also fostered a string of southern colonies in the hopes of maintaining a year-round route to Utah. Called the Mormon Corridor, these colonies led southward through Utah to the Las Vegas lead mission, to the San Bernardino mission, and on to the port cities of San Diego and Los Angeles.

Above: *Long before taking the oath of office as president, James Buchanan wanted to replace Brigham Young as governor of the Territory of Utah. Accepting the accusations of Judge W. W. Drummond that the Mormons were conducting illegal and un-American activities, Buchanan relieved Brigham Young of his duties as territorial governor and, without investigation, ordered the U.S. Army to escort the new territorial governor to Utah. Courtesy, LDS Church Archives*

Facing page, top: *Utah's second governor, Alfred Cumming, was one of the few territorial governors who attempted to understand the Mormon community. Despite the "Utah War" and the U.S. Army escort that brought him to Utah, Cumming was respected by the Mormon leadership, who were later disappointed when he left for Georgia after the Civil War broke out.*

Facing page, bottom: *When they began their march to Utah from Fort Leavenworth on July 18, 1857, the Tenth Infantry Regiment was under the command of General William S. Harney, who later accepted a different assignment. The regiment did not receive another commander until September when Colonel Albert Sidney Johnston took command of the troops near Hams Fork on the Green River. A late start, the delay in receiving a new commander, and the Rocky Mountain snows prevented the regiment from entering Utah on schedule.*

Some colonies, such as Cedar City, settled in November 1851 to develop iron production, were established for special purposes. Other towns were founded as missions to Indians, and Fillmore was settled as the capital of the newly formed Utah Territory. Nevertheless, the most important and persistent need compelling Mormons to found new colonies was the need for arable land. Most settlement sites had minimal land, water, and timber. As these resources were stretched to their limits, the only way to provide for the additional thousands of newborn children and inflowing immigrants was to found new colonies.

First settled were the desirable locations along the western edge of the Wasatch Mountains. Outliers such as Manti, settled at Ute Chief Walker's request, and Parowan in southern Utah were also settled early. Second, towns were founded in mountain valleys beyond the earliest settlements. Gradually the area of settlement was extended until it was deemed desirable to locate at more remote and difficult spots.

In these colonization endeavors church leaders used central planning of new colonies, complete with the issuance of calls or assignments to settlers. The procedure for town founding usually began with announcements carried in the *Deseret News* requesting volunteers for a projected colonization enterprise. If the volunteers were insufficient or there was a lack of skills in essential crafts and trades among the volunteers, "calls" would be issued. Calls to fill out the colonization lists often came at General Conference, or sometimes they came from the local bishops.

Before leaving, colonists were instructed in what to bring and when and where to assemble. Departures were usually set for fall so that the colonists could arrive in time to build mills, forts, meetinghouses, and irrigation systems, and to make preparations for spring planting. Before embarking on their journey, settlers received sermons emphasizing what was expected in terms of secular pursuits and in brotherhood and cooperation. Each colony was under the supervision of an appointed leader or leaders who organized the migration, kept the inventory of tools and supplies, coordinated work details upon arrival, and directed religious activities. Under collective effort canals were dug, roads built, a meetinghouse constructed, a school organized, gristmills made operational, a post office set up, and elections held. Within a remarkably short time a colonizing mission would create a village from what had been salt grass and sagebrush, and most colonists would stay on to worry a living from the unfriendly lands they had been sent to occupy.

In each community land was given freely to every adult male colonist through drawing lots; natural resources such as water, timber, and mill sites belonged to the community and were regulated in the community interest by the appointed religious leaders. Each Mormon town resembled every other Mormon town. Most were based on agriculture and related trades. Social life focused on religion and education, with the town square and its church as the center place for community life. The strong communitarian system and the village settlement pattern helped facilitate social and educational opportunities. The unity and cooperation of the Mormon system soon caused resentments among the rising tide of non-Mormon travelers through the region and among the small but growing number of non-Mormons who chose to settle in the area.

Nearly all nineteenth-century Mormons had the experience of colonizing new settlements. Mormon immigrants to Utah could look forward to an initial stay in Salt Lake City, and then they would be expected to make their way to villages where laborers were needed or where land was still available. Almost all witnessed the seeming miracle wrought as soon as a new colony was established: satellite towns grew up spontaneously in the vicinity until all available settlement sites were filled. In all, more than 500 Mormon settlements were established in the nineteenth century, and fewer than 50 were abandoned. When one considers the nature of the climate and terrain in which this settlement activity took place, this is a remarkable record. Under the acknowledged

leadership of Brigham Young, the Mormons traveled across uninhabited desert from oasis to oasis to occupy vast tracts of the American West from Mexico to Canada, but the center of all this activity remained Utah and Salt Lake City.

The organization of the Mormon Church had functioned as the instrument of government for Mormons since January 1845, when the Illinois legislature repealed the Nauvoo Charter. Seeking the maximum possible autonomy in political, legal, religious, and economic affairs, and not knowing whether their new homeland would be Mexican or American territory at the end of the Mexican War, the Mormons followed an honored American frontier tradition and set up their own form of government in Utah. However, in their combining church and state they violated another American tradition. The so-called "theodemocracy" the Mormons established was a church government with almost absolute power exercised by church leaders though tempered by the principle of common consent. But in practice, member approval of issues and elected officials was almost always unanimous and perfunctory.

Initially, Brigham Young had left John Smith and two counselors who presided over the High Council in charge of government in Salt Lake City as he returned to Winter Quarters. The High Council performed all the functions of government, including passing laws, executing laws, and trying legal cases.

Upon his return the next spring, Brigham Young assumed the leadership, laying out a series of far-ranging economic and political plans for the development of Deseret. A practical, down-to-earth man, always direct and to the point, he was sometimes perceived by his critics as tyrannical, countenancing no opposition. Rumors even surfaced about blood-atoning Danites, a group of Mormon men reputedly prepared to enforce Brigham Young's autocratic will with violence. These, however, belong to legend and folklore, for there is no historical evidence that the Danites existed after their organizer and leader was excommunicated by Joseph Smith in Missouri in 1838.

The accomplishments of the Mormon Church government were impressive. In the two years of its duration it filled executive, legislative, and judicial functions; passed laws for protection of citizens and provided the ways and means to construct forts, roads, bridges, public buildings, and civic projects; inaugurated a system of currency; and initiated a movement for creation of either a territorial or a state government for Deseret.

On May 3, 1849, Dr. John M. Bernhisel left Utah to carry an application for territorial government to Washington, D.C. In the meantime a meeting was called to plan for a constitutional convention. This assemblage decided to form the State of Deseret. A committee drafted a constitution, an election was soon held for the legislature of the proposed state, and Almon W. Babbitt was sent to Washington to carry the General Assembly's petition for statehood. The political realities of the moment doomed the statehood ambitions, but as a part of the Compromise of 1850 Utah was given territorial status on September 9, 1850.

The State of Deseret government, however, had already begun functioning in March 1849. Like the earlier theodemocracy, it featured prominent churchmen in most elective and appointive positions. Brigham Young served as the governor of this quasi-official government, which rather successfully settled legal disputes, chartered the University of Deseret (which was to become the University of Utah), organized a militia, and made rules and provisions to control and conserve the natural resources of Deseret.

In 1851, when the Territorial Administration appointed by President Millard Fillmore took over, Brigham Young assumed the office of Territorial Governor and Superintendent of Indian Affairs, marking the shift from the quasi-official State of Deseret to the official government of the Territory of Utah. Among the others appointed by Fillmore were three

non-Mormons, whom the Mormons regarded as carpetbaggers, and three Mormons. The Mormon Church continued to dominate Utah political affairs, as Church General Authorities remained the source of first approval for every political nomination in Utah. The members of the Territorial Council and House of Representatives were nominated by church authorities and unanimously elected with no opposition slate for years. One legislative session had such thorough accord that no negative vote was recorded on any action throughout the entire session. The territorial delegates and many other officials in Utah from city councilmen to legislators were quasi-ecclesiastical figures. They were selected by church leaders and, in some instances, set apart—a Mormon Church Priesthood function.

It is little wonder that such practices appeared to be a flagrant violation of American political principles to non-Mormons, who were used to a much more pluralistic and individualistic political and social system than that prevailing in Utah. On the other side of the coin, to Utah Mormons the voting for a handpicked slate of church candidates without electioneering was simply an expression of confidence in trusted leaders. They did not feel any particular need to separate matters of church and state. Mormons were confident that their chosen leaders were vitally interested and involved in

Above: *Having discovered the approaching U.S. Army while en route to Utah from the east, Orrin Porter Rockwell (seen here) rode quickly into Salt Lake City and up Little Cottonwood Canyon where the citizenry was celebrating Pioneer Day (July 24th). The news of an invading army shocked and angered the Mormons, who immediately began to muster the Mormon militia, the Nauvoo Legion. Photo by Savage and Ottinger, courtesy LDS Church Archives*

Above left: *This ennobling sketch of Colonel Albert S. Johnston was published in* Harper's Weekly *in 1857, about the time of the Utah Expedition. Johnston did not agree with the newly appointed governor, Alfred Cumming, who wanted a peaceful end to the so-called "Utah insurrection." Courtesy, Utah State Historical Society*

Facing page: *The sego lily, a beautiful yet simple flower, has an edible bulb root eaten by the first Mormon settlers during the first years of settlement. Courtesy, Utah State Historical Society*

Page 65: *This photo of the bugle corps of the United States Army under the command of Colonel Albert Sidney Johnson was taken around 1858 in Utah. Courtesy, LDS Church Archives*

economic and political aspects of Utah life and that the decisions they made would be for the community's best good. But one-party rule, centralized economic planning, and the open practice of polygamy announced in August 1852 were most vexing to non-Mormons. These "gentiles" also continued to feel that the key to Brigham Young's personal rule was intimidation and terror.

Mormons, however, generally had trust and confidence in him. He ruled absolutely, but more by being preeminently a man of the people than by use of force. People sought his advice on even trivial issues. He oversaw the planning and execution of policy in minute detail. Annual visits were made to all the Mormon towns, where he met with local officials and discussed their concerns. On these tours of his Kingdom he was always readily accessible to his people regardless of their station in life. Brigham Young had the commitment and loyalty of the vast majority of the Mormon people, and they followed him almost as if by instinct.

During the first four years of Utah settlement, three forms of government had been implemented—the church, the State of Deseret, and the Utah territorial government—and in each Brigham Young was the leader. Probably the Mormon people who lived through these transitions could not detect any difference in the way they were governed from one to the next. But Broughton B. Harris, Lemuel Brandebury, and Perry E. Brocchus, the three non-Mormon territorial officials who arrived in 1851, found it difficult and uncomfortable to function in the theocratic setting, and they began to call upon the federal government to correct this aberration—this un-American system. It took the Utah War of 1857 and many difficult years of antagonism to bring satisfaction to the non-Mormon critics.

When the first non-Mormon officials, whom Yale historian Howard R. Lamar described as "political hacks," found their hopes and ambitions thwarted, they left Utah to carry to Washington complaints about the Mormon Church's overshadowing control. These were just the first of many complaints that were to come to the attention of the federal government in the next several years.

The open avowal of polygamy in August of 1852 subjected Mormonism to additional criticism and political strain. In 1856 John C. Fremont, the first presidential candidate of the newly formed Republican party, coupled polygamy with slavery as the "twin relics of barbarism." Democrat James Buchanan, elected in 1856, was eager to show that the Democratic party's support of popular sovereignty on the slavery issue in the territories did not carry over to protection of polygamy in Utah Territory.

During the winter of 1856 territorial officials began to complain that they had no real authority and that the Mormon Church administered the territory to suit itself, sometimes to the detriment of the federal government. On March 30, 1857, Judge W.W. Drummond left Utah Territory and wrote a letter of resignation to President Buchanan, charging that the Mormons were defiant of federal authority and that Brigham Young ruled the territory as a dictator. He recommended the appointment of new territorial officers in conjunction with the sending of an army to Utah to uphold their authority. Although the many specific charges of Drummond and others were for the most part wholly unfounded and grossly exaggerated, they did show that neither Mormons nor non-Mormons had been able to bridge the cultural gap separating the two factions in Utah. Buchanan, predisposed to act against the Mormons, accepted the complaints at face value and determined to appoint new officers complete with military support.

Delays in implementation developed as the president found it difficult to find a man willing and able to replace Brigham Young as governor. He also found that military officers were reluctant to assume command of his proposed army march so late in the year. Finally, Alfred Cumming of Georgia agreed to accept an appointment as governor on July 18, 1857. The 10th Infantry Regiment then marched out of Fort Leavenworth. Destination: Utah. Object: to install Governor-designate Cumming. General William S. Harney, commander of the regiment, found urgent responsibilities in Kansas, and so, belatedly, Colonel Albert Sidney Johnston assumed command of the army that was already marching toward Utah.

Word of the approaching army was delivered to Brigham Young on July 24 as he and 2,587 Mormons were assembled in Big Cottonwood Canyon to celebrate the 10th anniversary of their arrival in Utah. Since Young had received no official notification of his removal as governor, he chose to mobilize the militia and the civilian population to resist the "invading force."

Militiamen under such resourceful officers as Lot Smith and Robert Burton rode east to see to the safety of incoming Mormon immigrants and to spy on the federal troops. Missionaries were summoned home, and the colonists at outlying sites such as San Bernardino, Las Vegas, and Carson Valley were called back to Salt Lake. Fortification of Echo Canyon was begun as stone walls were built rimming the tops of cliffs overlooking the canyon road. Mormons posing as immigrants gained firsthand information about the attitudes and intentions of the soldiers by fraternizing with them. What they heard was alarming, for the soldiers talked in most belligerent terms of their desires and intentions toward the Mormons.

These reports convinced many Mormons that the army intended to destroy them.

When Captain Stewart Van Vliet arrived in Salt Lake City on September 7 to make arrangements for provisioning the troops for the winter, Brigham Young warned him he could expect no help from the Mormons. Rather than let the enemy possess their improvements and possessions, they would lay waste to the land, burn homes, fields, and businesses.

Mormon militiamen thoroughly familiar with the countryside reinforced the Mormon intention to resist by conducting a persistent, bloodless guerrilla war against the federal army. Cattle were stampeded, wagons and supplies were burned and confiscated, range that army cattle might forage upon was burned. Under the cover of darkness fearless riders galloped through the army camp, stampeding horses and mules and causing consternation. Virtually anything short of shedding blood was employed to delay the army. The tactics worked, for the army bogged down in unseasonably cold weather and deep snow near Fort Bridger.

When Colonel Johnston caught up with his troops, they were ordered to head to Fort Bridger, which the Mormons had purchased from Jim Bridger two years earlier. Because armed mountain men would not permit the Mormons to take possession of the fort when they first attempted to do so, the Mormons built Fort Supply about twenty miles away. The Mormon Legion preceded the army to both forts and burned them to the ground. Colonel Johnston was thus compelled to set up winter camp near burned-out Fort Bridger at a site he called Camp Scott. The nearly 2,500 men and the hundreds of civilian camp followers settled in for a cold, miserable winter.

Brigham Young had hoped that if the army could be kept out of Utah until June of 1858, a peaceful settlement might be reached. In February his hopes were raised when Colonel Thomas L. Kane arrived in Salt Lake, having traved from Washington, D.C. under the pseudonym of Dr. A. Osborne, coming by sea to California and on to Utah as an unofficial negotiator. From Salt Lake he proceeded to Camp Scott to urge Governor Cumming to go to Salt Lake under Mormon escort to meet personally with Brigham Young. Cumming accepted and found that he was received with respect. He and Brigham Young agreed that the troops could pass through Salt Lake, but a permanent campsite would be established a day's journey away in Cedar Valley. Salt Lake would be emptied of citizens except for men detailed to light fires if the soldiers on their passage through should molest any property.

After these preliminary agreements were reached, Kane returned to report to the president while Cumming returned to the army to await the arrival of peace commissions that could bring an official pardon to Brigham Young and the Mormons and thus conclusively resolve the stalemate. The commissions arrived in Salt Lake on June 7, and on June 12 they announced that the differences had been settled. In return for amnesty the Mormons accepted the establishment of a federal military fort in their midst. On June 26, 1858, the army passed through the abandoned city to establish Camp Floyd in Cedar Valley, forty miles to the southwest of Salt Lake. Although the Utah War with its peaceful conclusion had displaced Brigham Young as governor, elected Mormon officials continued to seek and accept his advice on matters of state, even though he now held no formal political office.

The war, known to Mormons as Buchanan's Blunder, did not directly bring about any loss of human life, but indirectly it had some tragic results for immigrants of the Fancher Party traveling through southwestern Utah. Furthermore, it imposed a heavy burden upon the Mormons that caused a strain in relationships with federal officials for years.

In the fall of 1857 the Fancher Party, an immigrant company of non-Mormons from Arkansas, began traveling through Utah along the southern route to California. Unfortunately this was a time of extreme tension in Utah, due to the federal army's approach. One Mormon leader, Franklin D. Richards, had ordered that Utah settlers were to save their food and supplies for whatever eventualities might come with the war. The Mormons were ordered not to sell or trade as much as a kernel of grain to strangers. Mormon refusal to trade angered the immigrants, who then began to commit unwise acts aimed at antagonizing the Mormons. On occasion they took what they wanted. They swore at and otherwise verbally abused the Mormons. Some boasted of participation in the persecution of Mormons in Missouri and Illinois. Others threatened that when they reached California they would send back an army to assist Johnston in crushing the Mormons. Mormons and Indians both reported that the members of the Fancher Party poisoned water holes and gave some poisoned meat to unsuspecting victims.

Tensions were also worsened by the delicate relationships between the Indians and Mormons in southern Utah. One of the charges against the Mormons was that they stirred up Indians to commit depredations on non-Mormons. Mormons had maintained relatively good relationships with Indians. In fact, the Indians classified whites as "Mormonee" ("Mormons" or "friends") and "Mericats" (non-Mormons who were, therefore, suspect).

Good relations began with the fortunate fact that the Salt Lake Valley was a buffer zone between the various tribes and not the regular habitat of any tribe. This meant that the Mormons were not yet encroaching on the territorial claims of any group. As they moved out of the Salt Lake Valley to take up additional settlement sites, the Mormons intruded on tribal territory in nearly any direction they moved. But the full implications of settlement in the Great Basin did not occur to the Indians until the Mormons were too numerous to be driven out.

The Indians did not generally inhabit the mountains or deserts when they had a choice but rather chose those lowlands where water and land combined to produce heavy grasses and, thus, abundant game. These were precisely the same areas the white settlers spotted as ideal for agriculture. Even though the Mormons generally distrusted and feared Indians and were shocked by their poverty and life-style, they had a different attitude toward Indians than most frontiersmen. The *Book of Mormon* spoke of a group of once-enlightened people of Hebrew descent who had become wild, dark skinned, and undisciplined through sin. However, the book promised a special destiny to "Lamanites" (Indians) through conversion to Mormonism. Believing this, Mormons made extraordinary efforts to befriend and convert the Indians.

Generally, Mormons welcomed the opportunity to do missionary work among the Indians and followed conciliatory policies toward them in order to gain their love and confidence. However, Mormons were ambivalent in their attitudes toward the Indians, for they heard tales of their atrocities, saw them kill one another, experienced their theft, and were repelled by what they regarded as their squalor. So the widespread animosity of frontiersmen towards the Indians was shared by Mormons, but it was tempered by their teaching, beliefs, and a keen sense that fairness and justice ought to apply to all people.

When Mormons moved onto Indian lands in Tooele Valley, Utah Valley, and San Pete Valley, they began plowing and fencing and did not offer to pay for the land. Disagreements ensued and warriors were killed. In one engagement of militia in Utah Valley, thirty-five Indians were killed in a nine-day campaign. But, for the most part, Brigham Young worked to maintain harmonious relations, and settlers and Indians fraternized and aided each other.

This peaceful coexistence was occasionally marred by outbursts of violence on both sides. From 1853-1854 the so-called Walker War was fought, and the Tintic War occurred in 1856. Both "wars" were provoked by continuing encroachments of whites on tribal lands and by acts of reciprocation by Indians. Both were more skirmishes than wars,with some loss of life on each side followed by eventual resolution. In the Walker War twelve whites and an unknown number of Indians were killed, and the Tintic War, which was really one confrontation, resulted in the deaths of three whites and several Indians. But there were no persistent campaigns urging extermination of the Indians, and Mormons usually pursued a benevolent policy toward them. Violence was not common, and when it occurred it was on a limited scale.

In 1857 the Mormons were anxious to placate Indians and hoped to make use of them as allies if the Utah War became a shooting war. Due to the two recent Indian wars, Mormons were fearful of retribution by Indians on Mormon settlements if the Mormons were not cooperative in some of the Indian desires. The Indians knew of the Utah War and Brigham Young had told Captain Van Vliet that he would no longer "hold the Indians by the wrist."

Under these circumstances, the Fancher party was inadequately advised about the alienation of the Indians. Nevertheless, the Fancher party made it southward past Cedar City to the lush and favored campsite at Mountain Meadows on the Old Spanish Trail. Indians had been threatening to attack, and the Mormons at Cedar City were stirred up by the insulting actions of the company as it passed through Iron County. On Sunday, September 6, 1857, at a special High Council meeting, a discussion was held about what to do relative to the company that had recently caused so much consternation.

Mormons were already acting to stir up the Indians and incite an attack. A resolution was adopted to send James Haslam to Salt Lake to ask Brigham Young what to do. Without awaiting word, an Indian attack was launched on Monday

Thomas L. Kane created a long and enduring friendship with the Mormons by encouraging President James K. Polk to call the Mormon Battalion when war broke out with Mexico in May, 1846. During the so-called "Utah War," Kane traveled to Utah to negotiate the terms of peace between Brigham Young and Johnston's army. Courtesy, Utah State Historical Society

morning, September 7, which resulted in the death and wounding of some in the Fancher Party. They quickly circled their wagons and a siege began. The Indians turned to their Mormon instigators, demanding help to consummate a victory over the beleaguered immigrants. When three men from the besieged camp seeking aid were killed by Mormons, the local Mormon leaders decided they could not wait for Brigham Young's advice, which arrived September 13, and urged that the company be saved even if it took all the men in southern Utah. Under a flag of truce John D. Lee, who had been called to Mountain Meadows to manage the Indians, convinced the immigrants to lay down their arms in return for a promise of safe conduct back to Cedar City. The fifty-four Mormon militiamen who were at Mountain Meadows on Friday, September 11, acting under military orders, then killed the disarmed men while the Indians killed the women and older children. Altogether 120 immigrants were killed. Seventeen children under two years of age were spared and ultimately, through federal appropriations, were returned to their relatives in Arkansas and Missouri.

Federal attempts to apprehend and punish the participants were foiled by the tight-knit Mormon society, which closed ranks and protected its members. Lee was apprehended in November of 1874 and, following two trials, was executed in March of 1877 by a firing squad at the scene of the massacre.

The tragedy at Mountain Meadows was a bizarre aberration, but it did happen and it will not go away. To Mormon and non-Mormon it was a grievous event, and to Mormons it has remained a painful burden that went against every principle of their faith.

Another carryover of the Utah War was unlike the burden imposed by the Mountain Meadow Massacre. Camp Floyd, established by the army, came to be an economic bonanza for the Mormons. The fort provided opportunities for contracts for goods and services of all kinds. When Camp Floyd was abandoned in 1861 with the outbreak of the Civil War, some $4 million worth of surplus goods was sold to Utahns for a small fraction of their actual purchase value.

The year after Camp Floyd closed, Fort Douglas was established on the foothills east of Salt Lake overlooking the city, thus restoring the outward symbols of the sovereignty of the United States. From this point until statehood, Mormons were made very much aware of the federal presence, which was now represented by Colonel Patrick Edward Connor and the California Volunteers stationed at Fort Douglas. They put the Mormons on notice, particularly through their newspapers, the *Valley Tan* and the *Union Vedette,* that they would not be left alone again. Americans were not going to allow the Mormon people, who were so different in values and aims, to pursue their unique society, even though they lived hundreds of miles in any direction from the nearest non-Mormon territory. The Mormons' economic cooperation, political unity, and polygamy would continue to be sources of controversy and political conflict for years to come.

When the Mormons first arrived in Utah, Ute Indians believed they could continue their lives unaffected by the newcomers. However, as the settlers moved out of the Salt Lake Valley and onto traditional Indian lands used for living and hunting, the Utes became alarmed. Chief Wahkara, shown here with his brother, Arapeen, led the Ute in a war that lasted a year, ending with a document of peace signed by Wahkara and Brigham Young.

Pioneer Society and Culture

Opening a frontier was never easy. Building forts, houses, public buildings, and barns; plowing and planting; building fences and putting in roads and mills was backbreaking work. If the work was not enough, the loneliness from being cut off from the cultural and social institutions that enriched the lives of those in more established areas increased the burden for pioneers on almost all American frontiers. Often few institutions of government and law enforcement were available, and even schools and churches were few or nonexistent. Despite these considerations the Great Basin was chosen as the Mormons' new homeland in order to gain isolation, so that these displaced people could attempt without outside interference to build their model of the ideal society. Under these circumstances, a conscious effort was made to provide the amenities of cultural life for the Utah Mormon pioneers.

The strong sense of community they had cultivated con-

The Ebenezer Beesley Band gathered in the studio of Savage and Ottinger for this group portrait in about 1868. Musical bands were valued highly by nineteenth century Utahns, so much so that most Mormon communities could boast of a fine musical band not long after settlement. Beesley, who was a noted Salt Lake City businessman and musician, would later serve as the conductor of the Mormon Tabernacle Choir. Courtesy, LDS Church Archives

Above: *In 1862 Commander Patrick Connor, pictured, and the California volunteers marched into Salt Lake Valley with orders to establish a fort and protect the emigrant roads in and around Utah. Connor chose to establish the camp on the foothills east of Salt Lake City, from which he could also monitor the activities of the Mormons. Courtesy, LDS Church Archives*

Facing page, top: *Named after Stephen A. Douglas, Lincoln's presidential rival, Fort Douglas, located east of Salt Lake City, was established in 1862 to protect emigrants on the overland trail. The Mormons were not enthused by the army's presence so near Salt Lake City, but did enjoy the army dollars spent in the city. Courtesy, LDS Church Archives*

Facing page, bottom: *Photographer Charles W. Canter took his cumbersome camera equipment near Echo Canyon and photographed this Mormon emigration train in 1867. Courtesy, LDS Church Archives*

vinced the Mormons that it was better to do things together through cooperative effort. It was good for people to live close together in towns rather than scattered on individual farmsteads. Lone genius was not highly honored. Among these remarkably orderly and unified people, dissent was frowned upon. The finest accomplishments of mankind in their eyes were those of the community and not those of the individual.

From the outset cultural life centered on the community. Mormons did not rush off individually in pursuit of precious metals unless called to do so on behalf of the church. They founded towns cooperatively and in doing so drew lots for farm and town properties. The general layout of Mormon towns was characterized by broad streets, a church square, farms outside of town, brick construction (where and when possible), and houses set back from the sidewalks. The wide streets had ditches running on both sides with water used for culinary and irrigation purposes. Lombardy poplars stood in stately rows along the streets. North-south and east-west streets all intersecting at right angles and often even having the same street names from one town to another were a common characteristic.

In the colonization phase, a fort was almost always the first structure built. As it went up, the settlers lived in wagon boxes, tents, and dugouts. When the first permanent homes were built, they were often log houses, and many continued to stand in use in barnyards or as outbuildings for years. Due to considerations made in selecting a town site, most Mormon towns were located near a canyon that became a favorite recreational site for outings and picnics, but that on a more practical level supplied water, timber, and mountain pasturage. Even so, conveniently accessible lumber was usually limited, and so adobe became a common building material.

In this harsh land not particularly blessed with natural resources for farming, the Mormon commonwealth quickly and in defiance of nature became a land of small farming communities. Wheat, maize, oats, potatoes, peas, and beans were the predominant crops in early Utah. Brigham Young stressed agriculture as the essential base for the developing Mormon Kingdom. He had expressed his determination to cut every thread tying the Utah economy to the outside world. Even had it not been his desire to sever economic ties, the isolation of Utah meant that the Mormon people had to be largely self-sufficient in the production of foodstuffs. The flow and timing of immigration required a surplus of food each year. The thousands of new arrivals often had spent their savings on the journey to Utah and were nearly destitute upon their arrival. They had to be fed until the next season, when they might participate in the new seasonal harvest.

The production of food therefore came before any other economic need or consideration. Since wheat, vegetables, hay, and livestock, rather than gold or silver, were felt to be key products in making a people wealthy, suggestions were often circulated for improving farming. The Deseret Agricultural and Manufacturing Society was organized to experiment with different varieties of crops and livestock to determine which might do best in this new land. Lucerne (alfalfa) and fruits of various kinds were found to do well and were encouraged in various ways. Cotton production and the silk industry were also experimented with in Utah's Dixie to enhance the prospects for self-sufficiency.

The early years on the remote frontier in Utah were rather primitive. Homes were simple and unadorned, trade was minimal, and famine often threatened. Heavy goods such as iron and nails, high-bulk items including bolts of cloth and rolls of paper, and fragile products such as window glass and china were all in high demand in early Utah. However, the prices for such goods were exorbitant, due partly to shortage and heavy demand but mostly to the high cost of transportation.

Very soon the supply of these items that had been brought to Utah by the pioneers was nearly exhausted. In most instances people did without, since they were unable to produce replacements themselves and were too poor to order new ones from the states. In a seemingly miraculous manner the problem of supplying some scarce necessities was temporarily overcome. The gold discovery in California in January of 1848 was followed by President James Polk's announcement to the nation the following December that precipitated the gold rush of 1849. The California-bound gold-seekers streaming through the Salt Lake Valley were eager to pay hard cash

for foodstuffs, repairs, and fresh livestock. They sometimes bartered scarce merchandise for goods and sometimes, in their eagerness to get to the goldfields, abandoned whole wagonloads of merchandise that was scarce and dear in Utah. At best, however, this was only a stopgap solution.

Lacking financial institutions and subsisting on an extreme scarcity of hard cash, Utahns also benefited temporarily from the gold and silver infused into the isolated economy by the gold-seekers. This, however, was not enough to provide for the capital formation necessary to establish the manufacturing that could make Utah self-sufficient. The growing demand for Eastern goods soon drained the hard cash and contributed to an adverse balance of trade between Utah and the states.

Above: *The arts were not ignored by the Mormon pioneers, who began organizing cultural societies, musical groups, and theatrical associations shortly after arriving in the Great Basin. The Salt Lake Theater, completed in 1862, was an expression of the pioneer community's appreciation of the arts. This photo of the Salt Lake Theater was taken in the 1890s after a number of remodelings of the interior. Courtesy, Utah State Historical Society*

Facing page: *St. George was once the winter home of Brigham Young in the 1870s. In the distance is the St. George Temple, the first such structure completed by the Mormons on the Wasatch Front. The orderly and well-organized streets, homes, and trees can be seen from this view. Courtesy, LDS Church Archives*

It seemed then that the only permanent solution lay in building up manufacturing in Utah. For most of the nineteenth century the Mormon Church did everything possible to encourage the growth of manufacturing. Early efforts included a paper factory; a sugar plant; iron manufacturing; the making of glass products; furniture, nail, silk, and tanned-leather plants; and woolen and cotton mills.

For a people financially barely able to transport themselves across the plains, it proved very difficult to save enough to finance such ambitious industrial development. For a time a circulating medium was provided by gold coins minted by the Mormon Church from several thousand dollars in gold dust brought back by men sent by Brigham Young to California to prospect for the church. From time to time various printed currencies were also used, backed by items of value such as cattle. Military posts—Camp Floyd, established in 1858, and Fort Douglas, in 1862—also paid cash for supplies and services. This proved another windfall to the Utah economy. But it was the Mormon tithing system that became the biggest commercial and financial institution in early Utah. The Mormon institution of tithing provided the capital necessary to launch the various industrial enterprises undertaken through church backing.

In each community a local Bishop's Storehouse was established to accept contributions to the church. It was expected that all faithful Mormons would contribute 10 percent of their increase. Much of what was contributed in the early period in Utah was in the form of commodities—whatever the individual might have produced. These commodities could be used for the poor; the surplus could be marketed or it could be sent to another community where production was down or times hard. If the bishop needed men to work on a road, canal, or public project, he could pay workers in tithing scrip. The holder could then present it at the tithing office for goods or he could exchange it with others for goods or services. If it was exchanged for his services, for example, the holder could then present the scrip at the tithing office for beef, flour, or whatever.

The tithing office also provided services similar to modern-day banking transactions. For example, if a man were going to be traveling through Utah, he could deposit items at the local tithing office in exchange for tithing scrip. Then as he traveled he could exchange his deposit credit in his local tithing office, represented by the scrip, for goods along the way, thus eliminating the need to transport so much with him on his journey. Or he could make a deposit in his local tithing office and make transfers so that someone residing in another part of the territory could withdraw without actually having

to transport the product.

The tithing system greatly facilitated exchange and also involved itself in taxation, public-works projects, welfare, warehousing, general distribution, retail and wholesale merchandising, and cooperative management and banking. Through it the church leaders could also control economic development by diverting surpluses from one activity and allocating them to another, more favored activity. Tithing contributions were also used to support colonization, to redistribute local products, and to build a surplus for investment in manufacturing.

Despite the success of the tithing system, Mormons in time increased their desire and demand for imported goods. Even though Brigham Young favored local manufacture and strongly opposed importation, the demand for imported items increased. An increasingly brisk trading business fell almost by default into the hands of non-Mormons. As the transcontinental railroad inched its way across the nation toward Utah in the 1860s, it was clear that its arrival would facilitate an increased trade in imported items. Brigham Young therefore determined that if the merchandising of outside goods was inevitable, it should be controlled by Mormons.

Beginning in 1866, the Mormon Church supported a boycott of non-Mormon stores. By early 1869 Brigham Young had put together an elaborate plan for a church-sponsored mercantile system. A community store was to be formed in each town as a local retail outlet. Stock was to be issued in such small denominations that all could invest as stockholders. The mother store of this system, known as Zion's Cooperative Mercantile Institution (ZCMI), was to serve as the primary importer and wholesaler of goods. The ZCMI system was to be a community-owned and -managed retail outlet for imported and home-manufactured goods in every Mormon town. With Mormons asked to patronize only the cooperative stores, the ZCMI system was bound to flourish. In all, more than 150 local cooperative stores were established in all parts of the Mormon Kingdom. Eventually the wealthier citizens came to monopolize the shares of stock, and the stores lost much of their cooperative nature.

The substantial profits accruing to the ZCMI cooperatives were reinvested by the Mormon Church in the founding of industries. Manufacturing in textiles, sawmills, shoe shops, dairies, furniture factories, broom factories, and other areas expanded. Nevertheless, Mormons became increasingly involved with the gentile world. The hope of building a society that was economically self-sufficient was never quite fulfilled. In time many Mormon-developed industries fell to the relentless competition of the outsiders or were taken over by non-Mormon interests.

In spite of all the energy directed toward self-sufficiency for pioneer Utah society, there was still opportunity for an active social life. Much of this focused on church and educational activities, but even the recreational outlets—music, dance, dramatic presentations—were closely affiliated with Mormon Church endeavors. Considering the poverty of the people and the stage of settlement they lived in during much of the nineteenth century, cultural life in Utah was rich, ambitious, and rather advanced.

Brigham Young once said, "If I were given the task of civilizing people, I should straightaway build a theater for the purpose." Indeed he did just that in Utah! One feature of early Utah recreational and cultural life was drama. Very early

many communities established active dramatic associations. The first building used for cultural activities in Utah was the bowery built in 1847 on Temple Square. In 1852 cultural performances were moved to the old Social Hall, on Social Hall Avenue between South Temple and First South streets. Then in 1861-1862 the Old Salt Lake Theatre was built, and it became one of the most famous cultural landmarks of the American West as well as the social center of the territory. Its completion assured that, as the Mormon people found the time and means for entertainment and socializing, the arts and letters would find expression.

Another form of relaxation that found great favor among the Mormons was dancing. Holiday observances usually ended with dances that might last until 2 or 3 a.m. Even the Salt Lake Theatre did not take a back seat to dancing. Its design permitted the covering of the orchestra seats with a floor that allowed for conversion to a large dance hall. It seemed that everyone from Brigham Young down enjoyed dances, provided there were not too many risque dances such as the waltz on the dance program.

Music also played an important recreational and cultural role in pioneer Utah. It symbolized the Mormon determination in even the most depressing circumstances. William Clayton's hymn "Come, Come, Ye Saints," became a song of inspiration and defiance in the face of obstacles. William Pitt, an English convert to Mormonism, had organized Pitt's Brass Band in Nauvoo. It also entertained and cheered the Saints across the trail from Illinois to Utah and continued to cheer them in the valley for years to come. Music performed by brass bands, military bands, orchestras, and string bands, and renditions by choral and choir groups entertained and heartened Utahns on numerous occasions.

Choral performances have always been a part of Mormon Church worship. The Mormon Tabernacle Choir came to set the standard for musical renditions and organizations. Conducted in the nineteenth century by such talented musicians as Charles J. Thomas, George Careless, Ebenezer Beesley, and Evan Stephens, the choir grew in talent and reputation.

Today the Mormon Tabernacle Choir probably best represents Utah's cultural achievement. The nearly 400 voice performing group is the official choir of the Mormon Church. In 1929 it began a series of weekly broadcasts over CBS which became the longest continuous coast-to-coast series in American radio broadcast history. The choir began recording with the Philadelphia Symphony Orchestra in the 1940s and their combined rendition of "Battle Hymn of the Republic" won a Grammy Award in 1959. It has also made several acclaimed national and international tours and has performed at presidential inaugurals.

The visual arts did not match the cultural level attained by the theater and music. Though represented in Utah, they were not widely supported. Some talented Utahns of the nineteenth century were sent by the Mormon Church to France, where they were expected to develop their skills in order to decorate the walls of Mormon temples. Much of this type of art was didactic and directed toward the functional end of inspiring and promoting faith.

It could also be said that Utah pioneer architecture was not distinguished. Much was borrowed and adapted. Early on, adobe was the main building material. The homes were functional but not particularly unique architecturally. Log houses were also common in early Utah. After 1860 brick became a much more commonly used building material, and homes began to be more elaborate, but the architecture remained mainly borrowed and adapted.

Nineteenth-century Utahns also did not produce great literature. However, since Mormons were encouraged to keep journals and written records, there is a surprising amount of writing for a pioneering people. Much of the writing, both published and within the journals, was polemical and defensive. The Mormon poet Eliza R. Snow led in the production of poetry; much of it was devotional. Newspapers were everywhere a popular reading item. Beginning with the *Deseret News,* first published in 1850, and extending to local papers and the later gentile papers, the newspapers were important dispensers of information.

Brigham Young had insisted that "the people must have amusement as well as religion." As a result, citizens of the territory, whether they lived in Salt Lake City or isolated Mormon colonies, could participate in a variety of cultural and social activities. On long winter nights when the farm work was minimal, people might be found at local literary or poetry societies. They might attend debating or discussion societies, join drama groups, attend dramatic presentations or musical performances. The talented and desirous had many opportunities to participate; the others, many opportunities to be entertained.

The planned closeness of life in small-town Utah fostered a rich social and cultural tradition that would have been unattainable on scattered individual farmsteads. Town life promoted defense, schools, religious activity, moral progress, cooperative labor, and cultural activity. Pioneer Utahns continued the acute social consciousness first developed by Mormons during the Kirtland and Missouri era of Mormonism. However, some found this way of life oppressive. It was difficult for a dissenter to go his own way, but nevertheless some did. Among the most notorious of Utah's wayward was Butch Cassidy. Born Robert LeRoy Parker, he was raised in the central Utah town of Circleville. Utah's most famous outlaw, Parker turned to the Wild Bunch, where he became famous as Butch Cassidy.

There were other ways of dissenting, such as leaving the practices and beliefs. Some "Jack Mormons" (non-practicing members) who apostatized stayed in Utah despite intoler-

Above: *The railroad altered both the social and physical landscape of Utah, bringing increased goods, services, and opportunities to the once isolated Mormon commonwealth. Here, two silhouetted figures pose in the man-made channel through the Rocky Mountains. It is somewhat ironic that the territory of Utah, with its desire for isolation, would be the meeting place of the transcontinental railroad. Photo by James Crockwell, courtesy, Brigham Young University Photo Archives*

Facing page: *A party of Mormon women and children separate silkworm cocoons from mulberry leaves, which were used to make silk cloth. Mulberry trees were planted throughout the territory in hopes of developing a silk industry. Photo by George Edward Anderson, courtesy, LDS Church Archives*

Even though only a few could be considered men or women of letters, early Utah did have its promising literati. Sarah Elizabeth Carmichael was one of Deseret's fledgling young poets in the 1860s. Photo by Savage and Ottinger, courtesy, Brigham Young University Photo Archives, Anthony Street Collection

ance from the Mormon faithful. The most sizable defection came with the Godbeite heresy of 1869-1871. William S. Godbe led a group of prominent Mormons who opposed the economic programs of the church leadership. He also advocated rapproachment with federal officials and the gentiles residing in Utah. In October 1869 Godbe and others were excommunicated. It was Godbe and his followers who opposed Utahn agrarian isolation and who met in Corinne in July of 1870 with Colonel Connor to found the anti-Mormon Liberal Party.

The cities and villages and Mormon way of life were certainly distinctive. But the American westward movement began to catch up with Utah. When it did, non-Mormons in significant numbers began to arrive and to exert an influence on Utah's society and culture. A second Utah, consisting of military forts and mining and railroad towns, was emerging to challenge the Mormon dominance of society.

As early as August 1849, Captain Howard Stansbury of the United States Corps of Topographical Engineers arrived in Utah with a surveying party to explore and map. His findings and those of subsequent government explorers influenced later stagecoach and railroad routes through Utah. Overland freighting, the stagecoach, the Pony Express and the telegraph all served to put Utah more into the mainstream of travel and communication. But it was the coming of the transcontinental railroad, completed at Promontory Summit in May of 1869, that more than any other event opened a new era in Utah. The railroad tied Utah more closely to the economy and culture of the nation and ended the isolation of the Mormon Kingdom once and for all.

The sudden influx of people coincident with the coming of the railroad added a whole new dimension to life in Utah Territory. Though there had been a few government officials, merchants, former Mormons, and drifters in Utah, the population had remained predominantly Mormon until well into the 1860s.

In 1862 the Third California Volunteers, a United States military company, was sent to Utah under the command of Colonel Patrick Edward Connor to protect overland mail routes during the Civil War. Connor was stridently anti-Mormon and made it his personal undertaking to reshape Utah along less unique lines. In the pages of the *Union Vedette* he sought effective ways to diminish the Mormon influence in Utah.

Connor strongly opposed Brigham Young's economic priorities. It had been claimed that gold and silver were to be found in Utah. If so, widespread prospecting was bound to unearth it. The resulting rush of prospectors, miners, and suppliers would overwhelm the Mormons and institutionalize more traditionally American ways in Utah.

In 1863, after Mormon ranchers had discovered silver in Bingham Canyon, Connor actively promoted prospecting. Thereafter, gold and silver were found in Little and Big Cottonwood canyons, in Parley's Canyon, and on the western slope of the Oquirrh Mountains at Ophir and Stockton. In 1875 rich galena ore was found at the Horn Silver Mine in Beaver County, which led to the founding of the boom town of Frisco and the completion of the Southern Utah Extension Railroad into southern Utah in 1880. Also in 1875 silver was discovered in sandstone near Leeds, resulting in the founding of Silver Reef. The mining industry had been opened in Utah.

Precious-metal production remained limited and provided only a minimal return prior to the completion of the transcontinental railroad. Its completion in 1869 dramatically increased mining activity and attracted the thousands of nonMormons to Utah that Connor had hoped for.

Soon the number of miners in the territory was significant. To supply their wants and needs merchants and traders flocked into Salt Lake City and other places where mining activity was becoming hectic. The boom towns in the mining districts inhabited by the miners and their suppliers were worlds apart from the farm towns of the Mormons. In life-style the narrow main streets offered a variety of amusements unknown in the Mormon towns. Physically, these boom towns consisted of ramshackle unpainted structures situated in a random fashion along the twisting narrow canyons that constituted the streets. Significantly, the gentile population of Utah increased by more than 400 percent in less than ten years. This infusion of non-Mormons soon provided graphic evidence that the political system, the public social services such as schools and hospitals, and diversified religious worship were woefully inadequate in Utah.

The railroad had also introduced into Utah gentile-dominated railroad towns that vied with Mormon communities to become transportation centers. In 1869 Corinne, the first Utah town settled by non-Mormons, began its short and colorful career as a transportation and trading center. But Mormon-built extensions, such as the Utah Central Railroad linking Salt Lake City to the transcontinental line and bypassing Corinne, shortened Corinne's existence. Nevertheless, Corinne had introduced into Utah a railroad town with its gentile influences.

Prior to this influx of population, non-Mormons in Utah tended to be small in number, mostly federal government officials and their wives, who were usually cultured and of relatively high social standing. Most adhered to the Episcopal faith. The Bishop Daniel S. Tuttle, who served the Utah Episcopal community from 1867 to 1885, was among the first to recognize the need for an alternative school system for the non-Mormon children. As a result, he established St. Mark's Day School in 1867, and he later founded other schools in communities besides Salt Lake City.

It was not only in education that Mormons tended to provide for their needs within their own system. In health care as well, they seemed unaware that the needs of non-Mormons were not being met. Mormons, preferring midwifery and the healing of illness with prayers and home remedies, had established no health-care facilities in Utah. In 1872 Bishop Tuttle established St. Mark's as the first hospital in the territory.

Many of the soldiers stationed in early Utah at Camp Floyd and Fort Douglas were Roman Catholic. When railroad and mine workers began to arrive, many of them were also Roman Catholic. Initially, itinerant priests performed services for these people. Even though several others had preceded him, the Reverend Lawrence Scanlan became the best known and the most vigorous Roman Catholic priest. From 1873 until his death in 1915, he directed Catholic activities in Utah. Because he and his followers were not very evangelical in their activities, the Catholics generally had good interchurch relations with the Mormons. Like Tuttle, Scanlan saw the need for building schools and hospitals as well as orphanages and, of course, churches. With the completion of the railroad and the increase in mining activity, the Catholic congregations scattered widely throughout Utah grew considerably and became the largest religious body in the territory after the Mormons' majority.

Very early in Utah's development resident merchants, who were often Jewish, arrived. They were the first non-Mormon ethnic people to come to Utah in significant numbers. Services were held in Salt Lake City for the members of the Jewish merchandising and trading families as early as 1864. The relationships between Jews and Mormons were generally satisfactory other than when Mormon exclusionary commercial policies bore down heavily on Jewish and other non-Mormon trading firms.

Presbyterian and Methodist missionary work began in 1869, marking a new era both socially and religiously for Utah. Religious affiliation became more than ever a basis for differentiation. The Catholic, Jewish, and Episcopal churches served mainly members of their own faith already residing in Utah. The evangelical churches sent ministers to Utah not because they had significant membership needing pastoral care but more as missionaries to convert the Mormons. The position of the Protestant evangelical religious groups was so decidedly anti-Mormon that social tensions were inevitable.

When the evangelical ministers found themselves isolated in a sea of Mormonism without a base from which to work, they emulated the works of Tuttle and Scanlan and began building schools. However, unlike their predecessors, these schools were not primarily to provide education for gentiles but to better educate young Mormons and woo them away from Mormonism. Within 25 years evangelical Protestant groups spent more than $1,500,000 in an effort to provide a superior education in Utah. They opened 75 schools and 53 churches and, in the process, did provide superior education.

However, in the 1890s the church schools began a rapid decline. The territorial school system had started to provide free schools throughout the territory. The hope of educating Mormon children away from Mormonism had not been realized to any significant extent, and the depression of 1893 dried up contributions. Among the few survivors of the evangelical Protestant schools are Wasatch Academy at Mount Pleasant and Westminister College in Salt Lake City. Church schools, such as Judge Memorial High School, were estab-

lished by the Catholics mainly for members of that faith, and have continued to survive and do well.

The quality of life in pioneer Utah was enhanced by the activities of the various religious denominations. Experiences in a more pluralistic society were educational and broadening. The territory now had social services such as hospitals, orphanages, and some quality schools. Moreover, the Mormons also began to open hospitals and to provide other social services of their own.

Change and expansion had brought outside capital to Utah. Jobs and prosperity had increased. Even though Utah had from the beginning been uniquely more urban in its pioneer phase than other Western territories, the changes had served to enrich urban life. Cultural interests were in some respects more refined, and there was greater support for the fine arts and for social services. Undeniably, the railroad had brought great change to the territory. Some of it was welcomed, but some was not. In order to minimize the unwanted impact, Brigham Young in 1874 introduced the communitarian economic system known as the United Order of Enoch to his faithful followers.

In order to unite the Saints in temporal and spiritual affairs and to ward off the gentile influence, producers' cooperatives were founded in a variety of forms in more than 200 Mormon communities. Some of the orders simply founded a cooperative factory and continued to live and work as they had before. Orderville, in southern Utah, became the most rigid and unique of the orders. The residents ate at a common dining hall, wore homemade clothing of the same material and the same pattern, and shared nearly equally in the work and returns of their cooperative ventures. While some orders failed within a year, the Orderville United Order, as well as some others, remained a financial and spiritual success for several years. For the most part, though, the movement did not realize the goal of insulating the Mormon commonwealth from the national economy and society.

When Brigham Young died in 1877, his successor, John Taylor, sought to achieve coordinated marketing policies and to promote manufacturing through the formation in 1878 of Zion's Central Board of Trade. The purposes included cooperative price fixing of products sold to exporters, promotion of general business activity, minimizing competition, encouraging local manufacturing, disseminating information, and in general improving the economic well-being of the Mormons. The Board of Trade flourished into the mid-1880s, when the antipolygamy crusade peaked. Suddenly the board ceased

functioning without explanation, but its demise is most likely attributable to its key members having been forced underground to avoid arrest for practicing polygamy.

It seemed that none of the innovative and concerted Mormon efforts could reverse the great changes brought by the railroad. A more pluralistic society had arrived in Utah to stay. There were many denominations now represented with congregations and churches, mixed Mormon and non-Mormon attendance in schools, and entrenched social-service institutions. The expanded urban life was more cosmopolitan, both in the advantages afforded and in the vices that came as a part of urban society. Wide-open gentile towns, some of them mining towns, others commercial or trade centers, dotted the Utah countryside. These were dramatically different from the quiet farming communities the Mormons had founded.

The two diverse societies touched at some points, of course, but they generally kept their distance from each other for some time. The conflicts between the two Utah societies kept the territory in turmoil over economic, political, social, and religious issues until the 1890s. Although the two life-styles competed and barely tolerated coexistence for many years, eventually they came to coalesce and complement each other.

Above: *In 1885 an unidentified Utah mining community displayed these two banners across its main street announcing "Liberals! Election Day Monday Aug. 3." Organized in 1870 by such anti-Mormon notables as Fort Douglas Commander Patrick Conner and Salt Lake businessman and ex-Mormon, William Godbe, the Liberal Party, with its Washington contacts, developed into a formidable political body by the time this photograph was taken. Courtesy, Brigham Young University Photo Archives*

Facing page: *Roman Catholic sisters of the Holy Cross established the Holy Cross Hospital in Salt Lake City in 1875, beginning a continuing tradition of devoted service in Utah. Photo by Charles W. Canter. Courtesy, LDS Church Archives*

Americanization and Statehood

Despite federal military intervention in Utah in 1857-1858, Mormons remained firmly in control of the territorial legislature and the judicial system. Without a doubt, the Mormon Church continued to dominate political, social, and economic life in Utah. However, this very domination cost it dearly in its desire to have Utah admitted to statehood. Six times from 1849 to 1887 Utah's bids for statehood were rejected. Of all the issues keeping Utah a territory, polygamy came to be the item that most polarized Utah politics and intensified the non-Mormon opposition to Utah's admission to statehood.

National interest in the Mormon question in Utah went back at least to August 1852 and the public announcement of polygamy within the Mormon Church. Actually, polygamy had been introduced as a Mormon doctrine in a secret July 1843 revelation commending the practice to faithful Mormons. From the outset polygamy had proven to be controversial and divisive even within the inner circle of loyal

In the mid-1870s Brigham Young encouraged his secretary, George F. Reynolds, to appeal his conviction of bigamy as a means of testing the constitutionality of the anti-bigamy laws. Two years after Brigham Young's death on January 6, 1879, the Supreme Court upheld the lower court's decision and Reynolds was imprisoned. Some 25 years later Reynolds posed for this group portrait with his sons. Courtesy, LDS Church Archives

Above: *Emma Hales Smith has been a misunderstood figure in Mormon history. Suffering untold sadness and grief because of her husband's beliefs, Emma privately opposed the principle of plural marriage. After the martyrdom of her husband, Emma chose to remain in Nauvoo instead of going West to Utah. Courtesy, Utah State Historical Department*

Facing page: *Bishop Aaron Johnson and his wives posed in front of his home in Springville in about 1875. Johnson served in the first territorial legislation assembly and as the bishop of Springville during the community's first 19 years, from 1851-1870. True to the faith and calling of a nineteenth-century Mormon church leader, Johnson practiced polygamy—however, his practice of the "principle" was highly unusual, having married more than a dozen women. Photo by Anderson and Crandall, courtesy, Heritage Prints—Rell Francis*

Mormons. After the death of Joseph Smith, in June 1844, some groups and individuals left Mormonism over this very issue. Polygamy, however, remained an open secret until the 1852 public announcement of the practice. Open admission of the existence of polygamy shocked and outraged middle-class Victorian America.

Most studies of the Mormon institution of polygamy agree that its practice was limited to men of upstanding character and some financial means who could gain the consent of the earlier wife or wives. Nevertheless, those Mormons who did not participate actively in polygamy usually were committed enough to the faith to support and defend all doctrines and practices. This different way of Mormon life led to conflicts with leaders in the non-Mormon community. Eventually the practice of polygamy became a major issue for reformers throughout America.

John C. Fremont, the Republican candidate for president of the United States in 1856, promised that if elected he would stamp out the "twin relics of barbarism": slavery in the South and polygamy in Utah. James Buchanan, the Democratic nominee who defeated Fremont, met the challenge in Utah by sending an army in 1857 to put down an alleged rebellion and to reassert federal authority in the Utah Territory. When the Republican party won the presidency in 1860 with Abraham Lincoln, the predominantly Republican Congress remaining after the Southern secession proceeded to pass the first federal antipolygamy law, the Morrill Antibigamy Act of 1862, sponsored by Representative Justin S. Morrill of Vermont. This law struck at the two major issues offending non-Mormon Americans—the temporal power of the Mormon Church and polygamy.

During the growing rampant individualism of the emerging "gilded age," the central direction given to Utah's economy by the Mormon Church leaders and the cooperative aspects of the ZCMI system, the United Order, and finally Zion's Board of Trade went against the popular notions abroad in the land. Most Americans believed that the government should have a limited voice in economic decisions, leaving the economy to the vicissitudes of the marketplace and to the individual choices of investors and industrialists. The temporal power of the Mormon Church, emphasizing cooperation and sharing as opposed to the competition and individualism so central to capitalism, seemed rather un-American to gentile capitalists.

Thus plural marriage was prohibited in the territories by the Morrill Act, and the Mormon Church was disincorporated and restricted to $50,000 in property ownership. However, because of his overriding concern over the outcome of the Civil

War, President Lincoln overlooked enforcement of the Morrill Act and it remained moot for years.

Despite the lack of governmental attention to polygamy in Utah during the Civil War and the immediate postwar years, there were two groups in Utah with close ties in Washington that spared no effort in keeping the Mormon question alive. One group consisted of the rapidly increasing contingent of gentile businessmen and federal-office appointees. The other influential group in regard to congressional policy toward Utah comprised the representatives of the evangelical churches.

The main source of influence for the non-Mormon minority in Utah was their contacts in Washington. These associations were most helpful only as long as Utah remained a territory. Non-Mormon Utahns, therefore, vigorously opposed statehood, using every possible occasion to remind governmental officials on the national level that the Mormon majority was self-contained and that it often ran roughshod over minorities, leaving them disfranchised and without an effective voice in Utah politics. The Mormon practices of cooperative economic activity, consensus politics, and polygamy were consistently effective targets for those wishing to delay Utah's admission to statehood. The practice of polygamy, however, provided antagonists with the most damning evidence that Mormonism was a bizarre aberration wholly incompatible with American concepts of religious and political acceptability.

With the end of the Civil War and the reconstruction of the South well under way, the Congress of the United States, now accustomed to using its power and exercising its will in the conquered South, could focus fuller attention on finding solutions to the Mormon question in Utah. Because Congress tended to trust the federal appointees in Utah and the non-Mormon evangelical representatives more than the suspect Mormons, it was especially easy to defer the question of Utah's statehood until a time when Mormons were properly Americanized and when true separation of church and state was achieved in Utah Territory.

As gentile businessmen and evangelical leaders attempted to make Utah morally, socially, and politically more compatible with American religious and political institutions, they dipped their brushes into each other's pots to better blacken the image of Mormon Utahns in the eyes of federal officials. The non-Mormon opponents of Utah's statehood aspirations agreed that the most effective means of rousing the American public and, consequently, their congressional representatives to action, was the polygamy issue. By the 1870s the completion of the transcontinental railroad brought increasing numbers of non-Mormons to Utah. There was also an increased apostasy from within the Mormon ranks, particularly from the Godbeites, led by Mormon apostate William Godbe, whose voice also increased the effectiveness of the anti-Mormon campaign. Perhaps as much as 10 to 15 percent of the territorial population was now non-Mormon. The settlement of the states' rights issues in the South in favor of federal control seemed to set a precedent also for imposing a federal solution on the Mormon question.

Non-Mormon critics now asserted that the Mormon effort to set up and maintain an exclusive political domination in the Utah Territory necessitated an irrepressible conflict similar to that over slavery but now to be waged between polygamous Mormons and the social and political system of the

United States. Politically, the Mormon Church government was hierarchical, ascending through priesthood offices to the Quorum of the Twelve Apostles and, ultimately, to the First Presidency, with the president at the very top over all. Within the Mormon belief in consensus government there was no room for political opposition. In selecting civil officers in Utah, the Mormons simply nominated those whose church callings indicated an aptitude and divine approval, usually nominating only one candidate for each office and then electing the nominee. The decision making processes among the elected officials often followed closely the practice of decision making in church bodies. There was little distinction made between religious and secular aspects of life: political matters were taken up in church meetings and religious matters were discussed in civil councils.

Because the Mormon Church school system was seen as another instrument of Mormon control, it also became a matter of concern for the non-Mormon minority in the territory. Federal appropriations for Utah Territory were never very generous, and their arrival was usually unpredictable. The chief, but limited, source of revenue proved to be property

taxes, with an additional amount raised from licensing bridges, roads, and other businesses. Rather commonly in these circumstances the Mormon Church called upon its members for labor contributions in order to construct civic improvements. Many buildings used for public purposes were built with local Mormon or even churchwide resources. Appropriations of the territorial legislature for education remained a mere pittance. Cities and towns proved as reluctant to tax as did the territorial legislature, and so the free-school movement made little progress in Utah. The typical situation was the tuition-supported, parochially established and directed community schools, which seemed adequate to Mormons but grossly inadequate to non-Mormons. The gentile minority naturally enough viewed with suspicion the Mormon dominance of educational affairs.

In 1869 the federal land system was extended to Utah, but still no federal lands were transferred to the territory for school purposes either then or at any other time during Utah's territorial period. Soon non-Mormons began to press for educational services that the Mormons were content to seek through their church. Following the passage of the Territorial School Act of 1874, both the territorial legislature and local governments increased contributions to the school system, but not nearly enough to satisfy the requirements of a free-school system.

Mormons expected that one day all civil government would fail, and that when this occurred the responsibilities their ecclesiastical government would take over would include education. The outbreak of the Civil War in 1861 seemed to signal the collapse of the American government. In preparation for imminent takeover, a new constitution for a proposed "State of Deseret" was drafted in 1862, and a full slate of candidates was chosen. When the petition to Congress for statehood under this constitution was rejected, the State of Deseret continued to function as a ghost or shadow government even though the territorial government remained in existence. Finally, in 1870 the shadow government faded into oblivion.

With Utah so divided between those of the Kingdom and outsiders, Patrick Edward Connor, commander at Fort Douglas, launched a vigorous and unrelenting attack upon the entrenched power of the Kingdom exemplified in the shadow State of Deseret government. His efforts resulted in the organization of the Liberal party in February of 1870 as a gentile party dedicated to unseating Mormon officeholders, from the territorial delegate to Congress on down.

In response the Mormons established the People's party, whose journalistic voices were the *Deseret News* and the new Salt Lake *Herald.* Mormon apostates countered with the anti-Mormon *Tribune,* whose name was later changed to the Salt Lake *Tribune,* as the newspaper of the Liberal party. National support for the Liberal party in Utah generally came from the national Republican party, and support for the People's party generally came from the Democratic party, which was more of an advocate of states' rights. Nevertheless, the national political parties existed only in the background of Utah politics until the 1890s.

The Morrill Antibigamy Act of 1862 had resulted in no convictions of Utah Mormons. Mormon control of probate courts, which claimed jurisdiction over criminal cases, made it virtually impossible to gain indictments or convictions of those arrested for polygamy. The Liberal party now made plural marriage its major political issue. Polygamy and the political struggle for control in Utah were tied together in one package by the Liberal party. In the 1870s this campaign began to have discernible effects.

As a result of the renewed federal interest in polygamy, in 1870 Illinois Representative Shelby M. Cullom introduced the Cullom Bill. The effect of its provisions would have taken the courts out of the Mormons' hands, imposed fines and imprisonment for polygamy and cohabitation, disfranchised polygamists, permitted wives to testify against husbands, and authorized use of the military to enforce the law. On March 23, 1870, the Cullom Bill passed the House of Representatives. It died in the Senate, however, when the railroad lobby and Southern senators from reconstructed and border states prevented its coming to a vote.

The debate over the Cullom Bill led to a mass meeting of 3,000 Mormon women in the Salt Lake Tabernacle. National suffragettes, who were pleased by the Utah territorial legislature's granting Utah women the franchise by an act signed on February 12, 1870, were shocked that these Mormon women would defend their right to participate in plural marriages. The protest of the Mormon women seemed to refute the popular national assumption that they were the unwilling victims of polygamy.

Despite its defeat, many provisions of the Cullom Bill were later revived to become parts of subsequent antipolygamy statutes. The first of these and the only congressional act dealing with the Mormon question in the 1870s was the Poland Act of 1874. Sponsored by Vermont Representative Luke P. Poland, this act moved jurisdiction in criminal cases from the locally elected and, consequently, Mormon-controlled probate courts to federal courts, where convictions against polygamists might be won.

The death of Brigham Young, on August 29, 1877, at the age of 76 brought to an end what gentiles considered an autocratic, 30-year personal rule of Utah. The Quorum of the Twelve under the presidency of John Taylor faced increasing external pressures and a growing desire among the Mormons for change and accommodation. Taylor, however, remained most adamant and inflexible on the polygamy issue.

However, a court case that was begun with the knowledge and consent of Brigham Young in 1875 as a test of the constitutionality of federal antipolygamy legislation finally resulted in an adverse Supreme Court ruling for the Mormons on January 6, 1879. This decision brought the new Mormon leadership under John Taylor to a crisis of sorts. Mormons had claimed that antipolygamy laws interfered with their First

Above: *Caught in the tide of persecution, John Taylor, the third president of the Mormon Church, went into hiding in 1885. Still in exile, he died July 25, 1887, at the home of Thomas F. Roueche at Kaysville in Davis County. Courtesy, LDS Church Archives*

Facing page: *In 1882 the United States Congress passed the Edmunds Bill, which made practicing polygamy both a felony and a misdemeanor. The bill also called for a temporary use of a commission known as the "Utah Commission" to supervise elections and approve only those voters who took an oath against polygamy. Courtesy, LDS Church Archives*

Page 87: *LDS Church President Wilford Woodruff posed with his two counselors, George Q. Cannon and Joseph F. Smith, on the church leader's birthday on March 1, 1894. When this portrait was taken, Woodruff had been church president for less than five years. During that time Woodruff steered the church away from economic and political downfall by formally announcing the Manifesto proclaiming that plural marriage was no longer an essential Mormon doctrine. Photo by Charles R. Savage. Courtesy, LDS Church Archives*

Amendment guarantee of freedom of religion. George F. Reynolds, once Brigham Young's secretary, had become a volunteer defendant in the case to test the Mormon claim. The first Reynolds trial ended in a mistrial for the acknowledged polygamist defendant. A second trial resulted in a conviction, carrying a fine and an imposed jail sentence. The case of *Reynolds* v. the *United States* was heard on appeal by the United States Supreme Court. The high court ruled that the Morrill Antibigamy Act was constitutional. The First Amendment simply meant that Congress could not by law regulate religious beliefs, but it could regulate religious practices. The Mormons were left without a constitutional defense for plural marriage, but they continued the practice under the premise of a higher law: that is, God's revealed law superseded man's law.

The *Reynolds* case established momentum for an antipolygamy crusade. The Republican party and its presidents from Ulysses S. Grant to Chester A. Arthur outwardly supported such a crusade. In 1881 and 1882 Congress was flooded with petitions and proposals on the Mormon issue. The crusaders were given the weapon they seemed to need with the signing on March 22, 1882, of the Edmunds Act, sponsored by Senator George F. Edmunds of Vermont.

The Edmunds Act contained many of the proposals of the defeated Cullom Bill and was itself chiefly a series of amendments to strengthen the Morrill Antibigamy Act of 1862. Its passage resulted in a major judicial crusade against polygamy. The Edmunds Act made the contracting of a polygamous marriage a felony, with a fine of up to $500 and up to five years in prison. Cohabitation was made a misdemeanor with a fine of up to $300 and a six-month prison term. Polygamists were denied the right to vote, hold office, and serve on juries. The established election procedure was eliminated. All registration and election officials were dismissed, to be replaced by a board of five commissioners appointed by the president of the United States to administer elections.

The election commission, or the Utah Commission as it was popularly known, consisting of three Republicans and two Democrats, arrived in August 1882. It immediately began applying the Edmunds Act in a broad fashion. In order to vote Mormons were required to take an oath denying that they lived with more than one woman "in the marriage relation." This phrase offended Mormons and provided an out for men who lived with more than one woman outside a marriage relationship.

Despite successes in reducing the number of Mormon voters, the Utah Commission's activity could not prevent John T. Caine's continuing election as territorial delegate to Congress or the filling of most local political offices by Mormons. The intended temporary status of the Utah Commission assumed greater permanency. On March 22, 1885, in the case of *Murphy* v. *Ramsey*, testing the constitutionality of the Edmunds Act, the United States Supreme Court upheld the disfranchisement aspects of the act but declared the test oath "null and void," since it exceeded the commission's authority. However, the Edmunds Act remained essentially intact. The federal court system in Utah, led by Chief Justice Charles S. Zane, now put into action a judicial crusade to arrest and imprison hundreds of Mormon polygamists in a concerted effort to stamp out polygamy once and for all. Posters offered substantial rewards for information leading to the arrest of prominent Mormons and lesser amounts for the arrest of any and all Mormon polygamists. Federal marshals were dispatched throughout the territory to track down and arrest offenders.

The first polygamy case under the Edmunds Act was tried by Judge Zane in October 1884. Rudger Clawson was indicted for both polygamy and unlawful cohabitation. Lydia Spencer, Clawson's plural wife, was summoned as a witness but did not appear. Lacking evidence, the first trial ended in a hung jury. The next day Lydia was found and seized. When she refused to be sworn as a witness in a second trial, she was sent to the territorial penitentiary for contempt of court. Rather than have her serve a prison sentence, Rudger Clawson requested that she testify, whereupon she admitted to being Clawson's plural wife. He was then found guilty and sentenced for both polygamy and cohabitation to a stiff fine and jail term. The precedents in the Clawson case were foreboding for all Mormon polygamists, since he was tried by an all-gentile jury, his wife was imprisoned until she agreed to testify, and he received a very severe sentence. Appellate court rulings in general upheld these precedents.

In defense against what they considered bad laws and against being considered guilty until they could prove innocence, Mormons worked out elaborate systems to avoid arrest. The so-called "underground" included surveillance, elaborate warning techniques, secret hiding places, mission calls, and outmigrations to Mexico and Canada. For the last two and a half years of his life, church president John Taylor was in hiding, moving from place to place and not daring to visit his wives and family. Despite all precautions, hundreds of other Mormons were arrested and imprisoned.

By 1885 the Mormons and the federal government had reached an impasse. The result was hard times for Utah's Mormon population. A flood of arrests of Mormon polygamists swelled the population of the territorial prison. The incarcerated now included Mormon apostles, stake presi-

dents, and bishops. In addition to those in prison there were numerous leading Mormon officials in hiding. Many church programs were abandoned temporarily or permanently, including the United Order. But the Mormons adhered with remarkable tenacity to their ways. The church continued to function, and the People's party retained its political control. In these circumstances the Edmunds Act was not meeting the expectations for a more comprehensive solution to the Mormon question. A law to break the seemingly absolute authority and sovereignty wielded by the Mormon Church was needed.

The Edmunds-Tucker Act responded to this need. This act, which became law on March 3, 1887, without President Grover Cleveland's signature, had devastating potential, since it was designed to destroy the Mormon Church economically and politically. Its provisions abolished women's suffrage in Utah and authorized the Utah Commission to administer test oaths. The hope was that the Mormons would disqualify themselves by refusing to take the oath, but nonpolygamist Mormons signed the oath and thus continued political dominance by the People's party.

This new legislation did prove effective in disbanding the Perpetual Emigrating Fund Company (PEF). The objective of this act was to prevent "ignorant aliens" recently converted to Mormonism from coming to Utah, due to a lack of financial assistance from the PEF. Thus they would be prevented from adding their support to the Mormon system. The act also removed some remaining obstacles to prosecution of polygamists by mandating compulsory attendance of witnesses at trials and requiring wives to testify against their husbands. Finally, the law disincorporated the Mormon Church and declared all its property in excess of $50,000 escheated to the United States. The office of Territorial Superintendent of Schools was replaced by a Utah Supreme Court-appointed commissioner in an effort to promote free public education. The forfeited property escheated to the United States from the church was to be used to benefit the territory's public schools.

The day following John Taylor's funeral, July 30, 1887, the federal government implemented the escheat provisions. The new church president, Wilford Woodruff, recognized that full enforcement of the Edmunds-Tucker Act would destroy the church. He therefore encouraged the submission of a new sixth petition for statehood with a proposed constitutional provision outlawing both polygamy and the "union of Church and State." House and Senate hearings considered this application at intervals for more than a year, but for non-Mormons nothing less than a formal and complete capitulation, tested over time, would do. Like its five predecessors, this petition was denied.

President Cleveland, upon assuming office in 1885, was more inclined to be cooperative and accepting of Mormon good faith on the issues of polygamy and separation of church and state, and he sought to foster an attitude of accommodation. He therefore appointed Elliot Sandford to replace the crusading Chief Justice, Judge Zane. Sandford encouraged Mormons to abandon the underground and to come in and accept moderate fines or imprisonments. Ultimately, more than a thousand Mormon polygamists were convicted under the various federal antipolygamy laws, most for the misdemeanor of illegal cohabitation.

Beginning in 1887, Mormon political dominance showed signs of breaking down. As the Liberal party experienced growing electoral success during the period of 1887 to 1890, some because of gerrymandering by the Utah Commission and some due to disfranchisement of Mormons, it sought assurance of continuing success. Liberals proposed legislation for Utah similar to an Idaho law upheld by the Supreme Court barring Mormons from voting whether they believed in polygamy or not. Despite the fact that thousands of Mormons already had been disfranchised, the Cullom-Struble Bill, coauthored by the sponsor of the Cullom Bill of 1870, was to be the means for disfranchising all Mormons.

While Congress considered the Cullom-Struble Bill, the

Supreme Court upheld the provisions of the Edmunds-Tucker Act dissolving the Mormon Church and escheating its property. Federal agents proceeded to seize church properties. Church president Wilford Woodruff considered his narrowing options. First, in 1889 he quietly withheld authority for performing plural marriages. Then the Endowment House, where many of the plural marriages had been performed, was torn down. Church representatives sought to dissuade national political figures from additional drastic actions against the Mormon Church. A delay in passage of the Cullom-Struble Bill was obtained, conditional upon an ending of the polygamy practice.

On September 25, 1890, Woodruff, acknowledging that he had found it necessary to act to ensure the "temporal salvation of the Church," issued a proclamation with the approval of his counselors and the Quorum of the Twelve that became known as the Woodruff Manifesto. In it he advised Mormons to refrain from contracting any marriage contrary to the law of the land. Because Secretary of the Interior John W. Noble would not accept the manifesto without a sustaining vote of a Mormon General Conference, it was submitted for vote on October 6, 1890, and unanimously accepted.

The bitterness and anguish over the Americanization of Mormon Utah was coming to an end. Nevertheless, Utahns watched once again as neighboring areas settled later and with smaller populations gained statehood. In 1889 Montana, with a population of 132,000, entered the Union. In 1890 Wyoming, with 61,000, and Idaho, with 84,000, were given statehood. Utah, with 208,000 people, was required to wait another six years while the nation evaluated whether the Mormon accommodation was genuine.

One necessary accommodation in addition to the dropping of polygamy was the adoption of national political parties in Utah. The Republican party was the nationally predominant party, but most church members were inclined toward the Democratic party. Ironically, politicians who had for years attempted to break the political influence of the Mormon Church were now asking church leaders to exercise influence in dissolving the People's party and establishing the Republican party, with assurances that Mormons would support the dominant national party.

In 1891 the church encouraged the founding of the Republican party and asked members to support it. Some church members were even assigned affiliation within the Republican party. The People's party was then disbanded. The non-Mormon members of the Liberal party were reluctant to disband, fearing that their growing voting strength would be disrupted and the party's voters would split between Democratic and Republican affiliation. The Liberal party continued until 1893, when most of its affiliates joined many Mormons in the Republican party.

As a result of the contrition shown by the Mormons in 1893,

shortly before leaving office President Benjamin Harrison granted an amnesty and pardon to all Mormons who had refrained from unlawful cohabitation since November 1, 1890. A year later Grover Cleveland, back in office for another term, restored civil rights to all who had been disfranchised under polygamy acts except those who had not complied with Harrison's conditions. Congress then agreed to restore all church properties seized by the government under the Edmunds-Tucker Act and passed enabling legislation to provide for a Constitutional Convention for Utah. A constitution was written in the 1895 convention restoring the franchise to Utah women, outlawing polygamy, and specifically providing for separation of church and state. On November 5, 1895, voters ratified the constitution and elected the first officials for the proposed forty-fifth state. On Saturday, January 4, 1896, President Cleveland signed the Utah statehood proclamation; and on Monday, January 6, 1896, new state officials, including the first governor, Heber M. Wells, were inaugurated. In Utah there was a profound sense of relief, marked by an enthusiastic celebration. A conflict of more than forty years' duration had ended. In order to thoroughly Americanize the Mormons to assume citizenship in a state within the Union, the federal government had succeeded in eradicating the outward appearances of Mormon distinctiveness. Polygamy, cooperative enterprise, and consensus politics were ended after a long and bitter struggle.

Above: *Members of Utah's first House of Representatives posed on the steps of the Salt Lake City and County Building in 1896. Photo by George Beard, Courtesy, Utah State Historical Society*

Facing page: *By 1885 the Utah Territorial Prison was bursting at the seams with convicted "cohabers." Many polygamists at this time were either in prison or in hiding. It is estimated that federal officers arrested more than 1,000 polygamists. Photo by Charles R. Savage, Courtesy, LDS Church Archives*

New Immigrants, Labor, and Progressivism

A gunfight between two horse thieves and a sheriff's posse in August 1895, in City Creek Canyon near Salt Lake City just a few months before statehood, supplied graphic evidence that the frontier had not completely disappeared in Utah. But once Utah gained statehood, it moved rapidly away from its pioneer heritage toward fuller integration into the American nation and greater social, economic, and political diversity. Still, it was another two decades before Utah's political assimilation was more or less complete. The long, difficult process preparatory for admission to the Union had changed the outward symbols of Mormon distinctiveness, but it had not fully Americanized the newest state. However, the achievement of statehood did constitute an important point of transition in Utah's unique history. Statehood marked the end of one era and the commencement of another.

Utah's first immigrants were Indians. The second were the Mormon pioneers. The third wave of immigration began during the territorial years as unskilled labor was needed to work the mines and railroads. This third cycle increased and peaked during the first decades of statehood. It consisted of

A Greek wedding party in front of the Holy Trinity Church in Salt Lake City involved the families of Farmakis and Anast some time in the 1920s. Courtesy, Utah State Historical Society

During the last two decades of the nineteenth century, mining became a major link in Utah's economy. There were so many smelters polluting the air that damaged crops were reported by farmers around Salt Lake City. This was the United States Mining and Smelting Company's copper smelter in Midvale, photographed around 1906. Courtesy, Utah Power and Light

the "new immigrants"—Southern, Eastern and Central Europeans who came to work in the mines and smelters and for the railroads. These newcomers proved significant in the ultimate Americanization of Utah.

Although assimilation of the new immigrants had its trying times, they assimilated better than the 20,000 or so Indians living in Utah when the Mormons arrived. The Walker War of 1853-1854 and the Tintic War of 1856 involved Indian resistance to assimilation. Later, other events further complicated Indian assimilation. In 1863 federal troops under Colonel Connor fell upon a band of Shoshone Indians near the Bear River in northern Utah and, in the resulting Bear River Massacre, killed about 250 Indians. In 1865 the Black Hawk War erupted. It consisted of a series of raids conducted over the four-year duration of the conflict.

The Black Hawk War was inspired by a young Ute who refused to be settled on a newly created reservation in the Uinta Basin. The militants attracted to his position attacked settlements from Sanpete County southward to Arizona. Brigham Young advised residents in southern Utah to "fort up." This consisted of abandoning small communities and congregating in larger, fortified towns. About twenty-five villages were temporarily abandoned as Mormon retaliatory raids were conducted by elements of the Mormon militia.

In Kane, Washington, and Iron counties, in the extreme southern part of Utah, the raids were sometimes called the Navajo Raids. In the 1850s the Navajos, a group of Indians unrelated to the Shoshone, Ute, Gosiute, and Paiute, began moving into the southeastern part of the state. They came to the American Southwest from Canada, probably arriving just before the first Spanish appeared in this region. They became primarily shepherds and farmers and introduced a rich cultural heritage that has survived removals and discrimination. In 1863 the Navajos were removed from their tribal lands to Fort Sumner, New Mexico, but they returned in 1868 to conduct raids against ranches and villages in southern Utah that continued into the 1870s. The white residents lost more than 1,200 head of livestock in these raids. In 1884 the land south of the San Juan River in San Juan County was incorporated into the Navajo Reservation, and today the Navajo is the most populous of all Utah Indians.

The Dawes Severalty Act of 1887 moved to encourage Indians to give up reservation and tribal life for assimilation into the broader American society. Several reservations, including the Uintah-Ouray in the Uinta Basin, were greatly reduced in size by allotting the head of each Indian family 160 acres of land. Each single person over eighteen years of age received eighty acres and everyone under eighteen got forty acres. The lands not allotted to the Indians were to be made available for white settlement. The Uintah-Ouray Reservation was opened for white occupancy in 1905. White settlers quickly moved in, creating several new communities, and in 1915 Duchesne County was created almost wholly from what had once been Ute Indian reservation lands. Many Indians were indignant and felt betrayed by the White Man's government. Some of the distressed Utes fled for the Great Plains, where they hoped for an alliance with the Sioux to resist further white expansion. But the 1906-1908 trek to the plains ended in failure. The frustrated Utes returned to the Uinta Basin, carrying with them a sense of failure and a loss of hope. Until the 1920s they remained Utah's nearly forgotten minority.

As part of the secularizing process in Utah, the Mormon Church abandoned some of its economic and political activities and transferred much of its once-dominant educational function to the state. Gentiles in some quarters continued their Mormon-watch, but the enthusiasm they once bore for rescuing the Mormons from their folly had subsided. The decline of church domination of political, social, and economic life and the rise of vigorous economic competition signaled a rise in the secularization of life in Utah. The economy of the state began to integrate more and more into the broader national economic patterns. The reliance people once placed on Mormon Church programs and agencies to meet social-welfare and community needs gave way to more conventional American practices of dealing with such problems by governmental action.

In 1899 the Mormon Church leadership concluded that the gathering of its membership to Utah was no longer essential; in fact, the gathering was often discouraged. Utah was now developing economically in the direction of commercialized agriculture, corporate mining, and manufacturing. Mormons still following the counsel of church leaders stayed on the land, so the growing demand for industrial workers had to be filled from elsewhere. New immigrants from southern and eastern Europe now came in response to the labor needs in a more industrialized Utah. Their role in supplying blue-collar labor helped change Utah from an agricultural to an industrial state. Their finally successful battles for unionizing mines, mills, and smelters led to a safer and improved lifestyle for Utah's industrial employees.

The laying of the railroad was begun in the 1860s and continued in Utah until about 1910. This work required many, many workers, which Utah's farm population did not have the time or inclination to provide, even though Brigham Young encouraged some Mormons to take jobs in initial railroad construction to reduce the need for gentile laborers in Utah. Railroad agents began recruiting workers from abroad. The imported workers were found in Italy, in the Slavic provinces of the old Austro-Hungarian Empire, on the Island of Crete, in mainland Greece, and indeed throughout southern, central, and eastern Europe. Those immigrants who made their way to Utah were but a fraction of the great migration of people who left Europe due to advertisements and agents who promised high wages in America. The new immigrants were also driven from their homelands to America by forces such as poverty, internal strife, and persecutions.

The rapidly burgeoning industrialization in America called for a plentiful labor supply. The new immigrants shouldered the burden of the blue-collar labor required in this industrial drive. In Utah this was most often work for the railroad companies or in the mining industry. In accepting such jobs in Utah, the immigrants pioneered a new way of life and added a new and vital dimension to Utah and its people.

Although the vast majority of the more than six million immigrants streaming into the United States in the first decade of the twentieth century ended up in large cities such as Chicago and New York, some, through inclination or response to labor agents, came west. Upon arriving at Ellis Island they were processed, given a slip of paper showing their destination, and directed to a train that would deposit them there. The new arrivals into Utah were quickly sent off to such places as Bingham Canyon, Helper, Murray, and Magna. In railroad and mining camps they were soon concentrated in sufficient numbers to form mutual-aid societies, religious congregations, and trade and communications networks that closely linked them to a society that virtually re-created a colony of the homeland.

Because of language, religious differences, customs, and sometimes a darker skin color than the earlier-arriving Northern Europeans, the new immigrants found that they brought out fears and prejudices among the older residents. Thrown back on their own resources, they often joined and supported labor-union movements and participated in strikes and protests when wages were cut, or when employers brought in new ethnic groups as scabs or strikebreakers.

The new immigrants originally lived apart from the rest of Utah. They pioneered a way of life dramatically different from that of the first Mormon pioneers. In doing so, they broke new ground in a significant way for all Utahns. The new immigrants were the first Utahns to earn their livelihood all their lives as industrial workers. In pioneering this new way of life, they suffered some of the most egregious injustices and indignities imaginable. But with courage and resourcefulness they fought and formed organizations for mutual help to reduce the awful toll of industrial accidents, to improve wages and housing, and to get fair prices and service at company stores.

Soon many of the children of the earlier Mormon pioneers, finding that they could not all make a living from the land, turned to industrial labor, and in doing so they discovered that the new pioneers had made industrial employment a satisfying way of life. The new immigrants also temporarily brought the balance of the Utah population in 1920 to very nearly 50 percent Mormon and 50 percent non-Mormon. Ironic as it may seem, it may well be that the Americanization of Utah was finally accomplished by the thousands of European immigrants who came for jobs and then settled in, adopting Utah as their new homeland.

Italians were the first of the new immigrants to arrive in Utah. Beginning in the late 1890s, Italians made their way to Utah to work for the Denver and Rio Grande Railroad as coal miners or railroad maintenance men. Once a nucleus of Italian workers was established at the camps of Clear Creek, Winter Quarters, Castle Gate, and Sunnyside in Carbon County, personal ties to Italy and correspondence with friends and family helped to bring other Italians to Utah.

Shortly after the Italians arrived as laborers, South Slavs, or Yugoslavs, began coming to work alongside the Italians in coal mining and railroad camps and at the smelters. Like the Italians before them, the Slavs found time away from their backbreaking toil to join fraternal organizations so that they might enjoy socializing in the traditional ways of the homeland.

As wives and sweethearts were brought to America, families were formed. Births and deaths and the new family life gradually helped to form a commitment to remain in the new land and to call it home. Many found a niche in Utah and stayed to raise children and grandchildren.

Following the Yugoslavs came the Greeks. Political turmoil, deprived conditions, poverty, crop failure, and labor agents such as Leonidas Skliris turned a small trickle of Greek immigrants into a flood after 1907. Skliris and other Greek labor agents, or padrones, enriched themselves by collecting a twenty-dollar fee for placing a worker in his first position and obtaining a signed contract written in English—a foreign language—promising to "irrevocably assign" a dollar a month out of any wage earned in the future. By 1910 more than 4,000 Greeks, mostly males, were residents of Utah attempting to replicate the home society. Through picture brides, journeys home in search of a wife, and occasional marriages to local girls, the intensely nationalistic Greeks were able to content themselves with life in Utah and commit themselves to remain.

The experience of the new immigrants added greatly to the diversifying of the character of Utah. Their lives in Utah were not greatly different from those of other new immigrants elsewhere. They suffered the loneliness of being far from home in a strange land. They had come intending to free themselves from poverty, but they soon found themselves exploited by labor agents, company stores, and indifferent employers. All were victimized by prejudice and discrimination. Accommodations for railroad crews, for example, were divided into "white men's camps" and "foreigners' camps." In the white camps separate railroad cars served for sleeping, cooking, and eating. In "foreigners' camps" one car served all three functions for the same number of men.

Whether working in mines or smelters or on railroad crews, the new immigrants found the hours long and the work backbreaking. They also encountered unfair practices, such as the short-weighting of the ore or coal they had mined. Some of the new immigrants were lynched, others were terrorized by the "new" Ku Klux Klan of the 1920s. When they organized to protest, they were often locked out of their jobs and saw new immigrant groups, pleased to find employment at any cost, brought in as strikebreakers. Although at first they tolerated living apart from the older settlers, isolated in labor camps, they gradually began to move to Utah's cities to establish businesses, gain formal education, and eventually enter the professions—thus becoming more visible members of a new Utah.

Utah's early mine and smelter workers found that work

was a constant hazard: there were many conditions that posed actual threats to their lives. Even though the wages at first seemed comparatively good, many workers came to feel they deserved much more. Early on they attempted to organize in order to speak with one voice so they might convince employers to improve working conditions, wages, and life in company towns. These organizational efforts were usually confronted by indifferent employers.

Even before the arrival of the new immigrants, the Mormon Church had responded in its own way to what was seen as the ills of industrial society. The cooperatives and United Order activities of the late 1860s and early 1870s were efforts to make workers the owners of the means of production. National leaders of the Knights of Labor, the earliest nationwide workingmen's organization to attempt to organize industrial workers, praised the Mormon cooperatives as models of how industrial society could justly be organized. Nevertheless, historical circumstances dictated that union organization in Utah would be almost entirely a gentile accomplishment.

Brigham Young was determined to keep Utah's economy independent from that of the nation, and he felt that lower wages would help. If wages were kept low, local manufacturers could better compete with goods imported to Utah by the

Page 96: *Entering the twentieth century was difficult for Utah. The abandonment of polygamy did not occur overnight, although many throughout the nation wanted it that way. During the first decades of the new century, there was a renewed emphasis by a number of Protestant groups to convert the Mormons to conventional Christianity. Courtesy, Bowling Green State University*

Below: *The Scofield mining accident still remains as one of Utah's worst mining accidents. Volunteers from Provo came with shovels to dig the graves. Photo by George Edward Anderson, courtesy, Utah State Historical Society*

railroad at much cheaper rates than those freighted in by wagon train prior to 1869. Also, Mormon leaders sought to keep church members out of organizations with national affiliation that were dominated by non-Mormons. Control over local affairs was seen as imperative and could be facilitated in this way. Then, as non-Mormons came to dominate labor-union activity in the 1880s, these organizations began to support Liberal party candidates for local political office.

The organizational efforts of the Knights of Labor also intensified feelings between the Mormon Church and union leaders. The Knights banned from membership persons who believed in or practiced polygamy. This rule made union participation impossible for practicing Mormons. Furthermore, the Knights were secretive in nature and were seen as confrontational rather than cooperative in their dealings with industrialists. Mormons were advised against affiliation with such organizations. The Knights also aimed to exclude Chinese workers, for they were seen as wage-lowering competitors. In August 1885 an unruly demonstration was held at Ogden, urging a boycott of Chinese businesses and the expulsion of all Chinese. The Mormon Church-owned *Deseret News* argued that it was unjust to drive out the Chinese. When the anti-Chinese activities of the Knights degenerated into acts of violence, including the killing of several individuals in surrounding areas of the American West, Mormon Church leaders concluded that violence and mob action were typical methods of union organizations.

It was for these many reasons, then, that Utah's new pioneers became the first to attempt to unify into organizations to gain decent wages and standards. Their conditions of employment were often disastrous.

In addition to low wages and unfair labor practices, the immigrants suffered from employers' seeming lack of concern for the health and safety of the workers. Too often there were tragic deaths and dismemberments as the result of industrial accidents.

Beyond the everyday accidents were two great mine disasters that occurred in early twentieth-century Utah. On May 1, 1900, about 250 men were in the Winter Quarters coal mine near Scofield when suddenly, at 10:28 a.m., a gigantic explosion ripped through the mine tunnels. Investigations indicated that 83 men were killed by the blast and 117 more were killed by poisonous gases produced by the explosion. Fewer than fifty men in the mine escaped with their lives. A massive effort was launched to find, remove, and identify the dead and to carry out a mass burial.

In addition to an outpouring of sympathy and an attempt to provide assistance to the widows and children, there was an investigation to find the cause of the tragedy. The Pleasant Valley Coal Company, despite claims that the loss of life could have been avoided had the mine been cleared of men before a charge was fired, was cleared of any responsibility.

In 1924 a second calamity killed 172 coal miners at the Castle Gate explosion. The combined effect of these two tragedies helped put the mortality rate in Utah mines at twice the national average during these early years of statehood.

Effective improvement in the conditions of work were slow in coming for various reasons. Loyalty to unions or union ideology was not well developed among the workers. Various unions competed for the loyalty of the workers and, partly as a result, there was never a sustained protest by the workers. Divided ideology and differences over which tactics to follow helped to minimize the concessions made by employers. Management also found it could play off one group of immigrants against another. For example, in the 1903-1904 Carbon County coal strike, which was led by Yugoslavs and Italians, management rushed in Greek miners to serve as strikebreakers. When the Greeks struck in 1912 against the Bingham copper mines and again in 1922 against the Carbon County coal mines, Mexican workers were brought in as strikebreakers.

There were frequent sporadic strikes in Utah in response to particular grievances, and major strikes occurred in 1901, 1903, 1912, 1922 and 1933. Concessions were always limited.

The most effective union in organizing sustained activity among the new immigrants of Utah was the United Mine Workers. Carlo Demolli, a charismatic Italian immigrant and labor organizer, came to Utah from Colorado in 1903 to help organize that year's strike against the Pleasant Valley Coal Company. From this time on Demolli remained a very popular figure among Utah's Italian immigrants. He was smuggled and protected from the local law-enforcement officials who sought his arrest to help the industrialists in breaking the strike. The company did quickly concede to some of the workers' demands, but it failed to recognize the union as the bargaining agent.

The 1912 strike at the Bingham mines was partly an attempt to free the Greeks from the domination of Leonidas Skliris. The strike again did not bring recognition to the union, but it did effectively break the power of Skliris. The 1922 Carbon County coal strike began as a protest against the short-weighting of coal. Union organizer Frank Bonacci led the United Mine Workers protest against the Kenilworth Mining Company. The outcome was again indecisive, as the company used strikebreakers to minimize concessions.

Two unions more radical than the United Mine Workers carried out unionization endeavors in Utah that concentrated mainly on the organization of coal miners. The Western Federation of Miners (WFM) was founded in 1893 at Butte, Montana, to represent metal miners and extraction workers. It moved its headquarters to Salt Lake City in 1898. After a three-year period its headquarters were moved from Utah. The WFM did not become a major force in the Utah mining industry. Many Utahns avoided the WFM because of its reputation for violence and radicalism. A second radical union was the Industrial Workers of the World, or the IWW, which made efforts to organize in Utah from 1912 to about 1915. The IWW reputation for violence and radicalism was effectively used against it, and no significant gains were made in Utah by Wobblies, as IWW members were called.

The event that continues to link Utah most closely with radical unionism is the Joe Hill case. A Swedish immigrant and IWW member known as Joel Haggelund, also known as Joe Hillstrom and Joe Hill, was boarding in Salt Lake City in 1914. During the evening of January 10, 1914, the Morrison grocery store on 8th South and West Temple was robbed. John G. Morrison and his son, Arling, were shot to death by the robbers. Witnesses claimed that Arling had wounded one of the assailants before he himself was killed. Later that night Joe Hill asked a Salt Lake physician to administer medical treatment for a gunshot wound. After an investigation Joe Hill was arrested, convicted, and sentenced to be executed.

There were many who protested the conviction and sentence. Some felt that Hill was discriminated against because he was a foreigner and a member of a radical labor union. Songs and poems written by Joe Hill, many while he was in prison, added to the sentiment for commutation of his sentence. Samuel Gompers, head of the American Federation of Labor, President Woodrow Wilson, the Swedish Ambassador, and many others of prominence urged Governor William Spry to commute the sentence to life in prison. Despite the pleas, protests, and much litigation, Joe Hill was executed by a firing squad at Sugar House on November 19, 1915. The Joe Hill case remains Utah's enduring connection with radical unionism.

The poverty and general plight of the new immigrants finally pricked the social conscience of many Americans and led to a campaign for reform urge that then went off in many directions. The concern of social workers, such as Jane Addams, for the new immigrants in Chicago led to the establishment of Hull House in an attempt to help the poor in that neighborhood. Such concerns stimulated a wave of reform that began in Eastern urban centers and then swept across America during the first two decades of the twentieth century. The Progressive Movement, as this wave of reform was called, involved a close examination of politics, conditions in the work place, food and drug processing and adulteration, corrupt and corrupting practices in big business, and a concern to protect the natural environment. At the national, state, and local levels of government, hundreds of pieces of legislation were passed to correct identified problems and to make America better and more moral.

Exposes of abuses found by the reformers were printed in mass-circulation magazines. Theodore Roosevelt referred to this type of journalism derogatorily as muckraking. The muckrakers called the attention of the people throughout the nation to slums, corruption-prone political processes, corruption in big business, graft, kickbacks, personal favors, and bribery. Much of this was true, but different circumstances gave the Progressive Movement different meaning in various areas of the country. Such was the case in Utah. The Progressive Movement touched Utah, but the meaning and results were somewhat different than in some other areas of the country.

Utah politics during early statehood and the Progressive Era continued to be muddled by the legacy of territorial days. Reform issues sometimes took a backseat to the felt need to launch and sustain a stable Republican party that could guarantee a reasonably balanced two-party system. The Progressive reforms in Utah sometimes swirled more around this consideration than around the need to root out what graft and corruption there may have been.

When Utah entered the Union in the winter of 1896, the nation was depression ridden. Farming and mining, the two main businesses in the new state, were not prospering at all in that first year of statehood. Wheat was 46 cents and corn 58 cents a bushel, hay was $4 a ton, and sheep were going for $1.50 a head. Many mines in the state were closed. Utah's one bumper crop was children, who, because of the declining support system of agriculture, were beginning to leave the state in large numbers to seek better economic opportunities elsewhere.

This photo of the first governor of the state of Utah, Heber M. Wells, was taken when he was a young man. Courtesy, Utah State Historical Society

In the special 1895 election for state officers, Republican Heber M. Wells was elected governor over Democrat John T. Caine and a third-party candidate. All major state offices went to Republicans; the two houses of the state legislature contained Republican majorities that elected non-Mormon Arthur Brown and Mormon Frank J. Cannon as Utah's first United States senators. This established a practice of choosing one Mormon and one non-Mormon to the U.S. Senate, which was followed until passage of the Seventeenth Amendment instituted the direct election of senators.

In the November 1896 general election, William Jennings Bryan, the Populist and Democratic candidate for president, won a resounding victory in Utah with more than 80 percent of the popular vote but lost the national election to William McKinley. William Howard King, a son-in-law of Mormon apostle Francis M. Lyman and a Democrat, was elected to the House of Representatives. The Democratic party also won control of both houses of the state legislature. The legislature then took fifty-three ballots to elect Joseph L. Rawlings to the U.S. Senate. In 1898 Brigham H. Roberts, a member of the Mormon Church Seven Presidents of Seventies (a general authority which oversaw missionary work) and a Democrat, was elected to the House of Representatives, but the House refused to seat him because he was a practicing polygamist. Party divisions also made it impossible to elect a senator, so Utah was unrepresented for two years in one of its two senatorial seats. A special election in 1900 chose William H. King to serve the remainder of B.H. Roberts' term in the House. This was the last major electoral victory the Democrats won in Utah until 1916.

Prosperity had returned to Utah and the nation by 1900, and the McKinley administration was generally given credit. Heber M. Wells was reelected governor in the 1900 general election, George Sutherland was elected to Congress, and, after 22 ballots, Thomas F. Kearns, a young and prominent mining magnate, was elected to the remaining four years of the unfilled Senate seat.

In 1903 the Utah legislature elected Reed Smoot, a Mormon apostle and Provo businessman, to the United States Senate to succeed Joseph L. Rawlings. Senator Smoot then proceeded to put together a powerful political machine that controlled Utah's Republican party for several years. Utah's second governor, John C. Cutler, elected in 1904, and the third governor, William Spry, elected in 1908 and reelected in 1912, were members of Smoot's machine, which became known as the Federal Bunch because of its many leaders who were federal officeholders.

There remained lingering problems of church and state relationships. Utah was young in political development, with a resulting instability in political loyalties. Mormon Church president Joseph F. Smith, Susa Young Gates, the most prominent Republican woman, and Reed Smoot were all concerned that Utah politics should follow the national pattern, which was Republican, at the turn of the century and for several years thereafter. Mormon-watching had remained a continuing mission of some Utah gentiles. A group of Salt Lake City ministers and lay non-Mormons protested the seating of Reed Smoot to the Senate. Hearings were begun under the chairmanship of Michigan Senator Julius Burrows, which continued through 1906. These centered on the alleged political power of the Mormon Church and on reports of continuing practices of polygamy in Utah. The Burrows committee on Privileges and Elections recommended against the seating of Smoot, but the Republican leadership supported him and Reed Smoot was able to retain his seat.

In 1904 the withholding of support by Joseph F. Smith for lackluster Senator Thomas Kearns proved decisive. A less independent gentile, George Sutherland, was elected by the Republican legislature. The Smoot controversy and the defeat of Thomas Kearns had some far-ranging ramifications. The Mormon Church hierarchy in 1904 made the performing of plural marriages an excommunicable offense and subsequently dropped two members from the Quorum of Twelve Apostles for refusing to comply. The defeat of Kearns, coupled with charges of improper church influence in Utah politics, led to the formation of the American party. This was, in effect, a revival of the old Liberal party under a new name. Former Senator Kearns used his stridently anti-Mormon Salt Lake *Tribune* as the flag-bearer of the new party. The American party won electoral victories in Salt Lake City and Ogden in 1905 and controlled those two cities politically from 1905 to 1911. In the process, it pushed through several progressive reforms, including the establishment of a city-commission form of government for Salt Lake City and the improvement of the urban transportation system.

Defection of Republicans to the American party threatened the balance Smoot and Smith had worked so assiduously to put together. After a defeat at the polls in 1911, the American party was disbanded, and most members returned to the Republican party. This solidified the Republican party, and the Smoot machine proved so effective that in the 1912 presidential election he as able to deliver Utah's three electoral votes to William Howard Taft over Progressive candidate Theodore Roosevelt and Democrat Woodrow Wilson, the winner in the nationwide election. Only Utah and Vermont among the forty-eight states gave their electoral votes to Taft.

The 1916 election signaled the decline of the Smoot machine. Simon Bamberger was elected as the state's first non-Mormon governor and one of the first Jewish state governors in the nation. The clean sweep of the Democrats in Utah in 1916 was their first significant victory since 1896. Although the Democratic win meant the decline of the Smoot machine, Reed Smoot himself remained as United States senator until the next Democratic sweep defeated him in 1932.

Joseph F. Smith, Senator Smoot, and their political allies who dominated Utah for much of the Progressive Era tended to favor business interests, but there was no offering by Utah business of kickbacks, bribes, or favors. Additionally, important Progressive legislation was passed by the Republican members of the Federal Bunch. In boss politics and graft, Utah could not hold a candle to the big-time cities. No business controlled the state as did the Southern Pacific Railroad in California, for example.

The fact that Utah's industrial economy was still very young and diverse during the Progressive Era helped to mitigate particular corporate or individual interests controlling the state. By 1900 prosperity had returned to Utah. Samuel Newhouse was able to capitalize on the commercial potential of the copper from his Highland Boy mine in Bingham Canyon to supply the metal as an inexpensive but efficient conducting wire to meet the needs of expanding home electrification. Daniel C. Jackling exploited the poor-grade copper ores in Bingham Canyon with open-pit mining and the refining of huge quantities of ore at the mills and smelters at Magna, Arthur, and Tooele. Thomas F. Kearns also made a fortune in mining, but mining of a different sort. The gold and silver from the Mayflower properties of his Silver King Mining Company at Park City formed the basis of his fortune.

Wealth came to Simon Bamberger through the building of an interurban railroad from Salt Lake City to Ogden and the development of Lagoon near Farmington as a popular fun spot. It was rivaled only by Saltair, built on the south shore of the Great Salt Lake in 1893, as a favorite recreational site. David Eccles made a fortune in lumber, utilities, and sugar, and then began a major bank operation, which became the First Security Corporation. The Denver and Rio Grande Railroad with its subsidiary, the Utah Fuel Company, which mined and shipped much of Carbon County's coal production, was a major corporation in the state. In 1897 Lucien Nunn came to Utah and set up in Provo Canyon the world's largest alternating-current transmission system to deliver 40,000 volts to the ore-processing plants at Mercur. His Telluride Institute became an important training, producing, and marketing center. In 1913 eighteen competing power companies were merged into the Utah Power and Light Company, which is to this day the predominant electrical utility in Utah. Yet none of these individuals or companies were able to wield sufficient influence in Utah politics to serve mainly their own interests.

No doubt abuses sprang up in Utah amid the frenetic activity and economic growth of the Progressive Era. Cities expanded in size and new suburbs were built. Utah was becoming not only more industrialized but also more urbanized. Even though there was substantial economic and industrial development during the first twenty years of the twentieth century, Utah actually was farther behind the nation than it had been in 1890 in the percentage of the labor force engaged in manufacturing. However, Utah did experience the commercialization of agriculture, the emergence of a substantial business community, and the development of corporate mining and manufacturing.

Purebred Hereford cattle and Spanish Merino and French Rambouillet sheep were imported and helped to improve quality and profits in the livestock industry. Stockyards and packing plants were built to fatten and process the livestock. The Ogden yards, built in 1906, grew to become one of the largest meat-processing facilities west of Omaha, Nebraska.

The practice of grazing the increasing herds on summer mountain pastures began to devastate the watersheds. The larger herds devoured and trampled the grasses. Runoffs of spring snow and summer rain caused serious erosion and disastrous floods in many localities. One of the major contributions of Progressivism was conservation of natural resources. Utahns generally gave strong support for various measures designed to preserve and protect valuable natural resources. Governor Spry and Senator Smoot were especially supportive of conservation measures. Many Utahns approved of national action to preserve forest and range lands and to develop water resources. Concerned about protecting the beauty of Utah's canyons and mountains, politicians and the public encouraged the preservation of Natural Bridges, Zion, Rainbow Bridge, and Dinosaurland as national monuments during the Progressive Era. Controlled grazing under United States Forest Service management and implementation of conservation methods eventually preserved the watersheds and mountain pastures.

The development of a local canning industry centered on the Wasatch Front helped to spur commercial agriculture. Utah farmers supplied fruit, tomatoes, and other fresh vegetables to canneries. The canning of condensed milk by the Sego Milk Company gave new portability to the products of Utah's dairymen, who saw their production go up with the increasing popularity of purebred Holstein cows. Cheese processing gave an additional stimulation to the Utah dairy industry. Since food and drug administration was a part of the Progressive Era's drive for reform, a state dairy and food commission was established in 1903, and laws were passed to regulate food handling and processing. One notable failure was a lack of effective regulation of the meat-packing industry. However, a State Board of Health with far-ranging powers was established. It had authority to deal with unsanitary conditions in general and to clean up water systems and supplies. The practices of veterinarians, physicians, optometrists, and barbers were also regulated by new state laws.

Utah's first constitution, written in 1895, is the only one the state has ever known. Although this constitution shows little influence from the long and stressful territorial experience, the lingering effect of Populism—the farmers' protest movement of the 1890s—is evident. The constitution provided for an eight-hour day for public employees, prohibited women and children from laboring in underground mines, and mandated health and safety legislation for industrial workers. It also uniquely and significantly provided for women's suffrage. The Progressives, however, found there was much more reform work to do, especially in the area of labor-related legislation.

Numerous small company towns housed the burgeoning immigrant population, often in unpleasant and unhealthful circumstances. Laws were passed to prohibit enforced patronage of company stores and to exempt employees from the mandate of living in company housing. Concern for mine workers was evident in legislation extending the eight-hour day to mine and smelter workers. No boys under fourteen or women of any age were to be allowed to work in mining and smelting. A state board for the arbitration of labor disputes was created, and blacklisting of employees was prohibited. Regulations concerning industrial employment pro-

This is the Utah Central Railroad engine #10 with crew, mechanics, and laborers in front of the Salt Lake Roundhouse. The numerous chimneys on the roundhouse roof were used to exhaust engine fumes while the motor was being serviced. Photo by F.I. Monson and Co., courtesy, Utah State Historical Society

vided for a minimum wage, increasingly stronger mine-safety regulations, and a strict workmen's compensation law. In 1917 the state legislature created a State Industrial Commission, declared unions legal organizations, and attempted to limit the use of injunctions in breaking strikes.

Even though some complained that Utah was backward and enacted little Progressive reform legislation, it can be demonstrated that a great bulk of Progressive legislation was passed regarding the conditions of industrial work and the treatment of industrial workers by big business. There was an obvious need for this type of legislation, and the state government responded. There was also some consumer legislation, such as the creation of a State Board of Bank Examiners. In the area of political reform, the party ballot printed and provided by political parties was replaced by ballots printed by a public commission and supplied to voters only at polling places under controlled conditions. The Initiative and Referendum were also passed to give voters the means of originating laws and rejecting laws the legislature had passed. Neither has been used very often.

Overall, Utah was perhaps about as progressive as circumstances dictated. Generally, Utah legislators responded to the Progressive Reform agenda by picking and choosing from the Progressive menu those measures that were most needed and would be most helpful in dealing with the rapidly changing conditions of statehood and life in the twentieth century. Joseph F. Smith, Reed Smoot, and, indeed, most other Utahns had hoped that Utah would be accepted by other Americans and that Utahns would be seen as loyal patriots and accomplished citizens who would uphold traditional American values. By the end of the Progressive Era, Utah was finally being accepted on these terms.

AUERBAC
REX
FURNITURE CO.

Decades of Transition: World War I to the 1980s

The peace that progressives had hoped for was ended by the events following the assassination of the Austrian Archduke Francis Ferdinand at Sarajevo in June 1914. However, the prosperity Progressives sought was accentuated as orders for the war effort in Europe poured into the United States. Utahns were as eager to enrich themselves as were other Americans. Agricultural and metal products were in great demand, and as a consequence Utahns realized a prosperity such as they had never seen before.

The American aloofness from the First World War came to an end in 1917. The United States' entry into the war gave Utahns the opportunity to prove that they were also patriotic. Along with other Americans Utahns planted liberty gardens, subscribed to Liberty Bond issues, volunteered for military service, and registered for the draft when it was instituted. Nearly 21,000 Utah soldiers saw military service during the First World War. Of those, 447 lost their lives before the armistice of November 11, 1918, ended the conflict.

The integration of the Utah economy into national patterns had come at an opportune time for Utahns to enjoy a healthy boom that lasted until the war's end. But the armi-

The new Utah State Capitol can be seen at the end of State Street in 1918. Courtesy, Brigham Young University

With the decline of the ecclesiastical dominion in Utah, a broader, secular network of commercial, industrial, and private interests began to influence the state. This transition can be observed in the growth and development of the State Fair Grounds. As commercial interests took hold of the state, the fairgrounds hosted a rash of new building. New manufactured goods, produce, livestock, and entertainment were all offered at the growing State Fair in 1917. Photo by L. Holland, courtesy, Utah State Historical Society

stice was followed by dramatic cuts in military expenditures. European farms also returned to greater productivity, thus greatly reducing the demand for American farm products. These circumstances brought an end to the wartime prosperity for many Utahns.

As early as 1919 the production of metals from the Utah mining industry dropped by more than 50 percent from the 1918 level. Mills began to close, and in 1921 the Utah Copper Company ceased production entirely. Mine and mill towns lost half or more of their wartime populations. Soon the effect of the depressed metal-mining industry was apparent in other areas of the economy. Coal mines, the electrical utilities, and the railroads were adversely impacted and began laying off employees. Layoffs and cutbacks created a general economic decline as overall purchasing power in Utah eroded significantly. Only gradually did recovery come in the Utah mining industry.

Some felt that on the farms conditions were even worse than in the Utah mining towns. It was not until the winter of 1920, however, that the depression hit Utah farms with its staggering blow. During the war Utah farmers had exerted every effort to feed American and Allied troops in Europe. They had taken up new lands and grown more food. By 1920 they had overproduced. The eventual consequence was drastically falling prices. Wheat prices dropped more than 250 percent from November 1919 to November 1921. Many farmers left their land to move to the city or left the state to seek jobs and greater opportunity. During the 1920s about 50,000 Utahns moved from the state. Many of those who left were the young and ambitious who hoped for a better life. Homes and yards in Utah came to be neglected and fell into disrepair, presenting a graphic statement of the general economic condition.

As Utah's two basic industries—mining and agriculture—suffered through difficult economic times in the 1920s, much of the rest of the American nation was beginning to enjoy a remarkable interlude marked by technological advances, social transformation, and a degree of prosperity.

While some sectors of the Utah economy continued to lag behind, other Utahns began enjoying changes that were revolutionizing their life-styles. Utah was now passing from the candle and oil lamp to the electrical age. Handy new appliances such as refrigerators, vacuum cleaners, electric irons, radios, and phonographs were becoming commonplace, easing lives and brightening leisure hours. The horse and buggy and the dirt roads of an earlier era were disappearing, replaced by the automobile and paved highways. Buses, trucks, and airplanes were opening entire new industries, making blacksmith shops a curiosity of the past.

Among the most exciting and most discussed inventions to hit America was the radio. The first commercial radio broadcast in America was aired in 1920. In 1922 station KZN in Salt Lake City opened, offering a half hour of programming each evening from eight o'clock to eight-thirty. In 1925 the call letters were changed to KSL. Station KLO opened in Ogden in 1924, and over the years many other stations have joined the Utah radio family to advertise and set standards for music, humor, and language.

The roaring twenties were the days of the flapper and the big-band sound. Dances at Saltair featured famous bands and that new sensation called the Charleston. In 1902 the motion picture was introduced, and by World War I there were movie theaters in Utah's major cities. Toward the end of the 1920s the talkies were introduced. Three Parry brothers from southern Utah began promoting their region as an outdoor studio for Hollywood movies. Tom Mix made the silent film *Deadwood Gulch* near Kanab in 1922. In 1939 John Wayne got his first big break in movies when he starred in the John Ford-directed classic, *Stagecoach*, filmed in southeastern Utah's Navajo country. Cedar City and Kanab became Utah's moviemaking center, facilitated by a thirty-three-mile railroad extension from Lund to Cedar City, completed in 1923, which improved access to the beauty of southern Utah's parks and mountains for both tourists and the movie industry. The filmmakers hired hundreds of Utahns as extras; rented rooms, livestock, and implements; and in many ways stimulated the economy.

Since the days when the land belonged to the Indians, Utah has been a crossroads of travel and communications. The Spanish explorers, mountain men, wagon trains, federal-government explorers, telegraph, Pony Express, stagecoach, and railroad all passed through Utah. By the end of World War I air transportation was added to the list of technological marvels that were changing lives drastically. Salt Lake City became an important crossroads city for transcontinental mail flights and for commercial passenger service. In 1926 airmail service, taking eight hours' flight time, was established between Los Angeles and Salt Lake City. The next year commercial air traffic began. The first hardy passengers dressed in flight suits, wore goggles, carried parachutes, and brought their own lunches if they felt their stomachs could tolerate food.

The general national prosperity and Utah's tentative prosperity in the 1920s were suddenly changed to an all-out Depression when the stock market crash of October 1929 signaled the onset of an economic downturn that hit harder and stayed longer than any in the nation's history. People who had suffered economically in the 1920s without asking for government solutions to their problems now came to believe that government should provide help in these more terrible times. Utah's industrial workers and farmers suffered severely; in fact, for many Utahns the Depression was worse than it was for most other Americans.

The basic Utah industries of mining and agriculture had never really recovered from the post-World War I depression. Both industries were tied firmly to the national and international economy. Demands were low through the twenties and dropped even lower with the Great Depression. To compound Utah's difficulties, severe drought struck the state in 1931 and again in 1934. Unemployment reached 35.8 percent in 1932. Per capita income dropped by more than half between 1929 and 1933.

Initially, President Hoover's attitude was that local agencies and charities should take care of relief. Utah's Democratic governor, George Dern, at first believed that the best thing that state government could do would be to reduce the tax load. Eventually President Hoover began to use some of the instruments of government at his command to combat the Depression. Gradually and somewhat reluctantly he began to launch programs of public works to build dams and highways and at the same time to provide employment. He also founded the Reconstruction Finance Corporation to help bolster the sagging financial structure of the nation by making federal money available, on loan, to the states. Governor Dern's Committee on Emergency Relief for Utah used much of the RFC loan money to buy food, clothing, and fuel for the needy. By March 1933 nearly 30 percent of Utahns were receiving aid from this source.

President Hoover's sense of how much direct relief could be given without damaging the character and independence of the people kept him from supporting or approving measures that would be truly effective against so great an economic calamity. In 1932 Franklin D. Roosevelt defeated Hoover in the presidential election. In his inaugural address F.D.R. assured Americans that they had nothing to fear but fear itself, and then he proceeded to initiate a wide variety of relief and recovery programs that became known as the New Deal. Utah's newly elected governor, Democrat Henry H. Blood, indicated at his inaugural that Utah would look to Washington for direction and aid in overcoming the Depression. He was not disappointed. Under acronyms such as FERA, PWA, and WPA, along with many other agencies, both direct relief and work relief were extended.

New Deal programs had a major impact in Utah. Only eight states received more help per person. One of the most popular New Deal programs to impact Utah was the Civilian Conservation Corps, which brought several thousand young men to Utah from all parts of the country to clear forest trails, fight fires, reseed grasses and trees, build roads, and do a wide variety of other tasks.

The Works Progress Administration (WPA) financed a variety of public projects in Utah from its inception in 1935 until it was phased out in 1942. Dams and canals were built, highways were constructed and maintained, and many public buildings were built and renovated. The WPA also afforded employment to artists, musicians, and writers on a variety of worthwhile cultural projects.

Millions of federal-relief and work-relief dollars helped put bread on the tables and clothes on the backs of Utahns. The expenditure of New Deal dollars stimulated spending and enormously impacted the well-being of Utah's retail merchants.

The Depression also had some long-term political effects in Utah. Senator Reed Smoot was defeated by Elbert D. Thomas, a University of Utah professor. The Democratic landslide of 1932 that ended Smoot's 30-year Senate tenure brought a Democratic victory that extended through the state legislature to local and county government. Henry H. Blood, elected in 1932, was reelected governor in 1936 and succeeded by Herbert B. Maw in 1940 and 1944. It was not until 1948, when J. Bracken Lee won the Utah statehouse, that a Republican governor was elected in Utah since Charles R. Mabey's election in 1920. Although in 1936 the *Deseret News* strongly supported Republican candidate Alf Landon for president and several Mormon Church officials denounced the New Deal, Roosevelt again won a landslide victory. Only five Republicans were elected to the Utah legislature that year. The New Deal overturned a general Republican trend in Utah politics and created a base of loyalty to the Democratic party that continued for many years.

The New Deal also brought a number of Utahns into national political prominence. Former Governor George H. Dern became Secretary of War in 1933. Ogden banker E. G. Bennett helped set up the Federal Deposit Insurance Corporation, which began operating in 1933, and Marriner S. Eccles joined the Treasury Department in 1934. The following year he became chairman of the Federal Reserve Board, remaining chairman until 1948 and on the board until 1951. It was Eccles who helped persuade Roosevelt that a federal compensatory fiscal policy was needed: government spending when private spending declined during depressions and taxing during inflationary periods. Eccles and the Federal Reserve Board became major shapers of federal taxing and spending policies.

Another outcome of the Great Depression was the initiation in 1936 of the Mormon Church Security Program, later called the Church Welfare Program. This system was modeled after a cooperative program developed by Pioneer Stake president Harold B. Lee that was designed to help the members of his stake on Salt Lake City's west side. Church congregations were to be part owners of producing cooperative farms that basically were run by volunteer workers. The products of the cooperatives were redistributed to the storehouses of local bishops and allocated by them to the poor within their congregations.

Despite all the efforts, the combined labors of local, state, federal, church, and private organizations failed to banish depression entirely from the land. Full economic recovery came only after war broke out in Europe late in 1939. In December 1941 America entered World War II. Then the enormous wartime demand for metals and agricultural products again brought prosperity to Utah. With the onset of war the relief programs were dismantled, and Utahns committed themselves to the task of winning the war against fascism.

Utah's men and women were called into the armed forces.

More than 65,000 Utahns served in the various branches of the military, and 1,450 gave their lives in the defense of freedom. Utah was also called upon to furnish war materials and to build defense plants and training centers. War-related industries brought full employment. To fill demands, thousands of women accepted wartime employment, and many additional people came to Utah to work in defense-related industries. In many ways family life was disrupted by relocation to a new area, military service, and defense employment of mothers. Rationing was imposed to save critical items—among them rubber and gasoline—for the military effort. With fewer consumer items available, many people invested their increased earnings in U.S. War Bonds.

The use of aircraft to transport military personnel and to carry bombs altered warfare significantly between 1918 and 1941. United States coastal areas now seemed to be potentially vulnerable to enemy attack. Secure inland bases were sought to store supplies, to train military personnel, and to serve as shipping centers. Existing installations such as Fort Douglas became headquarters of army operations for the Rocky Mountain and Pacific Coast states. Men from the eleven Western states were inducted into military life at Fort Douglas, which also served as a repair and salvage center for military vehicles and equipment. The Ogden Arsenal was a manufacturing center for bombs, artillery shells, and machine-gun belts, and it doubled as a distribution center. Hill Field, constructed between January and November of 1940, became an air defense, supply, and training base; it still remains as one of America's important national defense units.

A number of military and governmental installations were built in Utah. The Geneva Steel Plant was built on the eastern shore of Utah Lake between 1942 and 1943 at a cost of $200 million. Beginning in 1944, iron ore was brought from Cedar City and coal from Carbon County for smelting purposes. Geneva served to stimulate Utah's steel industry, which had until this time been centered mainly around Columbia Steel's Ironton plant, built near Springville in 1924. The Utah General Depot, now known as Defense Depot Ogden, was established as a major storage and distribution plant; the U.S. Naval Supply Depot at Clearfield was built to serve the navy as a general depot; and the Tooele Ordnance Depot was to receive, store, repair, and ship combat vehicles, small arms, and fire equipment.

The Kearns Army Air Base was established west of Salt Lake City as a training center for army air corps personnel, and Wendover Air Force Base became a gunnery range and a bomb-storage depot. The crew of the *Enola Gay*, which dropped the atomic bomb on Hiroshima in 1945, trained at

Above: *The signing of the Armistice on November 11, 1918, brought the young men of Utah back home. In Ogden, a large parade down Washington Boulevard welcomed the soldiers home. Courtesy, Ogden Chamber of Commerce and Hill Air Force Base*

Below: *Thousands of Salt Lakers crowded the streets celebrating the end of World War I on November 11, including this group riding on a Crawford Furniture Company delivery wagon. Photo by Sainsbury and Siddoway, courtesy, LDS Church Archives*

Above: *The LDS Church responded to the Great Depression in 1936 with the Security Plan, which eventually became known as the Church Welfare Plan. This was an intensive, churchwide organization in which each stake produced certain goods that were stored in the Bishops Storehouse in Salt Lake City, shown here, which were then dispensed to needy families. The families in turn worked for whatever was given to them. Courtesy, LDS Church Archives*

Top: *This 1925 view of the intersection of South Temple and Main streets in Salt Lake City features a statue of Brigham Young flanked by the earlier inhabitants of Utah, the Indian and the trapper. It is from this spot that the surveying of Salt Lake City and the rest of Utah commenced. Photo by Shipler Commercial Photography, courtesy, Brigham Young University Photo Archives*

Wendover. The Dugway Proving Grounds experimented with chemical warfare, and the Deseret Chemical Depot, twenty miles south of Tooele, became a storage and shipping center for chemical materials. The Bushnell Hospital at Brigham City was built as a treatment center for American soldiers wounded in action. Its staff pioneered in the use of penicillin in the spring of 1943. After the war it was closed for three years, but in 1948 it was reopened as an Intermountain Indian School run by the Bureau of Indian Affairs. Prisoner-of-war camps were also established in Utah to hold German and Italian prisoners.

After the war Hill Field, the Tooele Depot, Dugway Proving Grounds, and others continued to be significant features of the Utah economy. They employed thousands of workers as Utah became the home of missile-related industries and defense installations. By 1963 defense had become Utah's largest enterprise. Today Utah continues to rank near the top of the states in the proportion of the overall economy related to defense.

The end of the war found Utah on a course of economic development that was to change little until the late 1970s. New jobs and new prosperity had continued through the war's end. Opportunities had apparently brought about a permanent reversal of the outmigration of Utahns to other states. Many people now came to Utah to find work and to make homes. Government contracts and new industries further concentrated the state population along the Wasatch Front, where new building and new suburbs made Salt Lake City, Ogden, and Provo much like other modern American cities. Supermarkets and shopping malls sprang up, accessible by superhighways. Utahns now indulged themselves with televisions, hi-fi stereos, video games, and convenience foods—the blessings of modern twentieth-century American life. Growth and prosperity were in the ascendancy in Utah.

World War II also brought to Utah another wave of immigration, consisting of African Americans, Hispanic Americans, and Asian Americans. These final immigrants to Utah have sometimes been termed "unassimilated" minorities. The first black, James P. Beckwourth, arrived in Utah in the 1820s with the mountain men to trap extensively in Utah's mountain valleys in the employ of Ashley and Henry. In 1843 and again in 1845 John C. Fremont came through Utah, bringing with him a black servant named Jacob Dobson, who developed into a skilled frontiersman. When the Mormon Pioneer Company entered the Salt Lake Valley in 1847, three African Americans were included: Green Flake, Oscar Crosby, and Hark Lay. As Mormon immigrants arrived from the Southern states, some brought slaves with them. From time to time non-Mormons traveling through the Utah Territory introduced additional slaves. The first census taken in Utah Territory in 1850 revealed that there were twenty-four free blacks and twenty-six slaves. Ten years later there were thirty free blacks and twenty-nine slaves.

The Compromise of 1850, which granted territorial status to Utah, left the issue of the legality of slavery up to the people of the territory to decide. At first the Utah territorial legislature recognized and protected slave property. However, in 1862, after the start of the Civil War, the Congress of the United States prohibited slavery in the territories and thereby freed all slaves in Utah.

After the Civil War three regiments of black soldiers—the Twenty-fourth Infantry regiment and the Ninth Cavalry—were stationed in Utah. The Ninth Cavalry, serving at Fort Duchesne in eastern Utah, built a military post, protected settlers, controlled Indians, guarded stage and railway lines, and built and maintained roads. The arrival of the Twenty-fourth Infantry Regiment at Fort Douglas in October 1896 marked one of the first times in American military history that black troops were stationed contiguous to a large white community.

The African American population of Utah grew slowly, but by the turn of the century there were 678 blacks living in Utah. Most were concentrated in Salt Lake City or Ogden, where employment opportunities were more prevalent. The railroad center at Ogden offered the best prospect for employment for blacks and was the biggest employer until the outbreak of World War 11. Prior to the war the Depression years had proved especially difficult for Utah's black families, but World War 11 brought with it defense plants and military installations that provided employment opportunities. There were 2,400 African Americans from the south recruited to come to Utah to work at Clearfield Naval Supply Depot.

For the most part Utah's blacks found that they were left out of the mainstream of social and cultural life. Out of necessity, they developed their own churches, clubs, community centers, fraternal organizations, and newspapers. Utah's first black church was the Trinity African Methodist Episcopal Church in Salt Lake City.

In addition to being left out, blacks encountered discriminatory laws and practices. Until 1963 Utah law prohibited marriages between whites and blacks. Prior to the Civil Rights gains of the 1960s, blacks in Utah found they could not attend many public events on an equal basis. "Whites only" hotels, motels, and restaurants were common, and racial prejudice resulted in the lynching of a black man, Robert Marshall, at Price, Utah, in 1925.

Serving to exacerbate the racial problems facing blacks in Utah was the Mormon Church practice of denying the priesthood to black males. Finally, on June 8, 1978, Mormon Church president Spencer W. Kimball set forth a new church policy wherein all faithful, worthy men in the church could receive the priesthood.

Within Utah, national and local organizations offered a variety of assistance to blacks. In 1919 a branch of the NAACP was formed in Salt Lake City to work for legal and social reforms. Later a branch was created in Ogden to assist in the fight for human rights. In 1980 Utah's black population numbered about 10,000 and it was continuing to grow. Most lived on the Wasatch Front in Weber, Salt Lake, and Davis counties, where jobs with the federal government offer opportunities with little discrimination.

The first permanent Hispanic residents of Utah arrived around the turn of the century, coming from northern New Mexico and southern Colorado to work as sheepherders and ranch hands. Between 1910 and America's entry into World War I, a flood of Mexicans crossed legally or illegally into the United States. Many made their way to Utah, where they found work in the mines and mills or for the railroads. Utah's Hispanic population had increased tenfold from 1910 to 1920. During the 1920s additional Hispanics came to Utah as migrant farm workers. The Great Depression caused particularly hard times for the migrant workers. As unemployment increased and desperate people came to accept almost any kind of work at any price, the migrant workers found that white Utahns took their farm jobs. Under the circumstances, many of the migrant laborers returned to Mexico.

During and after World War II another great influx of Hispanic people arrived in the state. Many came to answer the sudden demand for workers in agriculture and industry. In the decade of the 1950s nearly 20,000 Hispanics entered Utah, and in the 1960s more than 20,000 were added to the population. Facing problems of substandard housing, inadequate health care, low wages, and language and cultural barriers, the Hispanics organized for mutual protection and equal rights. Utah's Hispanic populations has maintained many traditional holidays and customs. Preservation of the Hispanic cultural heritage is facilitated by the fact that over 80 percent of the Hispanics live in urban communities along the Wasatch front.

A third unassimilated minority in Utah consists of the 28,000 Asians from China, Japan, and the Pacific islands and those recently arrived from Southeast Asia. The first in Utah were the Chinese, who came in 1869 as employees of the Central Pacific Railroad. After the completion of the transcontinental line, some found opportunities in mining towns and some moved to Salt Lake City or Ogden to form all-Chinese neighborhoods and to become small-business owners. Between 1882 and 1952 Chinese Exclusion laws served to keep Chinese immigrants out of America. After the 1949 Communist takeover of mainland China, the ban was lifted, and many Chinese made their way to America from Hong Kong and Taiwan; some have found their way to Utah to become citizens.

During the first two decades of the twentieth century, the Japanese, who were not subject to the provisions of the Chinese Exclusion acts, made their way to America. By 1920 nearly 3,000 Japanese resided in Utah. Some worked in the mines at Bingham or the coal mines in Carbon County. Some became farm laborers, and others bought small plots of ground and became very successful truck farmers. During the Depression decade many of Utah's Japanese left to relocate in California or to return to their homeland. Fear of possible Japanese subversion on the Pacific Coast during World War II led to the tragic creation of Japanese Relocation Centers. At Topaz near Delta in Millard County one of these ten relocation camps in the United States was established. Beginning September 11, 1942, about 8,000 Japanese became involuntary occupants of tarpaper barracks. By the time Topaz closed on October 31, 1945, many of the internees had been allowed to leave the relocation center for various reasons—some to settle at places such as Tooele, where employment was available at the Tooele Ordnance Depot. After the closing of Topaz, many Japanese returned to California. By 1980 the Japanese population of Utah was about 6,000.

The long Vietnam War caused dislocation of people in Vietnam, Laos, and Cambodia. Perhaps as many as 132,000 refugees escaped to the United States in the months and years after the April 30, 1975 Communist victory. Over several years about 9,500 Vietnamese, Laotians, and Cambodians made their way to Utah to live with sponsor families until they could find work and a home. In Utah, as well as elsewhere in America, the Southeast Asians have found life very different, and they have suffered from culture shock. Many of the younger Southeast Asians, and most are young, have adjusted more readily to American life than the adults. As a group, however, the Southeast Asians have clung to their culture and beautiful crafts.

Some observers have suggested that from 1920 to 1980 there was little unique to Utah's history. In a limited sense this may be true, but history and culture do not consist simply of what people do. What they think and communicate to others is a vital part of cultural life. Their activities and the content of the activities have important meanings for the people who participate, both for the reaffirmation of their identity and for the definition of their place. Utahns, and Mormons in particular, have distinctive traits that have remained. The resemblance to other Americans is in some ways superficial. Mormons are still a unique people who cherish their uniqueness. Their cultural "Americanization" was more apparent than real. Utah's special historical legacy has helped ensure that it will not be a carbon copy of other American states.

Traditional pioneer skills and crafts such as quilting and canning have been perpetuated to give a distinctive quality to Utah's cultural form. Also deeply imbedded in Utah culture is a large repertoire of songs and hymns sung by Mormons, expressing their faith and conviction and praising their mountains, valleys, and traditions. Both their temples and their hills remain for Mormons symbols of the spiritual. Much of the Utah art and cultural expression, even holidays and celebrations, can be classified as didactic in tone and historical in orientation, presenting a ritualistic retelling of the story of the Mormon past both to entertain and to present a pageant of Utah's unique history. Utah has continued to have one of the highest birth rates in the nation, and Utahns have a strong sense of territoriality, a homing sense to return to their origins. A great emphasis is placed on family, genealogy, and family organizations. It is quite possible that Utah leads the nation in family reunions.

There also appears to be a continuing bias in Utah in favor of group over individual expression and achievement. The Mormon Church has remained a powerful agent in Utah. It can galvanize its followers into participation and response to combat disaster or to confront moral or political issues. Sometimes the response may seem to outsiders to be as indiscriminate and obstructive as Mormon responses seemed to nineteenth-

Utah's domed State Capitol building on a hill overlooking Salt Lake City. Ground breaking took place in 1911 and the building was dedicated on October 9, 1916. Courtesy, Utah State Historical Society

century gentiles. But the point is that the response to what Mormons perceive as the wishes of church leaders is remarkable. There is a continuing respect among Mormon Church members for the authority of their church leaders. Also, Mormonism is a faith that continues to exact a great commitment from its members in terms of contributions of time and money to church activities and enterprises.

By 1920 just over 50 percent of the Utah population was Mormon. By 1940 the percentage had reached 61 and it continued to grow, reaching 72 percent in 1970. In recent years the Mormon Church has displayed an increasingly open and lively interest in political matters that have been defined as having important moral dimensions. Examples would include the defeat in 1968 of a liquor-by-the-drink referendum, partly because of Mormon Church opposition. More recently there has been the church opposition to the Equal Rights Amendment. It appeared that by 1980 the Mormon influence was more evident and more powerful in Utah than perhaps at any other time in this century.

Utah's two senators, with Orrin Hatch's victory in 1976 over Frank E. Moss, were Republicans—Jake Garn was senior Senator, and Utah's two Republican members of the House of Representatives all ranked high among interest groups measuring the conservativeness of voting records. In 1986, Democrat Wayne Owens broke the Republican monopoly on Congressional seats with his election. There appears to be little ideological difference between Utah Democrats and Republicans, however. Both parties have reflected the basic conservatism of the Mormon Church. Party ideological differences are so few that often lifelong Democrats run on the Republican ticket in order to enhance their electoral chances. All Utah officials in the recent past-maverick Republican governor, J. Bracken Lee (1948-1956), George D. Clyde (1956-1964), Utah's only three-term governor, Democrat Calvin L. Ramplon (1964-1976), his handpicked successor, Scott Matheson (1976-1984), and Republican Norman Bangerter (1984-1992) worked closely with business to encourage development and growth within the state. All were boosters who advocated rapid economic growth through the founding of new business and industry. In general one would have to judge that they were successful in that the level of development and the rise in prosperity have been phenomenal. Utah's per capita income more than doubled from 1965 to 1975, though it continued to lag behind the national average. The population from 1940 to 1980 grew at a faster rate than the national growth rate. In that time the economy also become even more intricately interwoven into that of the national pattern and, indeed, even that of the world.

From World War II through the 1970s the Utah economy came to be based on government, manufacturing, mining, transportation, agriculture, tourism, and recreation. The federal government owns 64.4 percent of the land in Utah, and 20 percent of the employment in the state was with the federal government. Utahns remained ambivalent in their attitudes toward the federal government. For half a century most of the population yearned for statehood in order to throw off the yoke of Washington control. Since territorial days voters have displayed a distrust of Washington's meddling in local matters. Candidates for federal office have frequently appeared to be running against Washington and its influence.

Yet, on the other hand, there has been a pronounced eagerness among Utahns to secure Utah's share of reclamation, defense, and other federally funded programs, such as urban renewal, highway funds, and public works. Support for maintaining the funding of the Central Utah Project was a virtual litmus test for Utah politicians. Everyone seemed to recognize that the federal government had a great impact in the state, and most saw this as a mixed blessing. On the one hand the federal dollars helped increase prosperity and stimulated growth, made federal resources available, and helped preserve the environment; the trade-off was a growing federal influence and the fear that Utah was exchanging its hard-won and, of course, limited autonomy for prosperity.

In manufacturing, Utah moved more and more by 1980 to the processing of raw materials and the manufacture of finished goods within the state, as contrasted with the trend that dominated from 1869 until the 1940's of shipping raw materials out of the state for processing. World market conditions favored industrial and highly developed economies and Utah tried to adapt. Manufacturing more than tripled, as did the number of manufacturing employees from 1945 to 1980.

At the same time that manufacturing was increasing, Utah remained a raw-materials producer. Mining expanded, led by the Kennecott Copper Company, until 1977, when the mining industry fell on hard times, costing Utah thousands of jobs and millions of dollars in payrolls and tax base. It seemed for a time that the rich energy resources of Utah, such as oil, coal, natural gas, and tar sands, would more than offset the losses at Kennecott. Even though growth was experienced and coal mining, especially, saw a revival, that trend reversed itself, and the energy business became less a seller's market.

Utah's crossroads location has made the state a major link in national and international travel and communications. Trucking, railroading, air freight, and passenger service experienced great expansion by 1980, but they too were subject to the ups and downs of the economy. Salt Lake City was the hub-city for Western Airlines until its 1986 merger with Delta. Even so, transportation continued to infuse many dollars into the state's economy.

Agriculture, the economic lifeblood of Utah for so many years, underwent many changes after World War II. The number of farms decreased and their size increased. Rapid economic development and urbanization along the Wasatch Front seemed to pose a threat to Utah's farming future. Many farmers chose to sell their holdings rather than struggle to preserve their traditional ways. The great influx of people, along with manufacturing and transportation developments, caused farmland in Salt Lake County to decrease by nearly 25 percent in the 1970s. Agricultural acreage in Utah diminished by one and one-half times the national average during that decade as congestion and overcrowding replaced farms.

Tourism and recreation developed rapidly after World War II as people experienced prosperity and gained leisure time. Utah's natural beauty, her mountains and canyons proved valuable assets in the Utah Travel Council's promotion of tourism and recreation. Fishing, boating, hiking, camping and, perhaps most of all, skiing saw rapid growth and development. The Salt Palace attracted the Utah Stars of the soon defunct American Basketball Association followed by the Utah Jazz of the National Basketball Association as well as a professional hockey team, and it also drew many conventions. Visitors also frequented historical and cultural sites such as Temple Square, or they took in cultural events, including various theaters such as the Utah Shakespearean Festival at Cedar City.

Government attempted to keep pace with the state's rapid social, economic and population change and development. People expected much of their governments, yet they complained about too much govermnent and too much taxation. Attempts to meet the needs for improvements in education, highways, law enforcement, welfare, mental health, and environmental protection were only partially successful. A basic conservatism toward taxation meant that in education, particularly, needs were not well fund, especially from 1949-1965, and by then the state was in a catch up mode.

Through all the changes brought about by the efforts to bring Utah into conformity with national values and patterns and by the changes of the post war era, Utah still retained its strong individual identity as she approached the last decades of the twentieth century.

One of Utah's most spectacular vistas, Bryce Canyon National Park contains almost 40,000 acres of multicolored, eroded land forms. Iron and manganese oxides give the intricately carved formations their complex hues. The Indian name for this region means "red rocks standing like men in a bowl-shaped canyon." Photo by Mark E. Gibson

The Ute Indians, with their various bands, or divisions, covered a broad section of Utah and Colorado when the Mormon settlers arrived in 1847. Primarily hunters, the Utes used horses to travel long distances in search of game. Pioneer artist George M. Ottinger pictured this group of Utes at the foot of Ensign Peak overlooking the Great Salt Lake. Courtesy, Springville Art Museum

Facing page: *The high cost of outfitting thousands of European emigrants for the overland trail prompted Brigham Young to choose a cheaper form of transportation for these new Mormon converts: the handcart. Courtesy, Springville Art Museum*

Above: *William W, Major, like many nineteenth century artists, painted not as his eye saw it but as he thought it should be. Paying honor to Brigham Young, Major portrayed the church leader and his family surrounded by wealth and gentility. Courtesy, LDS Church Museum of History and Art*

Above: *This pastoral, late nineteenth-century scene in Utah of a farm near the Jordan River in the Salt Lake Valley was painted by Loras Pratt. Courtesy, LDS Church Museum of History and Art*

Left: *This detailed painting of Bishop Samuel Bennion's farm, near the Jordan River in Taylorsville, documents the various elements of an early Utah farm. Artist Don Weggeland spared no details, including a small train in the distance. Courtesy, Springville Art Museum*

Pages 120-121: *Pioneer Artist George Ottinger served as assistant fire chief and chief of the Salt Lake City fire department while working as an artist. This painting captures in vivid, exciting detail the sugar factory fire. The factory, which was built in 1854, was also used as a paper factory. Courtesy, private collection*

SUGAR REF
34

Above and facing page, top: *Salt Lake City, Utah, is graced by these heartwarming Mormon statues. Photos by Audrey Gibson*

Right: *Devastation caused by August 1999 killer force tornado. One man at this exposition site was killed and throughout the city 81 were injured. Courtesy,* Deseret News

Facing page, bottom: *The sight of Mormon temples, like this one in Manti, is indicative of the religious tendencies of the population: more than 70 percent of the state's population is Mormon. The Manti Temple, built in 1888, although not open to the public, is built on a hill and is visible for miles. Photo by Justine Hill*

Above: *The meeting of the rails at Promontory Point, Utah, in May 1869 was a major event in American and Utah histoy. All aspects of life in Utah were affected by the coming of the railroad. This color lithograph depicts a reenactment of this event from producer/director Cecil B. deMille's 1939 production* Union Pacific. *Courtesy, Paramount Pictures and LDS Museum of Church History and Art*

Facing page: *Salt Lake City's Peace Garden offers a quiet place of beauty and reflection. Photo by Mark E. Gibson*

中國和平公園

Above: *Eroded ravines have resulted in thousands of strange formations in stunning shades of pink and orange at Bryce Canyon National Park. Pictured here is Natural Bridge. Photo by Frank Tiller*

Left: *The Double Arch is one of the many geological formations in Arches National Park. Photo by Justine Hill*

Facing page, top: *The Cedar Breaks are another of Utah's breathtaking natural phenomena. Photo by Audrey Gibson*

Far left: *The endless variety of rock formations found in Arches National Park is evidenced in Balanced Rock. Photo by Justine Hill*

USA

Utah's Modern Emergence

The people of each generation and each decade stand on the shoulders of those who preceded them. They benefit from the constructive vision, and build on what has gone before. They must also rectify past mistakes and develop vision of their own, particularly where vision has previously been lacking. The Utahns of the 1980s and 1990s have fortunately had much to build on, but they have also faced challenges in building a vital economy, achieving wise political decisions, providing for the education of the citizens and for the protection of people and the environment, and for recreation and cultural amenities for the people.

With statehood, Utah's economy began to take on a look similar to that of most other states of the American west. As the Mormon Church backed out of controlling a cooperative economy with some communal aspects, the Utah economy emerged as being principally controlled by absentee eastern capitalist investors who made the major decisions affecting the state's basic economy structure. The largely extractive economy was centered in mining, agriculture, and railroad transportation, and controlled by Wall Street investors, making the Utah economy mainly dependent on Wall Street decisions. The economic decision makers generally ruled from New York or Boston without consulting their employees. Their terms of office were not limited by law nor were they voted on by many Utahns.

Utah was awarded the 2002 winter Olympic games on the first ballot of the International Olympic Committee in 1995 and Utahns in Salt Lake City celebrated the announcement wildly in front of the Salt Lake City – County Building. Courtesy, Deseret News

The state's economic scene changed dramatically with the Great Depression. As stalwart, hardworking people searched in vain for work, the New Deal, under President Franklin D. Roosevelt, operated on the philosophy that the federal government should be the employer of last resort. Work relief projects conducted under various New Deal alphabetical agencies helped restore the dignity of work to citizens and provided the means to build roads, bridges, campgrounds, trails, public buildings, sewer and water systems and reclamation projects. The New Deal created an economic shift wherein the Utah economy changed from being controlled from Wall Street to being controlled by Washington, D.C.'s public works and relief programs.

With the outbreak of World War II in Europe in the fall of 1939, federal dollars went to building military bases and other elements of a major military build up. This brought significant population growth and a dramatic increase in personal income and savings for Utahns. Wartime employment also increased Utah's minority population and the numbers of women in the work force. This wartime economy, in fact, made Utah even more dependent on federal contracts and thus even more under control of decisions from Washington, D.C. due to the great dependence on defense related employment.

Wartime anomalies also introduced much social disruption to families and this resulted in many social problems including increased divorce rates, increased unwed pregnancies, a rise in both juvenile delinquency and crime in general. These social issues continue to persist, although overall crime rates have been declining since 1994.

When the war ended in 1945, the federal government began shutting down defense plants and canceling defense contracts. Before the Utah economy experienced much negative impact from the cutbacks, international tensions led to the beginning of a Cold War between the so-called free world on one side and the Soviet Union and its allies on the other. America responded in several ways including increased military expenditures. Cold War military contracts fueled a continuing prosperity for the Utah economy, but the economic fortunes of the state rose and fell with shifts in military spending and the intensity of the Cold War. Utah companies that supplied goods and services to the military-industrial complex such as Thiokol, Sperry Rand, Hercules and

The population growth and economic prosperity generated by World War II military installations and military contrasts was evident in this picture taken from the air over Salt Lake City in the mid-1950s. Courtesy, Hill Air Force Base Logistics Command

St. George, that had a population of about 6,000 in 1960 is near 70,000 population in 2000. The white building in the center is the St. George temple which in 1960 was on the very southern end of town. In the second picture the red building in the center was at the southwestern edge of town in 1960. There was only one house even near by in 1960. Courtesy, Carolyn S. Hinton

Marquardt benefited greatly from defense contracts. By 1963 defense was Utah's largest industry.

Out of Cold War tension, the Atomic Energy Commission began open-air atomic testing at Frenchman and Yucca Flats in Nevada. These tests caused some lasting concerns for Utahns. Following a test in 1953, a large number of sheep in southern Utah sickened and died. The Cedar City, Utah sheep ranchers brought suit against the AEC, but lost their initial court case in 1956. In 1982 Judge Sherman Christensen refiled the suit on behalf of the sheep owners because the AEC had hidden information and there was strong evidence that some witnesses for the government had lied. The Tenth Circuit Court of Appeals in Denver, Colorado, nevertheless, reversed Judge Christensen's decision.

Other southern Utah residents, calling themselves Downwinders, alleged they or family members suffered leukemia and cancer due to radiation exposure caused by atomic testing. Former Secretary of Interior, Stewart Udall headed a team of lawyers that filed suit in 1979 on behalf of the Downwinders before federal judge Bruce S. Jenkins. The case, *Allen v. The United States,* did not come to trial until 1982. Finally, in May 1984 Judge Jenkins ruled in favor of the plaintiffs. However, again the Tenth Circuit Court of Appeals bailed out the AEC by overturning Judge Jenkins' opinion. In 1988 the United States Supreme Court turned down the Downwinders' appeal of the Circuit Court decision. Congress then stepped in to pass in 1990 the Radiation Exposure Compensation Act sponsored by Utah Senator Orrin Hatch and Utah Congressman Wayne Owens. The act apologized to the victims and established a trust fund to pay for some types of injuries up to a maximum of $50,000 per individual case.

Meanwhile, individual uranium prospectors such as Charlie Steen struck it rich. The AEC in 1948 began offering bonuses for significant discoveries of uranium plus a guaranteed price for high-grade uranium ore. These promises set off a frantic search for uranium throughout much of Utah. The greatest successes in finding uranium were at sites near Moab and Monticello in southeastern Utah. Charlie Steen, a down-and-out drifter, became an almost instant millionaire in 1952 when he discovered the Mi Vida Lode in Lisbon Valley near Moab. The Utah uranium boom continued until 1971 when the AEC ceased its heavily subsidized purchase program. By then miners and workers in the uranium industry were experiencing high incidents of cancer because the radium in the poorly ventilated diggings turned to radon gas which caused lung cancer. For years since, some uranium industry waste dumps have remained to challenge the ingenuity and resources of the Environmental Protection Agency.

By the close of the decade of the 1970s, Utah was beginning to move away from its economic dependence on Wash-

Alta, Utah's first ski resort remains one of the most popular. It will be the site of some of the ski venues of the 2002 Olympic games. Courtesy, Utah State Historical Society

ington, D.C. as it moved toward becoming a more mature commonwealth economy. The emerging economy depended less on the extractive mining industries, agriculture, railroading and on federal spending to sustain it. Reliance on federal spending slid back toward the national average of federal dollars coming into the state and dependence on federal dollars generally continued to decline throughout the 1980s and 1990s. Today Utah employers and Utah-owned enterprise accounts for much of the employment in the state, much of the wealth, and much of the continuing economic growth. Before the end of the 1980s a strong post-industrial and post-colonial economy based heavily in electronic and high-tech companies, supplemented by pharmaceutical and medical equipment companies, employment in Utah's public and private institutions of higher education, and tourism and the service industries, accounted for the majority of employment in the state. Although many service sector jobs such as motel maids and fast food services are low paying, contrary to some popular opinion, many service employees, such as lawyers, doctors, nurses, architects, and accountants are paid well.

Even some heavy industry such as Geneva Steel Mills, built by the government during World War II and sold after the war to Pittsburgh-based USX, is now locally owned. In 1987, Utahns, headed by Joseph Cannon, purchased, remodeled, and increased production and employment at Geneva. Ten years later the company filed Chapter 11 bankruptcy, but Geneva continues to persist today as a significant employer in Utah County.

Even though the transition to the new economy was sometimes painful, it has proven beneficial. The Utah economy in 1979 suffered, as did the national economy, from stagnation and inflation. Unemployment rose even further to reach 9.2 percent during the Reagan recession of 1983, but thereafter began a sharp decline. This new Utah commonwealth economy demonstrated great strength to sustain growth. During the 1980s, Utah was the ninth fastest growing state in the United States and it has maintained and exceeded that growth in the 1990s. Much population growth came to the urban areas of the Wasatch Front, but Washington County in southern Utah and Summit County east of Salt Lake City have shown the largest percentage increase in recent years. The vitality of the new economy was well demonstrated when during the Bush Administration recession of 1991-92 the Utah employment rate never reached five percent, which was well below the national average. Since 1993 the Utah unemployment rate has never exceeded four percent, and it has sometimes been below three percent. Much of this economic vigor stems from the new economic maturity, which no longer has to rely so heavily on outside private or federal decisions.

Part of the economic growth has come from the recreational and tourist industries. Utahns have boasted of "The Greatest Snow on Earth," and there are fourteen ski resorts in the state to take advantage of the snow and terrain. During the 1960s and 1970s the state placed a great deal of emphasis on the development of tourism and recreation. Given this focus and the winter sports assets of the state, it seemed logical to many to make a serious bid for the 1998 International Winter Olympic Games. The state's first bid was made in 1988, but when it was announced in 1991 that Atlanta, Georgia would host the 1996 summer games, it spelled doom to Utah's winter Olympic hopes for 1998. When it was soon announced that the 1998 games

Above right: *The E Center built in West Valley City partly to host various venues of the 2002 Winter Olympic Games. It is also home to the Utah Grizzles minor league hockey team. Courtesy, Carolyn S. Hinton*

Right: *Motorists have felt they have been considerably inconvenienced by I-15 construction and the many exit closures. Close quarters driving, 55 mile an hour speed limits and closures have resulted in considerable road rage on the part of some motorists. Courtesy, Carolyn S. Hinton*

would go to Nagano, Japan, the Salt Lake Olympic Committee, known as SLOC, began concentrating on gaining the 2002 Olympic games. Members of the committee attended the winter games in Lillehammer, Norway in 1994 to pitch their bid. Their trip was partly funded by the donation of $500,000 worth of tickets from Utah corporate newcomer, Delta Airlines, which had bought out Western Airlines in 1986. Committee members returned confident they had made a good impression. In June 1995 it was announced that Utah had been awarded the 2002 Winter Olympics in an unprecedented first ballot decision. The announcement sparked a wild celebration for many Utahns, although not everyone agreed that hosting the games would be positive.

Preparations for hosting the games were immediately put on a fast track. In 1997 the E Center in West Valley City was completed. It would host the new Utah Grizzlies hockey team but it was also built as a future venue site for diverse 2002 Olympic events. Before the year was out, the Olympic bobsled and luge track was also dedicated and named Albert's Alley for Prince Albert of Monaco.

Since the Wasatch Front was already experiencing major traffic problems caused by an average seven percent per year increase in traffic volume, it was determined that interstate I-15 needed reconstruction before Utah could hope to host the influx of visitors and traffic expected for the winter games. Bids were let in 1997 for a ten-lane freeway to be built at a cost of $1.59 billion that would be heavily subsidized by federal highway funds. An allied group of construction, engineering, and supply firms calling itself Wasatch Constructors won the contract and construction began in April of 1997. The project, taking four and one-half years to complete, is to be done prior to the 2002 Olympics. Construction has caused major traffic snarls, closures of sections, lanes, overpasses, and on and off ramps, accompanied by motorist "road rage." Delays and detours for motorists have lead to a well-deserved designation for Salt Lake County as one of the ten areas in the United States most adversely impacted by highway construction.

To compound disruption to businesses and motorists due to construction, the Utah Transit Authority undertook a $290 million project of its own to build a sixteen-mile light rail commuter line from Sandy in the south end of the Salt Lake Valley into downtown Salt Lake City. The official name for the line is UTA Transit Express, but it is known popularly as TRAX. The line was completed late in 1999 and is now operating very successfully. The fact that TRAX and the freeway construction have received federal funding has served to reverse the trend wherein Utah had fallen well below the national average for federal monies received by the state. For example, in 1994 Utah ranked 43rd among states in the amount of federal money received. By

Above: *The Utah Transit Authority assisted with federal funds built a sixteen-mile light rail commuter line running from Sandy into downtown Salt Lake City. Completed at a cost of $290 million in 2000 the system has exceeded expectations. Pictured here is a commuter train at the north end of the sixteen mile run as it passes in front of Temple Square on South Temple Street. Courtesy, Carolyn S. Hinton*

Below: *The two stars of the Utah Jazz, Karl Malone and John Stockton, in action. John Stockton has just driven the base line, drawing the defenders to him, before dishing an assist to Karl Malone for a lay-up. Courtesy, Southern Utah University, Gerald R. Sherratt Special Collections Library*

1999 Utah received $1.07 for each Utah tax dollar that went to Washington, D.C. This is much lower than the $2.11 Utah once received at the time that the state was heavily reliant on federal expenditures, but it is a reversal of the trend that prevailed from the mid-1980s to 1997.

Utah citizens in recent decades have witnessed significant achievements in other sport and recreational amenities besides winning the Olympic bid. The Salt Palace attracted the Utah Stars professional basketball team of the now defunct American Basketball Association (ABA), with its colorful red, white and blue ball and in 1971 won the ABA championship. By 1974 the ABA merged its strongest franchises with the National Basketball Association (NBA), leaving other franchises, such as the Utah Stars high and dry. Sam Battistone moved his NBA franchise from New Orleans to Utah where his team became known as the Utah Jazz in 1979. The Jazz had been a losing team when it arrived. During the 1981 season, lovable Frank Layden was hired as coach. In 1984 with newly acquired Adrian Dantley leading the way, the Jazz had its first winning record in franchise history and made the NBA playoffs. With some wise drafts, including picking its two stars, Karl Malone and John Stockton, the Jazz have made the playoffs every year since and is considered one of the NBA's soundest franchises.

In 1988 Frank Layden stepped down as head coach to become the president of the Jazz organization and was replaced by his assistant coach Jerry Sloan. In 1992, under new owner, car dealer Larry Miller, the franchise moved into a new arena, the Delta Center, which seats over 20,000 fans for a basketball game. The 1993 all-star game was hosted in the Delta Center and its success was capped for Jazz fans when Karl Malone and John Stockton were named co-Most Valuable Players for the game. In 1997 the Jazz won the Western Conference Championship but lost the world title to the Chicago Bulls in six games. The Jazz repeated as Western Conference Champions in 1998 but again lost the world title to the Michael Jordan lead Chicago Bulls in six games.

In addition to the Jazz and the Utah Grizzlies, a minor league professional hockey team, Ogden and Salt Lake City have

When it appeared that Utah Jazz basketball team was in danger of being sold to out-of-state interests who might move the team from Utah, local car deal Larry Miller bought the Jazz. He has enhanced the franchise by building the Delta Center as a 20,000 seat home for the Jazz. Courtesy, Southern Utah University, Gerald R. Sherratt Special Collections Library

had a long tradition with minor league baseball franchises. When Salt Lake's triple A franchise, the Salt Lake Gulls, left partly due to deteriorating conditions at Derks Field, the city could do no better than to attract an A independent franchise known as the Salt Lake Trappers. In order to attract another Triple A team, it was determined that Salt Lake City needed a new baseball facility. After much heated discussion it was decided to build the new park on the site of the old Derks Field. The Salt Lake Buzz, a triple A affiliate of the Minnesota Twins, began play at the new Franklin Covey Field in 1994.

Despite the several successful professional sports franchises, Utah sports, over the years, have been dominated by intercollegiate athletics. For example, the state has five universities competing at the Division I level in all sports but football; with three universities competing in Division I football. The Brigham Young University football team had built a reputation as a high scoring quarterback factory, but in 1984 it gained greater recognition as the BYU football team ended the season as the nation's only unbeaten major college team and was declared the mythical national champion by all three major national polls.

Notwithstanding its reputation as a quarterback factory that had turned out several National Football League stars,

After considerable controversy as to where to build a baseball facility that would attract a triple A baseball franchise, it was decided to build Franklin Covey Field on the site of old Derks Field. The facility was completed in time for the Salt Lake Buzz to play its 1994 home games here. Courtesy, Carolyn S. Hinton

Above: *In the 1984 Holiday Bowl Brigham Young University ended the season undefeated by beating Michigan and securing the mythical 1984 National Division I Football Championship. Courtesy, the* Deseret News

Above left: *University of Utah gymnastics team celebrates its tenth national championship and its fourth of the decade of the 1990's. Courtesy, the* Deseret News

no BYU or other Utah football player of any kind or description, had ever won college football's Heisman Trophy awarded to the outstanding player of the year. All that changed in 1990 when BYU's junior quarterback, Ty Detmer, was named the Heisman Trophy winner.

The University of Utah has also experienced great success in its athletic programs. In 1995 the university women's gymnastic team capped an incredible run of success by winning its second consecutive national championship, its tenth national championship over all, and its fourth of the decade of the 1990s. The team has continued to place among the top five in the nation each year since. Furthermore, in 1998 the University of Utah basketball team played the University of Kentucky for the National collegiate championship at the Alamodome in San Antonio, Texas, but unfortunately lost in a close game.

On a much less positive note, it was revealed in 1998 that the Utah Olympic organizers paid money and gave gifts to influence International Olympic Committee member votes. This revelation touched off controversy and investigations that resulted in the resignations of Dave Johnson and Frank Joklik from the committee. Tom Welch, head of the committee until he resigned in the summer of 1997 due to personal and domestic problems, was much criticized for his alleged role in the developing scandal. Several persons, including Tom Welch and Dave Johnson, have since been indicted for either giving bribes, misappropriating money, or accepting bribes. In an effort to offset the negative publicity surrounding allegations of bribery, Mitt Romney, who has a reputation for honesty, openness, and business sense, was appointed new head of SLOC. He got the committee back on track in attracting sponsor money and overcoming some of the negative effects of the scandal.

Utahns have long had legitimate concern about issues related to conservation and the environment. Unlike many westerners, Utahns during the Progressive Era generally approved of the setting aside and protection of national forest lands. Senator Reed Smoot was the senate sponsor of the 1916 bill that created the National Park Service. President Theodore Roosevelt, Chief of Forestry, Gifford Pinchot, and conservation measures were all generally approved of by Utahns. In the 1920s the city beautify and the city functional movement were well supported in Utah's urban areas. Public parks and recreation were seen as not only desirable but they appeared necessary. The reclamation movement of the Progressive Era enacted as the Newlands Land Act was bound to be popular in a semi-arid region such as Utah where lack of water is one of the most limiting factors to growth and development. When the Colorado River Compact allotting water to the Upper Basin states of Wyoming, Colorado, Utah and New Mexico and the Lower Basin states of California, Arizona and Nevada was signed giving Utah 23 percent of the Upper Basin's share of Colorado River water, Utahns hoped for Bureau of Reclamation built dams that would store and deliver water to sate Utah's thirst.

The most important and controversial issues that emerged from the proposal known as the Colorado River Storage Project called for dams at Echo Park on the Green River and at Glen Canyon on the Colorado River. The bill also authorized the Weber Basin and the Central Utah Projects. The Echo Park plan created immediate controversy for the proposed reservoir would flood the magnificent scenery of Lodore Canyon

and cover the Dinosaur National Monument. Utah born Bernard DeVoto was angered by the insensitivity of even suggesting the flooding of Lodore Canyon. His articles in opposition to the proposal stirred up environmental organizations to speak out. The Sierra Club led by David Brower and the National Park Service pressured the Director of the Bureau of Reclamation to drop the Echo Park Dam from the list, with Flaming Gorge Dam as a substitute. At the same time, the Bureau was authorized to proceed with the Glen Canyon Dam on the Colorado River.

Today, the Glen Canyon Dam with resulting Lake Powell sitting astride Utah and Arizona is controversial, as David Brower has suggested draining the lake in order to restore the Colorado River's ecology. In March 2000 there were counter demonstrations on opposite sides of the dam in support of preserving and in favor of draining Lake Powell. It, in reality, is not likely to be drained, regardless of the merits of arguments on either side. In order to drain the lake it would require agreement of both the states involved in the Colorado River Compact and Congress. Approval by the Upper Basin states, under existing conditions, is not a realistic expectation.

The Central Utah Project (CUP) to divert water from the Duchesne River to the Great Basin, although begun with enthusiasm when agreements were signed in 1965, experienced slow progress. Due to cost overruns, environmental concerns and court suits, in 1977 President Jimmy Carter put the CUP on his "hit list" of reclamation projects that would either be unfunded or face reduced funding because he considered them economically and environmentally unsound. Carter was severely criticized in Utah and other western states for his action. Putting the CUP on the "hit list" has proven to have a lasting negative effect on the Democratic Party in Utah. Political pressure caused the president to reconsider and to restore funding to the project. The Jordanelle portion of the CUP is finished but much of the rest of the project remains unfinished due to continued cost over-

Above left: *Lake Powell created by the Glen Canyon Dam backs water near to Rainbow Bridge National Monument. Some preservationists have suggested draining the Lake to protect such sites and to restore the Colorado River's ecology. Courtesy, Southern Utah University, Gerald R. Sherratt Special Collections*

Above: *In 1984 Congress passed Utah's National Forest Wilderness Act, the first in the nation. Among the wilderness areas created is the Ashdown Gorge Wilderness in southern Utah. The magnificent Flanagan Arch sits at the wilderness boundry. Courtesy, Southern Utah University, Gerald R. Sherratt Special Collections Library*

runs that have caused some water conservancy districts to withdraw.

Beginning with the Multiple-Use Sustained Yield Act of 1960, several acts of the national congress have mandated more environmentally responsible management of National Forest and Bureau of Land Management lands. The Wilderness Act of 1964 and the Endangered Species Act of 1966 are just two of a multitude of acts passed in the 1960s and 1970s requiring comprehensive management plans for use that impacts public lands.

Perhaps the most controversial environmental act for some Utahns has been the Wilderness Act, which directed the National Forest Service and the Bureau of Land Management to evaluate the suitability of roadless areas under their jurisdiction for wilderness designation. Utah's National Forest Wilderness Bill passed Congress in 1984 and set aside 750,000 acres of National Forest lands in the state as wilderness. It was the first statewide National Forest Wilderness Act passed in the nation.

Bureau of Land Management wilderness studies, on the other hand, have proven so controversial as to actuate an anti-environmental movement in some western states known as the "Sagebrush Rebellion." When law suits forced the Bureau to restore many acres of land to Roadless Area Review Study, westerners who favored development over preservation attempted to transfer ownership of public lands from the federal government to the states. In 1979 Utah Senator Orrin Hatch joined several other senators to sponsor a bill to accomplish the proposed transfer. It went nowhere and actually provoked a counterattack by environmentalist groups. In 1980 the Utah State legislature passed the Land Reclamation Act asserting Utah's ownership of federal lands within its borders. Governor Scott Matheson requested amendments to the bill to tone it down before he would agree to sign it. One amendment made the application of Utah's assertion of ownership contingent on a Nevada claim before the Supreme Court for ownership of public lands within that state. When the Supreme Court ruled against Nevada, Utah's Land Reclamation Act became a dead issue.

Utah's last Democratic governor in the 20th century. He was elected in 1976 and re-elected in 1980. Governor Matheson requested amendments to the Land Reclamation Act of 1980 which thwarted Utah's Sagebrush Rebels when the Supreme Court ruled against Nevada's claim for ownership of federal lands. Courtesy, Southern Utah University Journalism Guild

The long running debate over how much Bureau of Land Management land should be designated wilderness in Utah ranged from a proposed maximum of 5.7 million acres supported by most environmental organizations to a minimum of 1.2 million acres supported by proponents of development and a loosely organized group of conservative southern Utah legislatures led by Met Johnson calling itself the "Cowboy Caucus."

When Bruce Babbitt, Secretary of Interior in the Clinton administration, proposed increasing grazing fees on BLM lands to the average cost of grazing on nearby private lands, it touched off a controversy that led Met Johnson, a legislator from Washington County in southern Utah, to organize the "Cowboy Caucus," which carried on a crusade against almost any type of environmental initiative. It has even been alleged that the "Cowboy Caucus" caused personnel changes to be made in the Utah Division of Wildlife Management. Just the belief that this was so had a chilling effect on environmental proposals coming from state agencies.

In September 1996 President Bill Clinton delighted environmentalists and won the scorn and enduring wrath of many others, particularly in Garfield and Kane Counties in southern Utah, when he used the authority of the Antiquities Act of 1906 to proclaim creation of the 1.7 million acre Grand Staircase-Escalante National Monument in southern Utah. This new monument, the largest national monument in the lower 48 states, is situated on BLM lands that were part of the wilderness study area. President Clinton's proclamation effectively settled the issue for this large part of Utah's Bureau of Land Management wilderness study lands.

Utahns have long regarded their state as a cultural oasis in the west. Brigham Young fostered the arts during the pioneer period and the tradition he established has continued. The New Deal of the 1930s assisted in enhancing Utah's cultural accomplishments. In 1936 the Utah Symphony Orchestra was launched under a Works Progress Administration (WPA) grant. It has remained one of the finest symphony orchestras in America. The year after the founding of the orchestra, the Springville Art Gallery was begun as another WPA project and today the Gallery has developed until it houses one of the finest collections of western art in the country.

Since World War II, other major cultural developments have served to advance the arts in Utah. In 1962, founding director Fred C. Adams began the Utah Shakespearean festival in Cedar City. It has become one of the state's cultural gems.

Actor, director, Robert Redford, who named his Sundance resort in Provo Canyon after a character he played in a 1967 western movie entitled "Butch Cassidy and the Sundance Kid," used his Sundance Institute to launch and host the Sundance Film Festival. The festival opened in 1981 to offer promising artists the opportunity to exhibit their films. It is now considered second only to Cannes as the preferred premiere for new films. The showings are so well attended that the films show at Park City, Salt Lake City, Orem, Provo, and at the Sundance resort.

The generally favorable publicity Utah has received for accomplishments in the arts extends to the near 400 voice Mormon Tabernacle Choir, which began its "Music and the Spoken Word" broadcast on CBS Radio in 1929. The program continues to be broadcast each Sunday morning on radio and television. It is today the longest running continuous radio broadcast in history and is among the longest on television in America. The choir has sung at national and international events including presidential inaugurals. In 1959 the choir won a Grammy for its recording of "Battle Hymn of the Republic."

Fred C. Adams founding Director of the Utah Shakespearean Festival held annually on the campus of Southern Utah University in Cedar City. Courtesy, Southern Utah University Journalism Guild

Above: *One of the valued cultural institutions of Utah is its Utah Symphony Orchestra created during the Great Depression as a WPA artists project. It continues to be a major cultural amenity for Utahans at the turn of the century. Courtesy, Southern Utah University, Gerald R. Sherratt Special Collections Library*

Below: *An actor in costume at the Tony Award Winning Utah Shakespearean Festival. Courtesy, Southern Utah University, Gerald R. Sherratt Special Collections Library*

Left: *Popular actor and movie director Robert Redford who resides at his Sundance Resort in Provo Canyon is an environmental activist and he also sponsors the Sundance Film Festival held in Utah each year. It has gained national prominence. Courtesy, Utah State Historical Society*

Left below: *Robert Redford's Sundance Resort, which is run by the Sundance Institute, provides one of several scenic locations for the Sundance Film Festival screenings. Courtesy, Carolyn S. Hinton*

Below top: *One of the most important cancer research centers in the world is the Huntsman Cancer Research Institute that has been largely funded by the generosity of Jon Huntsman. The center is housed in this new facility on Medical Drive on the upper campus of the University of Utah. Courtesy, Carolyn S. Hinton*

Below: *Jon Huntsman the founder of Huntsman Chemical has generously donated hundreds of millions of dollars to the Huntsman Cancer Research Institute located on the Campus of the University of Utah. Courtesy, Southern Utah University Journalism Guild*

Utah also experienced a flowering of literature, a renaissance for its painters and artists, who no longer find it necessary to leave Utah to have an appreciative audience or to make a living. The Ballet West, the BYU Folk Dancers, and the Ririe-Woodbury Dance Company, among others, are acclaimed for their accomplishments.

Another amenity Utah citizens are favored with is outstanding institutions of higher education. The University of Utah Medical School, for example, is a national leader in cancer and heart research. In 1982 Barney Clark received an artificial heart developed at the University and implanted by a team of doctors at the University hospital. This was the first artificial heart transplant in a human subject in history. Cancer research has benefited greatly from the hundreds of millions of dollars generously donated by Jon Huntsman to create and fund the Huntsman Cancer Research Institute.

Although Utah has enjoyed many amenities and much favorable publicity, it has also had some negative, or at the very least, questionable publicity resulting from exaggerated claims by researchers, from natural calamities, from religious fanatics and from political controversy.

When two researchers at the University of Utah claimed they had discovered cold fusion, they received widespread publicity and some well-funded grants. In the end their claims proved exaggerated. The resulting negative publicity lead to demotions for some University administrators who had supported their claims.

Even though Utah's emerging commonwealth economy relied less on precious metal mining, coal mining remained a substantial element of the Utah economy. Technology, however, made it possible by the 1980s for fifteen miners to produce as much coal in a day as it took 250 miners to produce at the turn of the century. New technology, however, did not prevent a major coal mine disaster.

On December 19, 1984 the most deadly coal-mine fire in Utah history and the worst United States mine disaster since 1972 took the lives of twenty-seven miners in the Wilberg Mine fire in Emery County. There were twenty-eight people in the mine, more than double its usual crew, as they were attempting to break the twenty-four hour world-production record when fire broke out about 9:00 P.M. The smoke and gases quickly traveled 2,400 feet down the shaft to where the miners were working. Only one miner escaped. Eighteen miners and nine company officials were trapped and killed. Among the dead was Nannett Wheeler, the first woman to die in a Utah mine after women officially were given the right to work in underground mines in Utah in 1973.

After three days of effort the bodies were located, but the fire suddenly rekindled forcing rescuers to evacuate and seal the mine. The bodies were not recovered until December 1985, one year later and it was not until July 1986 that the federal Mine Safety and Health Administration (MSHA) could begin an investigation. Their finding was that the fire was caused by a faulty air compressor that was allowed to run unattended in a non-fireproofed area. MSHA in the end, issued 34 citations against the mine owners and operators.

At the same time the United Mine Workers of America severely criticized MSHA for failing to issue citations when it inspected the mine less than a week before the fire. A General Accounting Office investigation undertaken at the request of the Senate Labor and Human Resources Committee cited MSHA

In 1983 heavy spring run off created flooding in the streets of Salt Lake City. Over 3,000 volunteers turned out to sandbag State Street creating what was called the State Street River, which ran for over two weeks before cars could resume travel on State Street. Courtesy, the Deseret News

for allowing the Wilberg Mine to operate with outdated firefighting and evacuation plans, to operate with no fire-suppression devices, and to run a compressor known to be faulty.

A major natural calamity of another sort resulted from heavy accumulations of snow over the winter of 1982–83 followed by unusually warm spring weather that led to flooding. Crews of up to 3,000 volunteers built sandbag dykes that were as much as four feet high to divert flood waters from City Creek down State Street in Salt Lake City. For over two weeks the "State Street River" put cars off this heavily traveled street. The high run-off also caused rising water in the Great Salt Lake and Utah Lake to threaten buildings and highways. Pumps were even acquired by the state of Utah to pump water from the Great Salt Lake into the west desert to keep the lake level manageable. The floods of 1983 closed freeways in other areas of the state and created a slide at Thistle Junction that blocked a highway, the railroad track, and which eventually created a lake that rose to cover the town of Thistle, driving out its 22 families. The town of Thistle is no more.

More recently, Salt Lake City experienced a rare tornado of killer force. With winds up to 150 miles per hour, the tornado in August 1999, killed one man and injured at least 81 other people. Over 300 homes were damaged with 40 suffering extensive damage. The Delta Center, the home of the Utah Jazz, also suffered extensive damage.

In 1985 two people in Salt Lake City were killed by bombs contained in packages. Two days later a third bomb went off in a car injuring documents dealer Mark Hoffman. This bomb, which exploded accidentally focused the investigation on Mark Hoffman. He eventually plea bargained to avoid a death penalty. Hoffman is shown here at a court appearance. Courtesy, the Deseret News

A man-made tragedy occurred on April 15, 1999 when a mentally deranged man entered the LDS Genealogical Library and began firing a gun. Two people, a security guard and a patron, were killed and five others were wounded. This shooting, plus the shooting deaths of 15 people at Columbine High School in Littleton, Colorado five days later, led to a cry for banning guns in churches and schools. A bill was introduced into the Utah legislature, but when Legislators refused to pass gun restricts in churches and schools, a petition campaign producing high emotions on both sides of the issue was begun in an effort to get a gun initiative on the November 2000 ballot.

In 1985 one of the most bizarre forgery and murder cases in history began with the bombing deaths of Steven F. Christensen, a Salt Lake businessman and historical documents collector, and Cathy Webb Sheets, wife of a Salt Lake City businessman. There was speculation that these were mob hits directed against businessmen who involved mobsters in investments gone bad. Two days after the initial bombings, a third bomb exploded in a car occupied by historical documents dealer Mark Hoffman. He was injured but survived his extensive wounds. This third bomb helped focus the police investigation on Mark Hoffman. The first bombs had been an attempt by Hoffman to cover up a convoluted maze of forgeries of historical documents that Hoffman claimed were related to the history of the LDS Church. As evidence mounted against Mark Hoffman, he opted for a plea bargain to avoid a possible death penalty that might result from a first-degree murder conviction in a jury trial. Today Hoffman is serving a life sentence in the Utah State Prison.

The practice of polygamy by fundamentalists in defiance of Utah law has also caused some embarrassment to many officials and residents of Utah. Polygamy raids in the 1940s and 1950s attempted to put a stop to the practice but these succeeded mainly in tearing families apart and creating heroes among the fundamentalists. By the 1970s, some of the many fundamentalist groups were using murder and terror under a doctrine known as Blood Atonement, in an attempt to impose their beliefs on others. The most violent group included the family and followers of Ervil LeBaron. He and his followers are suspected of as many as 28 killings extending across the American west from Texas to Arizona and Utah to California. In 1980 Ervil LeBaron was convicted of planning the murder of a rival polygamist leader. LeBaron eventually died of natural causes while serving his prison term. Four years after LeBaron's arrest and conviction, Ron and Dan Lafferty, members of another fundamentalist cult, murdered their sister-in-law and her baby. Both were convicted and sent to prison, although Ron's conviction was overturned for a time because he was deemed mentally unstable.

More recently the practices of fundamentalists have captured headlines as accusations of sexual abuse, incest and sex with minors have emerged. In 1999 David Kingston, a fundamentalist polygamist, was sentenced to prison for sex with a minor and incest.

Unfortunately, many people outside of Utah have failed to see or understand the differences between mainstream Mormons and the fundamentalists who are not and cannot be members of the Mormon Church. The Mormon Church excommunicates anyone who believes in or practices polygamy, and most assuredly those who use or advocate violence.

Soon after statehood Utah began to resemble many other states in its political outlook and voting patterns. The Utah vote generally went the way of the national returns. Other than 1896 and 1898, this usually resulted in Republican victories except for those occasions such as between 1916 and 1918 when the Republican Party leadership forgot to attend to the desires of constituents and failed to deal with what the majority regarded as significant issues. When Republican governor Charles R. Mabey, who was elected in 1920, proved unable to provide effective executive leadership on taxes and recovery from the post World War I depression, Democrat, George Dern, was elected governor in 1924 and reelected in 1928. However, a Republican majority dominated the legislature and Utah's congressional delegation remained Republican except for Democratic senator William H. King.

The New Deal and World War II changed Utah's political landscape rather dramatically. The Democratic Party became the majority party and failed attempts at Mormon Church intervention to influence the outcome of elections seemed to indicate that Utah politics had risen above religious direction. However, after World War II some Mormon Church leaders such as J. Reuben Clark, Jr. and Ezra Taft Benson, resumed the attempt, with some success, to help the Republican Party in a major effort to reclaim the dominance that Republicans had held from 1898 to 1932.

The Republican resurgence in Utah began with Arthur V. Watkins' election to the U.S. Senate in 1946. That election also saw a Republican majority elected to the state House of Representatives for the first time in fourteen years. Some of the more extravagant hopes for restoring Republican political control were dimmed by the results of the 1948 election which returned a Democratic majority to the Utah legislature. But Republicans did elect maverick, J. Bracken Lee, to the office of governor over two-term incumbent Herbert B. Maw. Despite the fact that he was not Mormon, Lee received strong support from several highly placed Mormon Church officials. Lee was colorful, outspoken and controversial. He considered school teachers hired help rather than professionals, and in order to reduce taxes, he reduced teacher salaries to levels below those of neighboring states and below the national average. Despite a rapid increase in the number of school students, he continued to cut school funding. His proposal to find money for public schools and tax cuts was to eliminate Carbon College in Price and to return Snow College in Ephraim, Dixie College in St. George and Weber College in Ogden to the Mormon Church. In a November 1954 referendum, voters rejected this proposal.

By 1956 the Mormon Church owned *Deseret News* editorialized against Lee's reelection. Partly as a consequence, he was defeated in the Republican primary by George Dewey Clyde. Lee ran as a third party candidate but Clyde still won the race for governor against Lee and Democrat L.C. Romney.

The emergence of the Cold War in 1946 led to a right-wing anti-communist crusade in America that became known as McCarthyism. Named for Wisconsin senator Joseph R. McCarthy, McCarthyism began when Senator McCarthy charged in a speech in Salt Lake City that communists were rife in the State Department. Soon, some Utah politicians found they could benefit themselves by making unsubstantiated accusations of their own. In 1950 Wallace F. Bennett defeated incumbent senator Elbert D. Thomas in one of the dirtiest campaigns in Utah history. Bennett supporters, taking advantage of the fears produced by McCarthyism, smeared Thomas with charges about associations with communists and with subversive causes. Bennett was elected in a fairly close race.

In 1948 Reva Beck Bosone was elected Utah's first woman to serve in Congress. She was reelected in 1950 but in 1952 she was defeated by William A. Dawson who effectively used smear tactics, calling Bosone a dupe of "the Kremlin-controlled American communist party." A rerun of the Dawson-Bosone race in 1954 resulted in repackaged pro-communist charges against former Congresswoman Bosone.

Perhaps the most bizarre political fraud in Utah history was the Douglas R. Stringfellow case. Stringfellow, who was partially disabled, claimed he received his physical disabilities as a World War II hero. His oft repeated story was that he was a member of the Strategic Services, which operated covert behind the lines activities in Europe. According to his account, he was captured, severely beaten, and held in deplorable conditions without care for his injuries. When his story began to unravel and it was laid bare that it was a fabrication, he resigned from the 1954 congressional race only sixteen days before the election. His replacement, Henry Aldous Dixon, defeated former Democratic Congressman, Walter K. Granger, in a close race.

Although the Republican Party had made a major resurgence, for the most part the years from 1946 to 1976 were years of

Above top: *Utah Senator Orrin Hatch was elected to the United States Senate in 1976. In 1999, he announced his candidacy for the Republican nomination for president. He is the first Utahan to run for the presidency of either major national party. His candidacy was short-lived due to lack of campaign funding and lack of popular support. Courtesy, Utah State Historical Society*

Above: *Beloved president of the L.D.S. Church, ninety year old Gordon B. Hinckley, who proposed the new Mormon Church Conference Center and saw it through to a successful conclusion by April 2000, in time for the LDS April Conference sessions. Courtesy, Southern Utah University Journalism Guild*

political balance in Utah, although characterized by some abnormal political developments. One of the abnormalities was the 1958 U.S. Senate race. Arthur V. Watkins was elected Senator in 1946 and reelected in 1952. In 1954 this conservative Republican chaired the Senate committee looking into the activities of Senator Joseph R. McCarthy. When his committee recommended a censure of McCarthy, Senator Watkins paid a heavy price by way of enduring personal charges against his character led by McCarthy supporters. His health was even broken by the resulting stress. Former Governor Lee, a McCarthy partisan, challenged Senator Watkins for the U.S. senate nomination. When he lost, Lee again ran as a third party candidate and his presence on the ballot was instrumental in the defeat of Watkins by Democrat Frank E. Moss.

The 1976 election represented a major shift away from the political balance in Utah toward renewed Republican dominance. The balance had been preserved by the election of Democrat Calvin L. Rampton as governor in 1964 and his reelection in 1968 and 1972. Despite Rampton's success and popularity as Utah's only three term governor, the 1974 state legislature was the last to have a Democratic majority in either house and sometimes the Republican majorities have been overwhelming. Although Democrat, Scott M. Matheson was elected governor in 1976 and reelected in 1980, he worked with generally preponderant Republican majorities in the legislature and no Democrat has won the governorship of Utah since Matheson in 1980. One indication of the emerging Republican dominance of Utah politics in 1976 was presidential candidate Gerald Ford's lopsided victory over Jimmy Carter in Utah even though Carter carried the nation. Until this election, with few exceptions, Utah usually voted the way the nation went in presidential elections.

Since the election of Lyndon B. Johnson in 1964, three Democratic presidential candidates have won the presidency, Jimmy Carter in 1976, and Bill Clinton in 1992 and 1996. However, no Democratic presidential candidate has carried Utah since 1964.

Since 1980, when Utah gained a third congressional seat, Republicans have generally represented Utah in all three congressional districts. Exceptions have been Wayne Owens' victories in the Second Congressional District from 1986 to 1992 when he decided to challenge for the senate seat that had been held by retiring senator Jake Garn. Owens lost to Robert Bennett. In fact, no Democrat has represented Utah in the United States Senate since Orrin Hatch defeated Frank E. Moss in 1976. In the Third Congressional District, which was once considered one of the most Republican districts in America, conservative Democrat Bill Orton was elected in 1990, 1992 and 1994 before losing a very hotly contested race to Chris Cannon in 1996. Republican Jim Hansen has held the First

Congressional District seat since 1976 when he beat Congressman Alan Howe who was arrested and charged with propositioning a police decoy during the Democratic State convention.

In 1992, in what might be called the year of the women in Utah politics, Democrat Karen Shepherd defeated Enid Greene in the second congressional race. Republican, Olene S. Walker was elected the state Lieutenant Governor and Democrat, Jan Graham was elected the State Attorney General. In 1996 Walker and Graham were reelected, but in 1994 in a rerun of the 1992 race, the recently married Enid Greene Waldholtz defeated Karen Shepherd. Before she could stand for reelection in 1996 Congresswoman Waldholtz was forced off the Republican ticket for alleged illegal tricks carried out during both her losing 1992 campaign and her victorious 1994 race. These tricks were generally attributed to Joe Waldholtz, whom Greene had married shortly after the 1992 race and whom she was to divorce shortly after the 1996 disclosures of irregularities. Joe Waldholtz ended up serving a prison term for his involvement in the illegal tricks.

Partly due to Democratic Party mistakes such as Congressman Howe's arrest by a police decoy during the Democratic state convention in 1976, President Carter's putting the Central Utah Project on his hit list, party disunity, and running a pro-choice candidate for governor in 1992, to mention a few, Utah politics has changed from relative parity between the two major national parties to domination by the Republican Party. Danger lurks in this change; a new religion-based political alignment is replacing the system existing since statehood wherein members of all religions voted and affiliated in both parties. The tendency seems to be for active Mormons to affiliate with the Republican Party. This raises the possibility of a return to a religiously based party system similar to what existed in territorial days. Political research indicated that about 70 percent of the Mormon vote beginning with the 1984 presidential election has gone to the Republican Party. Conversely about 70 of the non-Mormon vote has been going to the Democratic Party. Since 72 percent of the state population is Mormon, the Republican Party, which became the majority party by 1976, is likely to remain the majority party. One danger that some believe has already been revealed is that a safe and dominant Republican majority will be so over confident as to ignore major issues that need to be addressed. For example, some have felt that there has been inadequate funding for education, and neglect of minority and women's issues. A good illustration comes from the heavy influence of conservative groups led by the Eagle Forum during the International Women's year event of 1977. These conservatives convinced many Mormon women that the organizers, actually moderates, were radicals. The conservatives passed their agenda including opposing recommendations to improve women's access to credit, to improve the workplace for women, and to assist women in combating job discrimination.

The interior of the lavish new LDS Conference Center taken during its first public use on April 1, 2000. Courtesy, Carolyn S. Hinton

In 1991 the state legislature passed one of the strictest pro-life laws in the nation and the state spent large amounts of tax money fighting a lost cause in the courts. The legislature has also pursued issues prohibited in the state constitution such as school prayer at high school graduations and in public meetings, as well as public decency on television. Contrary to the legislators' trend, the voters in 1994 defeated a state constitutional amendment that would have widened acceptable rules for teaching religion in schools.

Meanwhile, the Mormon Church officialdom, since 1954, has not intervened directly in partisan politics, but has vigorously involved itself in policy measures that are considered to be of a moral nature. These have included opposing the liquor by the drink issue in 1968, the Equal Rights Amendment in 1975, abortion on demand, and a referendum on pari-mutual betting in 1992.

School funding reached front and center during the 2000 legislative session as state teachers threatened to strike if the state legislature did not approve Governor Michael Leavitt's education package. Despite much hard feeling between legislators and the governor and legislators and the teachers, a funding proposal giving public schools a 7.2 percent increase and an average 5.5 percent teacher pay hike did pass.

Perhaps encouraged by the ease of his election victories in Utah's senatorial races, Senator Orrin Hatch in 1999 became the first Utahn to announce his candidacy for presidential nomination on either major national ticket. He withdrew after a poor showing in the New Hampshire primary and the Iowa caucuses. His withdrawal was also hastened because efforts to raise campaign funds proved difficult. It is also beginning to appear that mainstream Republicans may find it more difficult to gain their party nomination than to win the general elections. At the 2000 Republican convention, incumbent Governor Leavitt was forced into a primary race against a relatively unknown political newcomer by an uprising of right wing delegates. Tax rebel, Congressman Merrill Cook, who replaced Enid Greene Waldholtz in 1996, was also forced into a runoff against a Republican challenger. This is partly because Cook has appeared increasingly likely to lose in November to Democratic challenger, Jim Matheson.

During the last 20 years Utah has developed a modern, mature economy which has meant that Utahns are more in charge of their own economic destiny than when the economy was a colony of Wall Street or a colony of Washington, D.C. Utahns have demonstrated great creativity in the arts and letters, the state has experienced rapid population growth, it has overcome political turmoil and generally advanced the amenities and well being of the citizens of the state. Representative of the growth and maturity of the population and institutions is the opening of the new Mormon Church Conference Center at its April 2000 Conference. This facility, which the church has announced is for the use of the community, seats 21,000 people in comfortable padded seats. Additionally, Utah's tourism efforts have been so successful as to necessitate the beginning of a shuttle bus system to convey visitors into Zion National Park to offset ecological damage and to improve the visitors' experience. Despite the emergence of close to a one party political dominance in Utah since 1976, most holders of statewide offices and congressional seats represent themselves as moderates and most are honorable men and women who generally do not resort to some of the reckless tactics of the past. Perhaps this all means that Utah has arrived at fuller maturity as a culture, an economy, a society and as a political entity.

Above: *Governor Michael O. Leavitt was elected in 1992 and re-elected in 1996. He is attempting to win a third term as Utah's governor in 2000. Utah has had only one previous three-term governor. Courtesy, Utah State Historical Society*

Below: *Zion National Park has attracted so many visitors that the quality of the visitor experience and the ecology of the park were threatened. In May 2000 the National Park Service instituted a shuttle bus system in the Park. The new policy precludes anyone from driving further up the main canyon than the Zion Lodge. Courtesy, Carolyn S. Hinton*

Chronicles of Leadership

The foundation that supports Utah's economy is difficult—if not impossible—to describe in a few words. It is too diverse. And too fluid.

Tourism is now Utah's primary industry, bringing the state an annual income well exceeding one billion dollars. But, again, it is hard to describe briefly the state's scenic attractions. The Utah Travel Council has tried, envious of Montana's graphic "Big Sky Country" slogan, to find a catchy phrase that would fit neatly on a license plate or in a one-column newspaper headline. Licenses now boast of Utah's "Greatest Snow on Earth" to emphasize its winter wonderlands. Still, this one-season compromise leaves out the many other, year-round scenic and historic attractions.

Utah has always been diverse. When the Mormon pioneers arrived in what is now Utah in 1847, LDS Church president Brigham Young urged his followers to concentrate on agriculture and home industries that would provide food and fiber. They did, and thousands still do. However, trading with California-bound argonauts soon became a major industry. So did transportation, with the driving of the Golden Spike at Promontory, Utah, in 1869 to complete America's first transcontinental railroad.

The changing skyline of Salt Lake City in the 1980s reflects the growth and relative prosperity of the emerging commonwealth economy. Courtesy, Hill Air Force Base

ALLEN MEMORIAL HOSPITAL

The unique attitudes and personalities of the Western settlers have been indelibly imprinted upon each of the communities those pioneers helped to establish. These attributes are characteristic of the modern shopkeepers, teachers, and elected officials. Grand County and Moab (the county seat) are not excluded from these qualities. However, unlike most Utah communities, Moab was not settled by the Mormon pioneers. The early Mormon pioneers attempted a settlement known as the Elk Mountain Mission, but for various reasons the settlement failed—allowing the area to be settled by ranchers, farmers, prospectors, homesteaders, drifters and an occasional horse rustler. Three basic themes emerged from those early beginnings that have effected the business commerce through the present day. These themes are critical to recognize in order to understand the tremendous successes which have occurred at Allen Memorial Hospital.

The first theme would be daring independence. The early rejection of the Mormon's notion of planned communities with grid-like streets and uniform building lots, gave way to cattle trails and irregular parcels ranging from 40 to 160 acres. Newcomers were resented, yet cautiously welcomed, on conditions that they leave others alone—Indians and the harsh desert were challenging enough without inviting new ideas.

Secondly, the early Moabites were opposed to government and the taxes that came with it. The early settlers had carved out a home without the government's assistance, and they were not about to pay taxes for anything.

The third, and most enviable theme of the early settlers, was their perseverance in the face of adversity. Only the strong survived the challenges presented by the Native Americans who resented that white settlers assumed a right to possess their lands. Temperatures ranged 100° F to –20° F, and precipitation in this harsh land averaged slightly more than eight inches, annually. Before water wells, low precipitation years of less than three inches drove the weaker settlers away.

The modern day Moab community hosts a rather unique and diverse population, and the community seems split between the "locals," and "everyone else." Economically, Moab has seen a shift from a natural resource-driven economy in ranching, farming, mining and lumber, to a more tourist trade economy. Beginning in the early 1990s, the nation, and the world in fact, was attracted to Grand County's natural wonders-driven economy of white water rafting, rock climbing, jeeping, mountain biking, hiking and tourism in general. While locals have enjoyed the newfound income, they have guardedly endured any newcomers. One interpretation of the "everyone else" category is that *"...it is comprised of federal and State overseers (U.S. Forest Service, U.S. Park Service, Bureau of Land Management, etc.) of the public lands which surround Moab on all sides; those attracted to the splendid environment and outdoor life; a multitude of government agencies and service industries which have made Moab a regional service center; and retirees."*

CEO Chuck Davis has overseen many of the changes over the last seven years, including restoration and development of services in Grand County.

In 1993 the community opposed taxing options placed to a vote by the hospital board. Reminiscent of earlier times, property taxes and an optional one percent sales tax were defeated, despite threats that the hospital would close without the infusion of outside capital. The community voiced non-confidence in the board's administrator and their management. The core medical staff had eroded to one physician, one physician's assistant (PA) and a diverse collection of itinerant, part-time, contract and locum tenens physicians. As a result of the vote the hospital board was faced with two options—to close the hospital or turn the management over to someone the community could trust. Closing was the worst option. It would leave 7,500 permanent residents and 2.1 million tourists and visitors without fundamental health care services. The board chose to turn operations over to one of the largest hospital networks, HealthTrust, a spin-off of Hospital Corporation of America (HCA). Negotiations broke down after eight months and Rural Health Corporation was chosen as successor. They have been involved continually through to the present.

The hospital needed a miracle if it was to turn itself around without any financial support from the taxpayers. To remain operational, training, employee benefits, and equipment were cut from the budgets. Despite these cuts, the employees and providers continued to deliver safe, quality care. The employees proved to be the miracle needed to save the hospital and make it thrive.

An example of the resourcefulness and spirit of the employees was when the hospitals telemetry system failed. This is the system that monitors the vital signs of ICU patients. St. Marks Hospital (Salt Lake City) was replacing their telemetry and suggested that Allen Memorial network with them. The telemetry manufacturer, VitalCom, of Orange, California, designed a system that would link both hospitals. The system allowed the nurses freedom and flexibility to respond to emergencies, deliveries and routine patient care, without neglecting the cardiac patients. The system was the first technology of this kind used anywhere in the world, and was approved by the Food and Drug Administration in 1997.

The VitalCom system gave the hospital an opportunity to jump into telehealth. Its manager of information systems (Mike Foster, MIS) has tested in the top three nationally in his Microsoft Network test group. He has used his expertise in developing teleradiology, teledietician, teleconferencing, telemedicine with the Shriner's Hospital, and telemedicine for Children With Special Needs (University of Utah Health Sciences Center). He and the rest of the Allen Memorial team are currently exploring a telepharmacy model, which could revolutionize rural Utah patient pharmacies.

Revenues were $2.3 million in 1993; in 2000 the hospital revenues will be over $9 million. There were only 24 deliveries in 1993; from August 1999-August 2000 there were 119 babies delivered at Allen Memorial. Most surgery patients went out of town until a board certified general surgeon relocated to live among the area's outdoor activities. James A. Hoffmeister, M.D. has helped to restore the trust of the community, resulting in over 500 surgeries performed at the hospital each year. Dr. Hoffmeister is the co-inventor of the Dobb-Hoff Feeding Tube, an industry standard.

Confidence in the professionalism and quality of the employee staff has allowed the medical staff to grow to nine board certified providers. All registered nurses are bachelor's prepared, and most have pushed themselves to certification in advanced cardiac life support, advanced trauma life support and pediatric advanced life support. This is normally unheard of in rural hospitals. They are as unwavering as any settler—holding true to the diverse framework that once inspired this unique community—persistent, daring, and independent.

Allen Memorial Hospital: This 43 year facility is one of the oldest in the state of Utah. The next challenge facing Allen Memorial is to replace this building with a more modern structure.

ARCHITECTURAL DESIGN WEST, INC.

K.C. Schaub founded the firm that has evolved to become Architectural Design West. In 1889, he traveled from Switzerland to his new home in Utah, relying upon his formal European training, and began designing buildings. His architectural legacies include the dignified high-style Romanesque landmarks at Utah State University, the Eccles & Kearns Mansions, and the east doors of the Salt Lake City LDS Temple. To the company he founded he left his guiding principles of quality architecture and quality service.

Tony Wegener, chairman of the board at Design West, sees this history as basic to the firm's identity. "It is who we are and where we have been, seen as part of a continuum. You have to be doing something right to still be around after 111 years."

Design West has since grown and expanded. Today it is a regional firm organized into five electronically-linked offices. This brings the advantages of small, local offices as well as the benefits of the resources, expansive discipline base, experience, and design innovation of a large firm. There are now three offices in Utah, one in California, and one in Washington, employing over 60 people and encompassing a variety of disciplines.

Design West embraces strong core values. Scott Theobald, vice president, comments, "We believe people support that which they help create. We become very involved with our clients to ensure that buildings functionally and aesthetically serve their needs, and our work with clients is the common principle which sets us apart from others."

Architect K.C. Schaub established Design West in 1889.

With time, the name of the firm has also evolved. By the 1960s, the firm was named Schaub & Haycock, renamed Eugene Haycock & Associates, and in 1971 became Architectural Design West, Inc. This last change represented an emerging democratic spirit in the company.

Ink on linen drawing of Eccles Mansion in Logan, Utah.

Eccles Mansion today.

University of Utah student housing in Salt Lake City, Utah. It will house the athletes of the 2002 Winter Olympic Games.

Design West faced a very difficult period in the mid 1980s when three of the six principals, Michael Henderson, Richard Clyde, and Joe Oyler, were tragically killed in an aircraft accident. It was following this tragedy that Gary Acord, now president, left his own successful resort and custom home practice in Park City and joined Tony Wegener and Keith Sorenson at Design West.

Scott Theobald's view of the future is shared by the others at the firm. "More and more architects need to provide the complete package and assume responsibility for the client's satisfaction," he notes. "Design West is anticipating future demands for more quality and customized service with even quicker time frames. The profession has changed greatly since K.C. Schaub's day, but we like to think that the principles of quality he espoused will continue to serve Architectural Design West well.

Utah Valley Regional Medical Center - Women and Children's Center in Provo, Utah.

Old Main, Utah State University (USU), designed by Design West's founder, K.C. Schaub before the turn of the century.

CACHE VALLEY ELECTRIC CO.

Whether or not Henry Frederick Laub was a strong adherent of the philosophy proposed by Horace Greeley to, "Go west young man," will never be known, nor is it important. The fact is that some 68 years after Greeley's counsel was first advocated and when most of the East, the South, and much of the Midwest had already reached a degree of "civilization," H.F. Laub decided, in 1915, to stake his future in the still developing state of Utah.

The founder of Cache Valley Electric Company, a company that holds the oldest electrical contracting license in Utah—and more remarkably is still privately-owned by the same family—came out of Chicago, where as a young man he conducted trolley cars. In the early 1900s he began his electrical career as a hand with Keokuk Electric Light and Power Company in Iowa. He later moved over to the Commonwealth Edison Company in Chicago and in 1908 H.F. Laub was named superintendent of construction for the Electric Bond and Share Company. This position gave him his first exposure to the West.

As superintendent H.F. Laub transferred to Washington State, where he oversaw the construction of transmission lines, substations and other electrical work throughout Washington, Oregon and Utah. There was something about Utah he liked and he decided to venture out on his own by incorporating Cache Valley Electric in Utah, in the college town of Logan. H.F. Laub had committed himself to making a living in the still relatively-untapped electrical industry and Utah was where it would all take place.

The Utah that greeted H.F. Laub was nothing like it is today. The state capitol building (Utah had only been a state for 19 years) would not be completed for another year and Logan was a town of about 8,000 people. Logan and the encompassing Cache Valley were mainly agrarian. They were removed north of Salt Lake City, the closest resemblance that Utah had to a metropolitan area, by almost 100 miles of bad roads and undependable automobile transportation.

Crews at work on overhead lines. This photograph is typical of the way electrical construction was done in the early 1930s. At the time, Cache Valley Electric had already been in business for more than 15 years.

Logan City's Main Street in 1925, 10 years after Cache Valley Electric was founded. CVE's original location was in the middle of this block. In the beginning CVE not only did electrical construction, but was also a distributor and retailer of various electrical products.

During its formative years Cache Valley Electric busied itself with what electrical work it could successfully bid on and was also a dealer in electrical appliances. Some of the early projects included Pacific Fruit Express's massive plant in Nampa, Idaho and several schools in Utah, including work at Salt Lake City's University of Utah and the Utah State Agricultural College—now Utah State University—in Logan. During this period H.F. Laub constantly admonished those who worked for him to, "Never cheapen the product, which is us, and make sure that the customer gets what he wants—and

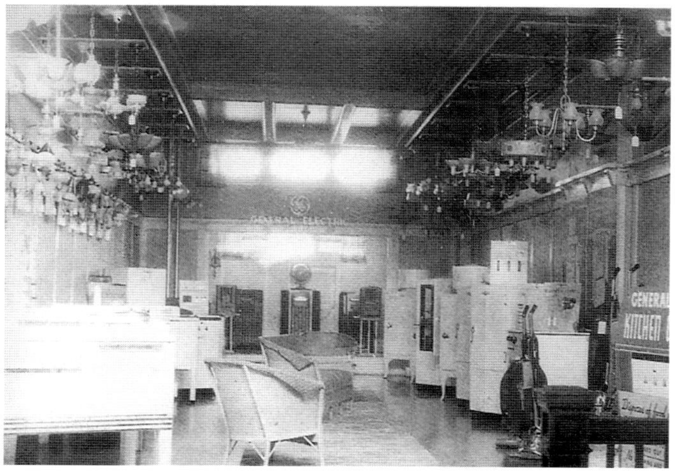

Upstairs display room at the original Cache Valley Electric showing the various electrical appliances and devices that were available to the public in 1926.

more." It was, and is, a principle that Cache Valley Electric has never abandoned. This philosophy also saw Cache Valley Electric survive and even prosper during difficult periods of the 20th century. The company, though a fledgling still, survived through World War I, the inflationary times afterward and finally the Great Depression. Former employees who served during some of these roller coaster years are most prideful in the fact that CVE has never missed a payroll.

In the 1940s Henry began to turn over control of the company to his only son Jack. These were strong growth years for Cache Valley Electric. The nation was recovering from the hangover initiated by the Depression and a war economy, where excellence in construction was a must, but the ability to perform at an accelerated rate without ignoring budget constraints, put companies like Cache Valley Electric in demand. CVE was the first electrical contractor to work at Hill Air Force Base in northern Utah. It also fulfilled the construction needs for the United States Navy at its Utah supply depot and built the electrical portion of the Bushnell Military Hospital and the Utah General Depot. The list of projects was becoming too numerous to name. It had found its niche and the appliance trade was abandoned. Cache Valley Electric was establishing itself as one of the premier electrical contractors in the West.

In the 1950s and 1960s Cache Valley Electric consolidated and expanded its position. H.F. Laub died in 1959 and Jack Laub assumed complete responsibility for the fortunes of the firm. In the 1970s he brought his sons Jack, Jr. and Jim onboard, and finally turned the reigns over to them.

One of Jack, Sr.'s final acts, in collaboration with son Jim, was to pursue opportunities with the steel industry. Military and other federal government contracts had become scarce, whereas heavy industries such as steel held opportunities that were, once again, in tune with Cache Valley Electric's expertise and ability to furnish a complete product in a demanding time frame and within budget. Cache Valley Electric moved from being an excellent regional electrical contractor to one with a strong national presence.

In 1985 Cache Valley Electric opened an office in Salt Lake City and has also expanded its operations to include teledata, service work and design building. *Engineering News Record* now ranks CVE as the 47th largest electrical contractor in the country. Though Cache Valley Electric now has a strong presence in the Midwest and the South, it is still headquartered in Logan and is in its third generation of family ownership.

As it enters its second century of business Cache Valley Electric takes pride in its history but also looks forward to continued growth in the future. CVE's major asset is in its ability to cultivate an excellent work force and stay ahead of its competition.

In its early years Cache Valley Electric was a distributor and retailer of several types of electric appliances and devices. This is an example of an early promotion for an electric lighting plant. Note that the demonstration would be done by wagon and not by a more modern conveyance. This advertisement ran circa 1923.

Although still headquartered in Logan, Cache Valley Electric no longer has offices in Salt Lake City, Phoenix, Denver, Blytheville, Arkansas and Charleston, South Carolina. This is a picture of the company's Salt Lake City office.

CASPER'S ICE CREAM, INC.

Casper's Ice Cream, Inc. was born at the Thornwood Dairy Farm in Richmond, Utah with Olonzo David Merrill & Sons, proprietors. The farm was located near the Gilt Edge flour mill about one mile north and three-quarters of a mile west of Richmond. Both of Olonzo's sons, David and Casper, graduated from Utah State University (then Utah State Agricultural College). When Casper graduated in 1925 his father said, "these cows put you through college, now do something with them, because we are not making any money bottling milk." Casper decided to start manufacturing ice cream. His first ice cream mix was made in a 10-gallon milk can. Soon after starting the business Casper was called to serve a mission for the Church of Jesus Christ of Latter-day Saints.

David had just returned from his mission and consented to operate the business until Casper returned. David installed ammonia compressors for freezing the ice cream. He constructed an ice pond in the Fall of 1925, harvested about 100 tons of ice that winter, stacked it in a cubical pile and built an ice shed around it. The ice was then covered with sawdust as insulation. In the Summer of 1926 he used the ice and salt to pack around ice cream for delivery. There were no refrigerated trucks at that time. He wrote in a letter to Casper on January 2, 1926, "I've done a little experimenting with a new specialty that I think will be a good seller. I take a brick of vanilla ice cream and mark it (into squares). Then I shove a stick into each section and after three or four hours in the hardening room I cut the sections marked, dip them in chocolate and roll them in nuts. I think I can sell them for 40¢ cents per dozen and make a good profit."

When Casper returned from his mission, David was ready to leave to pursue his engineering career. Casper's nickname was Cas and his friends would always say, "Cas, let's go." So he named the vanilla ice cream bar coated in chocolate and rolled in nuts, earlier invented by David, the "Casco®," changing the "go" to "co." Later Casper started making an ice cream sandwich. For several years he also produced pints, quarts and half gallons for stores and home delivery. Many farmers would come to the flour mill to exchange wheat for flour and would often stop next door to purchase some ice cream. One gentleman said, "these kids of mine won't let me come to the flour mill without stopping to get an ice cream cone. Give them a single and me a double." Early on, most of the ice cream sales occurred at the Richmond Black and White Days, 4th of July celebrations and the county and state fairs in Utah and Idaho. Casper's wife Anna worked right along with Casper in production, plant cleanup, sales and home delivery.

Richmond plant, circa 1931.

Logan Plant, circa 1952.

In 1946 the farm was sold to the LDS Church for a welfare farm (except for 40 acres) and the ice cream plant was moved to a newly–constructed facility at 580 North Main in Logan. Casper enjoyed designing and building new equipment. He developed a new freezer and obtained a patent on it. The freezer was designed to "stretch" rather than "whip" the ice cream, thus providing a better body, texture and mouth feel to the ice cream.

Casper and Anna's four sons Richard, Ronald, Derwin and George all worked in the business from the time they were very young. Richard has stayed with the production part of the business except for a short time constructing commercial buildings in California. Ronald died in 1949 at age 19. Derwin received degrees in civil engineering from Utah State University and Iowa State University where he taught for 15 years. George received an accounting degree from Utah State University, worked for Hercules for a time and then became the exclusive sales person for Casper's Ice Cream in Northern Utah. Richard and Casper developed the chocolate and

The Casco® and the Fat Boy® ice cream sandwich.

banana fudgesickles (low-fat, low-air ice cream novelty bars) which were added to the product line.

The business changed from a proprietorship to a corporation in 1971. Casper, Richard, Derwin and George Merrill were the stockholders and incorporators. In the 1970s sales branched out from Utah and Idaho to include California, Washington and Oregon. Casper's niece Irma Jean Pack and nephew DeVar Pack headed up sales in California.

In 1977 Casper and Richard invited Derwin to leave teaching at Iowa State University and join the production end of the business. A family partnership, Casco Limited, was formed in 1977 to construct the new plant, purchase the equipment and to hold the secret manufacturing process for the new factory. Casper, Derwin and Richard were the general partners. Casper's grandchildren and son George were limited partners. The Logan plant was sold to Premium Ice Cream and the fudgesickles were franchised to Premium. A new manufacturing facility was constructed at 11805 North 200 East in Richmond about 1,000 feet northeast from where the business had its origins. Freeze tubes 500 feet long with continuous stainless steel belts were constructed to freeze the extruded Casco® and ice cream sandwich. To their knowledge this is the longest ice cream freezing tube in the world.

Over the years Casper gifted his stock to his posterity and in 1983 resigned as a general partner in Casco Limited. Richard and Derwin were major stockholders in Casper's Ice Cream, Inc. and jointly operated the manufacturing facility. Richard sold the business to Derwin in 1990. George remained in sales.

A quantum leap in ice cream sandwich sales occurred when the name was changed to Fatboy® ice cream sandwich. After a couple of years of boardroom discussion about the possibility of a cholesterol backlash over a name such as Fatboy, the name was adopted. Without much advertising, the Fatboy® has become a household name for connoisseurs of quality ice cream bars. In the 1980s sales continued to flourish as an additional marketer Lee Gaveris, began selling Caspers' products on the eastern seaboard.

Currently, Derwin's sons Ralph, Keith and Paul are in office management, manufacturing, and sales, respectively. Keith's robotic product-sizing equipment has helped move the company from a hand-operated facility to a modern, automated facility. Paul has a degree in human resource management and heads up sales, purchasing and employee training. Derwin's other two sons Kevin and Kyle have moved on to other pursuits. Kevin designed an automated peanut candy blending operation. Kyle was in a Utah State University Senior design group that designed a liquid nitrogen booster process for Caspers' mechanical freeze tubes. Bryan Rasmussen implemented and extended the design.

Richard's son Kendal is now in sales for Idaho and the Northwest. Richard's son Sherwin, formerly a shift manager, is now in sales for another company. George's sons Ronald and Micah are also in sales. Ronald opened up the Denver market and Micah is continuing the Utah sales program. Derwin's son-in-law Brent Kelly has worked in production, business planning and information systems. John Apedaile has worked in refrigeration, plant maintenance, new equipment fabrication and troubleshooting. Richard's son-in-law Mike Allen has been production manager for several years and Ralph's wife Diane has run plant sanitation. Ron and Valdi Lofthouse upgraded Caspers' accounting procedures, while Shane Peterson, Kyle Smith and many other key employees have all contributed to Casper's Ice Cream, Inc.'s success. Most of Casper's grandchildren and great-grandchildren have worked on the assembly line, in the malt shop and in sales.

Casper and his wife, Anna.

Sons of Casper and Anna: Richard, Derwin, and George.

Richard's major contributions have been in product development, quality assurance and customer relations. Derwin's has been in the Richmond plant's construction, the accounting system and the financial guidance of both Casper's Ice Cream Inc. and Casco Limited. George has saturated the Utah market with company products at a critical time in the company's history.

Company owners and employees are encouraged to be active in church and community affairs. Many have served key church assignments, missionary work and scouting. Derwin has served as the mayor of Richmond, Utah.

A retail malt shop attached to the manufacturing facility sells ice cream products at a low price and operates at a "break-even" bottom line. This provides employment for teenagers and a good place for citizens of the community to get a bargain in ice cream purchases. At the grand opening of the malt shop, ice cream cones were sold for 5¢, in memory of Casper and the prices of his cones in 1925.

Currently, the Casco® and Fatboy® can be purchased in many of the major U.S. markets including Alaska and Hawaii. The company philosophy has been to provide employment for future generations of Casper Merrill's family, avoid going public, avoid venture capital and to maintain the company as a family business. Family members are encouraged to obtain college degrees and experience working for some other company before deciding on a career with Casper's Ice Cream, Inc. Casper Merrill's grandchildren currently operate the company. His early dream of progressing from mixing ice cream in a 10-gallon milk can and selling at county fairs to distributing the Casco® and Fatboy® nationally, has been realized.

The Richmond plant, circa 2000.

DESIGN ANALYSIS ASSOCIATES, INC.

Design Analysis Associates, Inc. (DAA), a Logan firm incorporated in 1972, derives its name from its initial objective of providing the service of analyzing other people's designs for reliability, functionality, and testability. This analysis work brought out a great number of questions related to, "What design process created this mess??" Led by president William (Bill) I. Fletcher, the firm pursued a path of perfecting a design process labeled "Design by Documentation" throughout the 1980s and early 1990s. This design process proved to be very successful. By 1991 DAA's team had completed 163 significant design projects for high tech companies around the world. Further, Fletcher continued to spread the "design gospel" by teaching 80, two-week seminars on how to design by documentation. These seminars were used to market DAA's design services and were very successful in bringing in projects of all kinds.

However, in 1988 Fletcher and his associates could see the "landscape" starting to change significantly. Computer companies worldwide began to struggle, collapse or restructure. At this time, Fletcher began to fulfill a lifelong interest in the physics and application of sensors. With the help of a NSF grant, Fletcher and his son, Terrell, developed some extremely accurate pressure measurement instrumentation. Soon the *WATER*LOG® Division of DAA was organized and DAA began producing pressure products for water level measurement in streams, lakes, tanks, aquifers, etc. In 1989, the *WATER*LOG® Division was but a trace element in the environmental market. Now, in 2000, they are a major force in the industry.

During the growth years of the *WATER*LOG® Division, the product line swelled from one product to near 50 products. Also during this period, the High Tech Division continued to hold its own in the industry. It was decided to spin off this division in late 1998. In fact, the spin off simply resulted in a downsizing of the High Tech Division, because DAA still maintains a small high tech group that continues doing very specialized design work for a select few.

Fletcher hopes to retire soon and write another book about the practical application of engineering principles. Many of these principles are documented in his first book, *An Engineering Approach to Digital Design*. Fletcher gives full credit of DAA's success to the long-term loyal and industrious employees who have been part of DAA's nearly 200 completed projects. His son and other long time associates plan on keeping the legacy alive.

Selected Design Analysis WATERLOG® products.

CHRISTOPHERSON BUSINESS TRAVEL

The phenomenal economic growth Utah has experienced since the early 1980s is reflected in the state's travel industry. As a gateway city and economic hub of the Intermountain West, Salt Lake is responsible for more than its share of travel.

Christopherson Business Travel is a professional travel management company whose own growth reflects Utah's economic and air travel boon. But the company's roots and pioneering spirit go back even further, to founders Merrill and Lucille Christopherson.

The Christopherson's formed Provo Flying Service, Inc. in 1940, to train pilots for action in WWII. Their first plane was a Cub Cruiser purchased for $1,600. With a top speed of 100 MPH, it took three days to fly the plane from Pennsylvania to Utah. Provo Flying Service's first pilots trained in the plane and graduated in December 1940.

After the war, in 1953, the company remained dedicated to pilot training but added Christopherson Travel—one of the state's first leisure travel companies. The addition of leisure travel to the flying service helped them maintain the business as a viable travel agency for more than 40 years. The Christophersons retired in 1981, the same year the company's current owner Michael A. Cameron was hired as chief financial officer and acquired a part ownership.

Cameron eventually purchased the remaining interest in the company in 1990. He shared his vision for the future and would carve out a new niche that transformed Christopherson Travel into the multi-million dollar showpiece it is today. But his vision of growing the small company with $1 million in annual sales was difficult to achieve, especially amidst increasing competition, regulations, mergers and, more recently, competition from the Internet and airline commission cutbacks.

Purchasing Christopherson Travel had forced Cameron to assume large debt. He faced several challenges he had never experienced before. The company was taking a big risk as it transitioned from a profitable corporation into a travel agency with huge debt that was quickly losing money. Relief was needed. Cameron began to make waves. First came a move in March 1991 that profoundly redirected the company's emphasis and overall direction—a name change to Christopherson *Business* Travel.

Rather than continue trying to be all things to all people, Christopherson refocused exclusively on meeting the needs of the Utah business traveler. Meanwhile, the company's debt and financial losses were mounting. An evaluation of how businesses select travel agencies revealed a tendency to select based on personal relationships more than on any other means. In 1992 the company implemented an aggressive business plan that revamped sales, marketing and operations to accommodate the new direction.

Christopherson was determined to succeed in business travel. But to do so consistently and better than any other agency, Cameron recognized the need for the best, most experienced corporate travel agents. Later that year the company began identifying and aggressively recruiting the best agents in the market.

Christopherson's strategic maneuvering began paying off in 1995. Success continued with the grand opening of a second office, located in the downtown Salt Lake City business district.

Christopherson was then faced with another dilemma. How would the company keep its top-notch people and maintain the hard-fought battle it was winning as Utah's business travel leader? A variety of employee appreciation programs and internal policies were instituted to ensure its role as the most desirable travel agency for those special agents. Memorable company parties, sales incentive programs and travel giveaways are now commonplace at the firm.

"We see our agents as more than ticket bookers," Cameron said recently of his now more than 60 agents with an average of 16 years experience in the business. "They are a hand-picked 'dream team' of professional consultants who manage travel for large and small corporations. They're the life blood of this company."

Photo of a jet from the Salt Lake City International Airport runway.

A Christopherson Business Travel travel agent. CBT now has 60 travel consulting specialists with a collective 750 years of experience.

Christopherson has maintained success largely by embracing new technologies for the benefit and convenience of its customers and employees.

The new Salt Lake City airport.

February 9, 1995 was a day every travel agent will remember, when all major airlines implemented the first of their commission caps. The caps set a limit on commissions airlines would pay travel agents for booking airfare, in an effort to compete with no-frills airlines. So what did Christopherson do? Cameron gave his employees a raise to boost morale. To pay for it, costs were cut in other ways and sales and profitability increased through implementing new electronic ticketing and management procedures. Christopherson has maintained success largely by embracing new technologies for the benefit and convenience of its customers and employees.

In 1996 Christopherson joined BTI Americas, a national travel agency network. In 1998 BTI merged with WorldTravel Partners to become the third largest travel management company in the nation. At that time, Christopherson became the exclusive Utah affiliate for WorldTravel Partners.

The company reached another milestone in February 1998, when it opened its first client dedicated travel office on-site in CompHealth's national headquarters. September 1998 brought the company's purchase of Sun 'N Surf Travel, now operating as Christopherson Travel's third Utah office. Christopherson opened its first office outside Utah in July 2000 with the establishment of a branch in Idaho Falls. Today the company operates four travel offices and six on-site offices throughout northern Utah and Idaho.

Christopherson Business Travel has been selected for many business awards and citations of excellence. The Salt Lake Area Chamber of Commerce recognized Christopherson Business Travel as its 1996 Small Business of the Year. The Utah 100 Organization named the company one of the fastest-growing in the state for five years running. The U.S. Chamber of Commerce, in conjunction with Mass Mutual Financial Group, awarded Christopherson the 2000 Blue Chip Enterprise Award.

Christopherson Business Travel has grown to become Utah's third largest travel agency and the largest locally-owned business travel agency in the state. Today the business-focused agency employs more than 60 travel consultants handling nearly 600 customers from 10 offices throughout northern Utah and Idaho. Christopherson is poised to continue successfully serving the growing demands of one of Utah's most important industries.

CBT, established in 1953, has been doing business for 47 years.

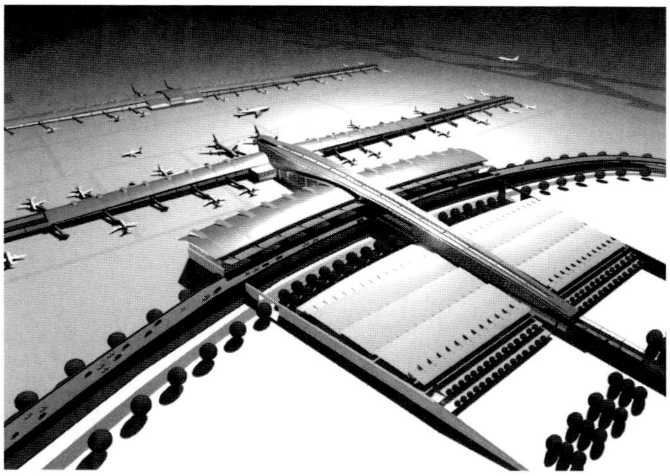

COLLEGE OF EASTERN UTAH

When the pioneers and immigrants who settled Carbon County began to establish towns, churches and schools, they also began planning for the future. In their vision of the future, education was very important—for their children, their grandchildren and for future generations. From this vision came the dream...an elementary school in every town...a high school for the county...and a college for eastern Utah.

The College was founded by an act of the Utah Legislature in February 1937. During the first week of October 1938 about 100 students enrolled in the first classes offered at what was then called Carbon College. The first president, Eldon B. Sessions, described the mission of the new college this way: "Junior colleges are now filling three needs. For some students they are a preparation for higher courses in universities. For others, they provide a two-year preparation for a definite vocation, and for a third group they are providing a balanced, general education."

The College grew slowly until World War II began. Then, vocational programs bulged at the seams as the government sent men and women to be trained in machine shop, auto mechanics, airplane engine mechanics, and as pilots and navigators. By 1943, training needs were met and enrollment dropped to only 27 full-time college students. However the 400 Carbon High School juniors and seniors who shared the facilities with the College kept the classrooms and halls filled with activity.

In 1944, Dr. Aaron E. Jones served as both president of the college and principal of the high school. In his first meeting with the State Board of Education, Dr. Jones asked for a separation of the college from the high school, and while the board agreed with the concept, the actual separation did not occur until 1959.

Grace S. Jones, eighth president, leads the commencement procession.

College of Eastern Utah, Price campus. Photo by Kimball Johnson

In 1953, the College faced its greatest challenge. At a special session of the legislature as a budget-cutting measure, Governor J. Bracken Lee proposed that Carbon College be closed and its lands and buildings sold. The citizens of southeastern Utah were outraged. Almost immediately efforts were started to save the college by forcing a popular vote to reverse the actions of the legislature. At least 30,000 signatures of voters were needed to place the item on the ballot, but over 56,000 were obtained. The results of the election in November 1954 were overwhelmingly in favor of saving the college: 78 percent of the voters rejected the legislature's decision.

In 1959 the State Legislature voted to place the College under the administration of the Board of Regents of the University of Utah. The transfer took place on July 1, 1959; at the same time the high school was separated from the college. Also that year, Aaron Jones retired as president and was replaced by Claude J. Burtenshaw. President Burtenshaw immediately began to make significant changes. The state legislature was asked to change the name of the college to College of Eastern Utah to better reflect the region served by the college. However, this change did not occur until 1964.

Allosaurus skeleton.

The fourth president of the college was John W. Tucker, who served during most of the '60s. An impressive building program was carried out during his administration. Until 1965, the original facilities had been changed only by the addition of the Geary Theater (1962). During a four-year period in the 1960s, five additional buildings were added to the campus. In 1969 the branch relationship of CEU to the University of Utah was ended when the Utah System of Higher Education was created and the college became one of the nine colleges and universities governed by that system.

Dean M. McDonald became president of CEU in 1969. He advocated the idea that CEU must assume the mission and goals of a community college. Under his guidance continuing education was established in Emery and San Juan counties. Building on support proved by residents in the communities of San Juan County, the CEU San Juan Campus was established.

In 1985 Michael A. Petersen was chosen as the seventh president of CEU. He pursued the goals of expanding higher education throughout southeastern Utah. The programs on the San Juan Campus were increased and classes offered in Grand County, culminating in the establishment of the Moab Center of Higher Education. The enrollment increased more rapidly than at any other time in the history of the College. President Petersen was successful in adding residential housing to serve just under 500 students and in acquiring the funding for the new Student Center.

The College of Eastern Utah moved into the new century directed by vision and leadership provided by Grace Sawyer Jones, the eighth president of the College of Eastern Utah. Under the leadership of President Jones the College has increased distance learning opportunities; gained significant increases in endowed scholarships; formalized ownership of San Juan Campus facilities; and entered into new partnerships with other universities, agencies, and school districts.

The CEU Prehistoric Museum founded in 1961 houses the largest collection of dinosaur tracks in the world, as well as eight dinosaur skeletons from the Jurassic and Cretaceous periods. Restored and recreated dinosaur skeletons are on display, as well as a magnificent Columbian Mammoth and Saber Tooth Cat. The Museum also has significant artifacts from the area's Fremont Indian culture. The Museum has over 600,000 curated items.

The CEU Prehistoric Museum, in partnership with the Bureau of Land Management, facilitates the Cleveland-Lloyd Dinosaur Quarry, which is the most productive Jurassic-period dinosaur quarry in the world, with 74 individual animals identified and on display throughout the world. The only known Stegosaurus footprints were discovered here, as well as a dinosaur egg containing a fossilized embryo.

The Prehistoric Museum director and staff, aided by hundreds of volunteers, are excavating fossils at multiple sites located throughout the southeastern Utah. The Prehistoric Museum staff and volunteers are also locating and cataloging rock art and habitational sites in the Nine Mile Canyon Area. This nationally accredited Museum is one of the finest in the nation.

Columbian Mammoth skeleton.

ECHOPASS CORPORATION

American Fork sits nearly a mile high in the Wasatch mountains, a scenic area adjacent to Utah's largest fresh water lake and only 30 miles from Salt Lake City. Once known mostly by tourists (its population almost doubled in the 1990s), it is now part of the center of high tech growth that includes Salt Lake City and Provo. It and Salt Lake City are also the major locations of a fast-growing company that enhances the ability of companies to communicate with their customers, Echopass Corporation.

Founded in the first quarter of the millennial year with a staff of 34, Echopass had more than 100 employees within six months, with expectations that that number would at least double by the end of 2001. By that same time, it expected revenues to reach $500 million and services to extend throughout the United States and into Europe and other parts of the world.

"We chose the Wasatch Front as the location for our premier development facilities because the level of education, commitment and enthusiasm of the community could offer us a dramatic advantage over the Silicon Valley environment," according to company founders Art Coombs, chief executive officer and Keith Barr, chief technical officer.

Echopass' technology provides its clients the capability to respond to their customers from a computer terminal, whether they phone, email, enter chat sites, send faxes, request web call back or use other communications media. This includes both inbound and outbound calls, ranging from requests for technical support to sales calls. There are no traditional telephones.

Thus far, there are two "Echocenters" to support this capability. More are planned, with sites elsewhere in the U.S. and Europe under consideration. These contain the interfaces and software that blend all of these communications devices. Research and development facilities are also in the area.

Each Echopass client is connected to an Echocenter with a secure, dedicated, redundant T-1 line that ensures reliable

Echopass telephone switching gear. Photo by Rick McClain

Echopass Corporation building. Photo by Rick McClain

service. Each has a local area network connected to its line.

The client's agents at its call center have computers and web access to the Echocenter. Once signed on, with a headset plugged into their computers, they can respond to or initiate both text and voice messages, by phone and by e-media. Moreover, each agent's sign-on carries authorization to direct calls to appropriately-skilled service technicians.

All capabilities reside in the Web connection and do not require clients to download any software to their systems. Thus, clients do not have most of the start-up costs associated with a call center or expenses for maintaining its infrastructure. Plus, from the single interface, they can manage a range of communication tools.

Echopass divides its services into three areas:

• Communications, including the interface, and administrative tools and reports to help clients track activity and administer their call centers effectively.

• Support, customer relationship management software that helps service agents track calls and their resolution.

• Sales, software that enables sales representatives to track their customer relationships.

To date, Echopass serves mostly small and mid-sized call centers, with between 10-250 agents, though some are larger.

The concept for Echopass developed early in 1998, with Coombs' and Barr's vision of more responsive customer care covering all phases of the relationships and all forms of communication. In March, as part of Sento Corporation, they launched the development and integration of their three service solutions.

It took more than a year to put the system into beta production. This began with 20 customer care agents in August 1999. Services went into full production three months later. In December, its first 150-seat, phone-free contact center opened, serving Network Associates and McAfee.

In March 2000, Sento spun off Echopass, which secured initial funding of $27.5 million from top venture capital firms.

Echopass server racks. Photo by Rick McClain

It also announced strategic agreements with Genesys and USWest (which became Qwest).

Echopass' first office was a small rental building in American Fork. Though it really had room for only 20 people, it housed 34, sitting anywhere the company could squeeze a table or desk. "It made for tight teamwork," the founders say.

In April, Echopass upgraded its first Echocenter to carrier class specifications, offering the combined features of traditional telephone and data centers. USWest announced it would resell Echopass Communications Services as part of its contact center solutions.

In May, a second service center using Echopass Communications Services opened, a 200-seat, high-volume, post-sales support facility in Evanston, Wyoming, for Sento. July saw the opening of Echopass Labs and a second Echocenter, a state-of-the-art development, integration and combined telecom and datacom center able to support 2,500 agents.

These centers, and those that follow, enable companies to open call centers in locations that normally could not support the significant telecom and bandwidth requirements. This facilitates opening such centers in smaller cities and creates hundreds of jobs. These companies can then focus on delivering high quality service to their customers. Echopass tools ensure that service agents can identify their clients and service them easily, without worrying about integrating a range of disparate products or about installation and maintenance.

Echopass emphasizes customer care. Its core values are integrity; accountability; respect for clients, vendors and each other; quality; and individual progression. Its mission is to be a prosperous organization focused on the long-term welfare of its clients, partners, employees and shareholders, and providing services that fundamentally improve the profitability and end-user satisfaction of the businesses it serves.

It chose its name to reflect its values. Explains Coombs: "There were a few variables that were important to me when naming the company. I wanted a name that meant something to those who founded the company, living on the Wasatch Front of the Rocky Mountains. The name also had to speak to the business services we envisioned. And, I was adamant about not paying someone else for a pre-registered web domain name.

First, Echo Canyon is a relatively well-known canyon in the Rocky Mountains between Salt Lake City and Evanston, Wyoming. Second, I liked the definitions of the words 'echo' and 'pass.' Echo means, 'Automatic reply, instant response, a natural communication phenomenon,' and pass means, 'A pathway; to deliver, distribute, or provide; to ratify, endorse or authorize; to succeed or do well.' I like the proactivity of the word 'pass.'"

Coombs adds, "We envisioned our clients' customers receiving instant replies to their questions regardless of media, without delays. Their ability to communicate would be instant, natural and effortless, and our services and tools would give them a passageway for that, to go far beyond their expectations. Finally, the domain name was clear."

Coombs recalls as a boy, driving from Salt Lake City to his family's cabin in the High Uintas. "We would go through Echo Canyon and my grandmother would briefly stop so my brothers, sisters and I could hear the echo of our voices. Spring, summer, fall or winter, the echo was always there.

"Our tools will be as solid and consistent as Echo Canyon. Echopass will provide a passageway for our clients to communicate with their customers instantly and automatically."

Millions of feet of cables interconnect the Echocenter and link it to Echopass' clients. Photo by Rick McClain

ENVIROCARE OF UTAH, INC.

The history of Envirocare began in the early 1970s when its founder Khosrow B. Semnani, had the visionary idea to dispose of low-level radioactive and mixed waste in an isolated desert in western Utah. In 1988, that dream became reality when Envirocare received its first license to permanently dispose of low-level radioactive waste. At the end of 1999, Envirocare had safely disposed of more than 667,000 cubic yards of waste material received from sites throughout the United States.

The Envirocare facility is located in Clive, approximately 80 miles west of Salt Lake City in the western Tooele County desert. The remote site, 40 miles east of Wendover, Nevada, is a virtually barren landscape.

In 1976, the Department of Energy (DOE) began the site evaluation process for a uranium mill tailings disposal project. The DOE spent eight years studying 29 potential sites, and determined that the Clive, Utah location presented the most suitable hydrogeological, ecological, and economic characteristics for long-term disposal of radioactive waste for the Vitro project. More than 40 miles from the nearest population center, the geology is stable and contains soil with very low permeability. And what little groundwater exists is too saline to be treated cost-effectively for human consumption or agricultural use.

Charles Judd, current president of Envirocare of Utah, was the first employee hired by Khosrow Semnani in 1988.

Khosrow B. Semnani, owner, founder and chairman of the board.

In 1984 the DOE began moving the tailings from a plant in Salt Lake City for permanent disposal at the desert site. Three years later, as the project was ending, Envirocare acquired the surrounding property and established the nation's first privately-owned commercial low-level radioactive waste disposal facility.

Envirocare's Radioactive Material License was first issued in 1988, allowing the facility to permanently dispose of Naturally-Occurring Radioactive Material (NORM). Two years later, in 1990, Envirocare received a RCRA Part B permit, creating the first licensed mixed waste (waste that is hazardous and radioactive) disposal facility in the United States. In 1991 the company received a permit to dispose of Low-Level Radioactive Waste (LLRW), and in 1993 the Nuclear Regulatory Commission issued Envirocare a license to dispose of 11e.(2) materials, including uranium and thorium mill tailings.

The forms of radioactive waste accepted by Envirocare typically include contaminated soil, building debris and other solid waste. This waste is the byproduct of various commercial and governmental operations people benefit from each day. Activities such as medical diagnosis and treatment, the development of new agricultural products and the manufacturing of many consumer products produce low-level radioactive waste that must be disposed of safely.

The Envirocare facility is licensed and regulated by 13 county, state and federal government agencies, including the

Aerial photograph of the Envirocare facility at Clive, Utah.

Environmental Protection Agency, the Nuclear Regulatory Commission, and four divisions of the Utah Department of Environmental Quality: Radiation Control, Solid and Hazardous Waste, Air Quality and Water Quality. These state and federal agencies monitor Envirocare's operations and inspect the site almost every day for compliance with established regulations.

Khosrow Semnani was 21 years old when, in 1968, he stepped off a bus in Salt Lake City with $47 dollars in his pocket. Nobody suspected—not even Semnani himself—that he would become one of the country's most innovative pioneers in the radioactive waste industry. Growing up in his native Iran, Semnani was convinced that education was the key to success. So, when Semnani graduated from high school he was determined to attend college in the United States.

Semnani left for America after spending two years in England learning English. A lengthy bus ride took him from Toronto to St. Louis to Salt Lake City, where he ran out of money. He attended Westminster College in Salt Lake City simply because they let him in. With no money for tuition, he paid his way as a janitor.

In just four years, Semnani graduated with a dual major in chemistry and physics. Two years later, in 1975, he received a masters degree from the University of Utah, where he worked for Dr. Henry B. Eyring, a distinguished chemistry professor. After graduation, Semnani worked for the Kennecott Corporation in Bingham, Utah until he was laid off during the copper depression of the 1970s. Although he found other work locally—first with the Thatcher Company and eventually as a chemist and physicist for Sperry Univac—the Kennecott layoff convinced Semnani to be independent.

At the time, public concern about the environment was increasing, and new federal laws were written to regulate the disposal of hazardous waste. Semnani saw an opportunity to dispose of the waste in the barren, salt-coated desert west of Salt Lake City. In 1980, still working for Sperry Univac, Semnani started lobbying the government. He acquired 640 acres of land in western Tooele County. He dug many of the trenches with his own two hands and a shovel. And he secured the federal Part 1 interim permit allowing him to dispose of hazardous waste. Semnani was in business.

Almost immediately, other waste disposal companies started calling, and Semnani sold this first operation to USPCI from Oklahoma. In addition to purchasing the site, USPCI gave him a position as a consultant and a 20-year contract with a percentage of the company's gross. In 1981, Semnani retired at the age of 34.

Semnani stayed retired for three days before seeking his next opportunity. After spending several years in various business endeavors, Semnani turned back to chemistry and engineering in the late-1980s. He had been following a three-year DOE project removing radioactive uranium mill tailings from an abandoned facility in Salt Lake County to a location in the Tooele desert not far from the hazardous waste disposal facility Semnani sold to USPCI.

Semnani had the idea to turn the land adjacent to the government site into a commercial facility that accepts low-level radioactive waste. The state would benefit from a site scheduled to be closed, Tooele County would receive another industry providing jobs and economic benefits, and the private owner of the facility would have a promising business opportunity. In 1988, after months of preparation, lobbying and securing permits, the country's first privately owned commercial low-level radioactive waste disposal facility was fully-operational. Semnani named his new company Envirocare.

An Envirocare employee performing a lab analysis at the Clive, Utah facility.

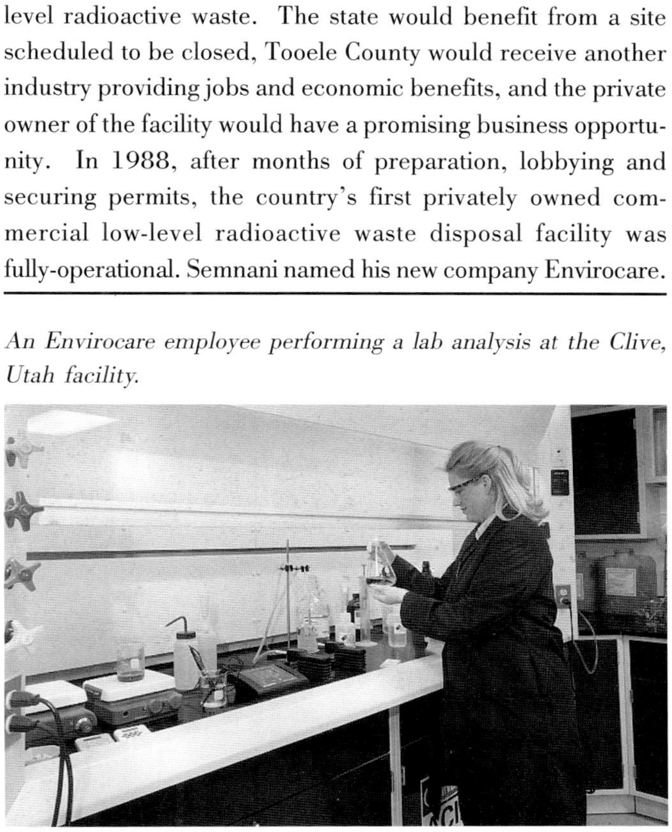

Headquartered in Salt Lake City, Envirocare is still the only privately-owned facility for disposing of low-level radioactive waste in the United States. In 1988, Charles Judd was hired by Semnani as the company's first employee. Judd is now president of Envirocare and the company currently employs more than 400 workers.

From day one, Envirocare has championed safety, customer service and communication. Each of the licensing and permitting processes included considerable stakeholder participation. Tooele County officials have joined Envirocare in a unique partnership, bridging the gap between commercial industry and the community. Customers wishing to dispose of their waste are confident in Envirocare's excellent safety record and commitment to meet regulations and public expectations.

Envirocare is a significant economic partner with Tooele County, providing both jobs and revenues. Each year the county receives a percentage of Envirocare's gross. In 1989, its first year of operation, Envirocare contributed $350,000 to the Tooele County budget. The county received $4.4 million from waste disposed at the facility in 1999. Envirocare's contribution exceeds the county's revenues from property taxes.

On a more grass-roots level, Envirocare is an active member of the community. Semnani has personally supported numerous local charities and equipped hospitals in Tooele. And the Envirocare organization has contributed millions to various community projects, including the Deseret Peak Recreation Complex located between Tooele and Grantsville.

Envirocare plays a key role in federal and private environmental cleanup projects, including remediation projects in residential and commercial areas. Various federal agencies have partnered with Envirocare to complete small and large-scale projects across the country.

An Envirocare employee takes a sample of radioactive material received at the facility.

A forklift operator transporting radioactive material received at the facility.

The Montclair/Glen Ridge, New Jersey cleanup, a Superfund project coordinated by the Environmental Protection Agency, is typical of Envirocare's important environmental projects. Through the 1940s and 1950s, several companies manufactured radium dials in these communities. The radioactive waste, stored on the property, was not removed when the companies closed down. During rapid growth in the decades that followed, developers used the soil on the lots vacated by these companies, not realizing the material was radioactive. The soil was used to build home foundations, driveways and parks.

In the 1980s, as records were reviewed, the state of New Jersey recognized the situation and the cleanup became a Superfund project. Dozens of families have been displaced from their homes—for months and even years—as their radioactive foundations, porches, and yards have been cleaned up. Envirocare received the waste from the Montclair/Glen Ridge project for more than 10 years, providing a solution for minimizing the real-time health risks for people in these communities.

Envirocare helps make environmental cleanup projects possible at a reasonable cost, saving millions of taxpayer and industry dollars. Envirocare is proud to participate in these significant efforts to reclaim land, water and resources in communities throughout the country.

A progressive and dynamic organization, Envirocare sets a high standard of excellence and accomplishment in providing a solution to the country's great waste management challenges, facilitating environmental cleanup projects, and giving back to its local community.

Envirocare is working diligently to fulfill its vision of becoming a full-service facility for the low-level radioactive industry. Serving both private and government customers, Envirocare is the leader in providing a safe and cost-effective solution for disposing of the country's low-level radioactive waste.

NIELS FUGAL SONS COMPANY

Although the tools and jobs have changed since 1924, the year that Niels Fugal founded his Utah construction company, the values that continue to make the company thrive remain the same. Now in its third generation, the Niels Fugal Sons Company continues to set the highest standards of service and integrity in the utility construction and telecommunications industry. With corporate headquarters at 1005 South Main Street in Pleasant Grove and a second office in St. George, the Fugal company and its 270 employees reach the entire western United States.

The son of Utah pioneers, Niels Fugal directed the company in its early years as it built early water distribution systems for communities throughout Utah and Idaho under contract with the Public Works Administration. The economic boom following World War II increased demand for construction, and in the late 1940s, Niels went into partnership with his sons, Neil, Boyd and Grant to form Niels Fugal Sons Company.

As technology improved and consumer demand increased, the company branched out into construction of natural gas lines. In 1947, the Fugal Company began installing natural gas distribution systems for Mountain Fuel Supply Company. More than 50 years later, the Natural Gas Division has installed systems in every area and community serviced by Mountain Fuel Supply Company, now known as Questar.

Founder Niels Fugal passed away in 1959 and his three sons continued to grow the business as technology advanced and demands changed. To keep up with the times, the company diversified into three divisions: Natural Gas Distribution, Telecommunications, and Network Services. The Telecommunications division is general contractor for US West now known as Quest, from Salt Lake City to Flagstaff, Arizona; its customers include AT&T, Sprint, MCI World Com and many other private and independent telephone companies. Through its Network Services division, the Fugal company offers a full range of voice and data-structured cable systems, including engineering, installation and testing to meet any communication and data network application.

The Fugal Company has installed thousands of miles of telelphone cable systems and currently holds the master contract for US West in the region south of Salt Lake City to the Arizona border.

Founder Niels Fugal, circa 1924.

With the retirement of the second generation, the third generation owners Daniel B. Fugal, chief executive officer, and Guy L. Fugal, president, continue to uphold the values of integrity, quality, leadership, teamwork and success. Under their leadership, the company has doubled revenues in each of the past five years.

"My grandfather was dedicated to doing the job right. His sons, Neil, Boyd and Grant, were taught well and they've passed this dedication on to us. We'll continue to provide the type of service that lives up to the reputation that our grandfather built," says Dan Fugal.

The present generation of Fugal management learned the business early. "It started out with a couple of Tonkas in the sand box and over the years we've built an impressive fleet with the newest and best maintained equipment," notes Guy Fugal. "But really, it's the quality of our people who get the job done, and we take great pride in exceeding our clients' expectations. Only today, the sandbox is a lot bigger, and so are the toys."

EQUITABLE LIFE & CASUALTY INSURANCE COMPANY

In 1931, in the midst of the Great Depression, with widespread unemployment and a sense of hopelessness pervading the land, a young doctor sat down at his desk and designed a plan to help restore the broken spirit of some of his fellow Utahns. The young man was Dr. Roderick Earl "Doc" Ross, founder of Equitable Life & Casualty, a company committed to being The Premier Life and Health Insurer for *The Ultimate Generation . . . Today's Senior Americans.*

As the Depression raged on, it became increasingly difficult for Utah families to meet expenses. Thousands were forced to surrender their life insurance policies, as every penny counted in surviving these incredibly hard times. Too many families were left with the burden of burial expenses upon the death of a loved one, without the means to pay. Doc himself had to borrow money to pay the funeral costs for one of his four sons who died unexpectedly.

Doc Ross, a discerning entrepreneur, recognized the need for an affordable way to help families through times of illness and bereavement. A caring, good-hearted man, he committed himself to action, and vowed to help lessen this overwhelming burden. He set out to organize a mutual aid association also known as a benevolent society. A benevolent society was composed from 500 to 2,000 people who each agreed to contribute $1 in the event of the death of any of its members. His objective became a reality with organization of The Wasatch and Summit County Benevolent Society in 1931. Doc, while managing the business, sold society memberships door-to-door. The society thrived, but Doc wanted to do more. He turned its operations over to its members to elect managing officers, making it an independent organization.

Roderick Earl "Doc" Ross, founder, 1935.

Earl Roderick "Rod" Ross, chairman, president and CEO.

In 1933, Doc organized the Community Mutual Aid Society of West Salt Lake County to serve a larger, more populated area. Doc convinced local banks to collect the dollar from each of his members. Membership cards were issued. Members would walk into the bank and contribute to the family of a deceased fellow. The bank would act as depository, free of charge. Doc Ross recruited good people to represent his mutual aid association and to sell memberships door-to-door. The dollar they collected was their commission. On a good day, a representative could earn seven or eight dollars. Ten percent of what was collected was used to pay for administrative, overhead and management expenses.

Equitable's home, 1948-1983. The historic Eagle's Lodge Building.

By May 1935, Doc had acquired 2,100 members. Earlier that same year, the Utah Legislature passed a bill that placed benevolent organizations under the jurisdiction of the Utah Insurance Department. The new law stipulated that members pay a premium of $1 per month. Doc invested $20 in 2,000 penny post cards. He recruited his wife and sons, Ray and Dave, to help him get these first premium notices out to the members. Through the family handwriting these first premium notices, Equitable was born.

On June 6, 1935, Doc incorporated the Community Mutual Aid Society of West Salt Lake County under the name of "Equitable Mutual Aid Protective Society," with its home office located in the heart of Salt Lake City. The name of the company was changed to "Equitable Mutual Life Insurance Company of Utah" on March 7, 1936 and again on May 19, 1938 to Equitable Life & Casualty Insurance Company. The company was headquartered in the historic Boston Building in Salt Lake's landmark Exchange Place.

In the 10-year period from 1940 to 1950, Equitable acquired nine companies, including Associated Life Insurance Society; Western Mutual Association; Mutual Protective Association; Olympus Mutual Aid Society; Voluntary Benevolent Association; Guaranty National Life Insurance Company; Mountain States Insurance Company; and Allied Mutual Life Insurance Company. Equitable was demutualized in 1947, becoming a stock company with the objective of earning profits for its shareholders. With this change came product diversity and growth which enabled risk coverage expansion to include life, health and income protection.

Family and succession were part of Doc's plan. Doc wanted his sons and daughters and their children to succeed him in managing and growing the company. Doc realized that the legacy he would leave his children had to include not only business knowledge, but also a commitment to caring; in essence, the spirit in which policyowners, agents and employees would think of themselves as being part of The Equitable Family. He wanted Equitable to be known as a "family business." Doc believed that the character of The Equitable Family would set the company apart and would be a significant part of its success.

By the mid-1930s, Doc had welcomed his sons Dave and Ray into the business to assist him. They carefully hired good people with strong work ethics, not unlike themselves, for positions in the home office. To represent the company, they selected honest, caring independent agents that would put policyowners first. Ray served as assistant general manager and director of agencies, recruiting, developing, and managing an independent agent sales force, until 1977. Dave was the secretary and treasurer and helped in managing the home office until 1978. Doc, as president, zestfully managed Equitable through his mid-70s, when he retired due to ill health prior to his passing in 1970.

Equitable's corporate headquarters, Triad Center, Salt Lake City.

Both Dave's and Ray's children also became integral to Equitable's management team and made significant contributions to the company's growth. Ray's son Earl Ross, served the company for 40 years, becoming chairman & CEO in 1987. Upon his retirement Earl was named chairman emeritus and serves as an honorary board member. Earl's four sisters also held various positions within the company and continue to serve as honorary board members.

Today, Doc's grandson, Dave's son Earl Roderick "Rod" Ross is Equitable's chairman, president and chief executive officer. Having worked for the company for over 30 years, Rod is committed to Equitable's future: "I'm proud to carry my grandfather's legacy into the future. Equitable remains dedicated to our pioneering vision of helping America's seniors and their families live happier and more financially secure lives. We put seniors first—always! We have embarked on an aggressive, yet disciplined, growth strategy, to grow bigger and better by focusing on what we do well. We continue to build on a tradition and our legacy of quality, integrity and success."

Equitable is a financially solid, nationally recognized leader in health care for senior Americans, licensed in more than 30 states. Equitable has achieved an impressive list of accomplishments:

• Equitable began offering Medicare supplement products the very year Medicare itself was implemented, over 30 years ago.

• In 1974, Equitable pioneered the marketing of Long Term Care insurance—long before others saw that protection against the catastrophic risk of extended health care would emerge as the critical health care financing issue of the 21st century.

Equitable since 1935.

Equitable agent gathering in 1958, (center top) Dave, Doc and Ray Ross

• In 1985, Equitable "broke the Medicare mold" by offering the first comprehensive home health care policy for seniors—allowing them to recover from illness or injury in the comfort of their own homes, not in institutions.

• Since 1988, the leading U.S. consumer magazine has rated Equitable's Long Term Care and Medicare supplement policies in the Top 10 in the country in each of their industry surveys—the only company nationwide with that distinction.

The bedrock of Equitable's financial strength rests on a strong capital base and conservative investment portfolio. This gives policyowners peace of mind, knowing that the company has the long-term ability to keep its promises, and to be there for them when needed. This financial strength enables Equitable to meet the changing needs of customers, while engaging in an increasingly competitive marketplace.

From the very beginning, Doc Ross' plan was to leave a legacy to the Equitable Family—agents, policyowners, employees and loved ones. He launched the company with a mission that transcends excellence, "...to do well by doing good." Doc's legacy and his mission live on today.

Equitable Life & Casualty—the second oldest and one of the largest insurance companies domiciled in Utah—has never been stronger, and its future never brighter.

PRO STEEL SECURITY SAFES

ProSteel Security Safes is truly an example of the American Dream. Founded in 1947 as Provo Steel & Supply Company, ProSteel still operates under the same philosophy today as its founder, F.L. (Shorty) Shurtliff did 53 years ago. ProSteel exists to serve its customers and to earn their respect and repeat business.

F.L. Shurtliff started the business with $600 and an idea that a quality metal working shop supporting the construction industry of Provo, Utah was just what the state needed. It wasn't long before other cities and states saw the need for Mr. Shurtliff's services and soon he was providing steel handrails, stairwells, and structural steel to the rest of Utah as well as southern Idaho, western Colorado, and southern and eastern Nevada.

In the early '60s, F.L. Shurtliff was fortunate enough to land a contract with the original Tropicana Hotel and Casino in Las Vegas, Nevada. This transaction propelled the company overnight from a small job shop to a major supplier of structural steel products.

It was during this period that a friend of F.L.'s came to the plant to have some equipment repaired, and commented that he needed to purchase a safe to store his guns and valuables. Ever the opportunist, F.L. told the gentleman that he could build him a safe that would do just that. In February 1977, Provo Steel & Supply Company began manufacturing gun safes.

Just as his structural steel business grew by providing quality products and services, the safe business was founded on the same principles. Similar to his original business, the security safes were sold and marketed by word-of-mouth. Sales and deliveries were transacted from the back of a pickup truck. The safes were sold as an accessory product to complement his existing business, and it wasn't long before the demand for these safes consumed the company's entire manufacturing capacity. With his business at a crossroads, F.L. chose to concentrate solely on the safe business.

As the business continued to grow, F.L. realized he needed a business partner to support his new customer base. In 1977, his son-in-law, Stan Shaw joined the business. With F.L. as his mentor, Stan soon took over the day-to-day operations of the company.

Soon a dealer network was established and safes were being sold throughout the United States. In 1982, Larry K. Johnson was added as sales manager. Larry continued to establish the independent dealer network, and it wasn't long before Browning, located in Morgan, Utah, began to inquire about the possibility of marketing the ProSteel Security Safes to their dealers. An agreement was reached and in January of 1983, ProSteel became the exclusive supplier for Browning Safes.

In 1989, Stan Shaw and his partners purchased the business from F.L. Shurtliff. Equinox Capital acquired ProSteel from Stan Shaw in 1999, and today the company is operated by CEO Steve Rodger and president Dale M. Szuminski.

The business has grown through major retail chains such as Bass Pro Shop, Gander Mountain, Cabellas, and Gart Bros., as well as through the original independent dealers and distributors. Today, Browning/ProSteel has established themselves as a leader in firearm security.

ProSteel still believes, as it did in F.L. Shurtliff days, that its primary source of competitive advantage is the commitment, enthusiasm, and ingenuity of its employees.

While still fully-committed to the firearm security business, ProSteel is currently developing new products for home and commercial security as well. "We believe that new products and markets are the lifeblood of all successful companies," says ProSteel President Dale M. Szuminski.

The Provo Steel & Supply Company established in 1947, and known today as ProSteel, still follows the philosophy of F.L. Shurtliff. "Our vision is to create value in the eyes of our customers, and to continuously improve our methods and processes in pursuit of perfection," says Szuminski. From the days of F.L. Shurtliff to today, ProSteel is positioned to succeed in all of its future endeavors.

ProSteel's current Manufacturing Plant, located at 1400 South State Street, Provo, Utah.

GODFREY TRUCKING, INC.

Godfrey Trucking, Inc. was founded on a vision by an entrepreneur, but in order to know the man you have to know the history.

Richard M. Godfrey had trucking bred into him. His father, Wayne M. Godfrey, hauled coal via truck from the coal mines in Carbon County, Price, Utah to Murray, Utah, 120 miles over the Solder Summit Pass, three times a week in the 1940s.

After graduating from Olympus High School in 1956 Richard (Dick) went on to wrestle at the University of Utah. He was a very tenacious, intense person. Dick learned how to work hard on the family farm with his grandfather Wilford Earl Godfrey and family. After marrying Katherine Diane Davis on February 11, 1961, Dick worked for Hercules Rocket Division at Magna, Utah. While he attended the University of Utah, Dick was enrolled in the Electrical Engineer program and was recruited by Pan American Airlines.

Pan Am hired Dick and one of his good friends Merrill Thompson to come and work for them at NASA in Cape Canaveral, Florida, on the Minute Man missile project. As a bonus they could attend Brevard Engineering School, one of the top engineering schools in the country.

So, the Godfreys, with their one-year old daughter Traci, and the Thompsons, with four-year old son Jeff and two-year old daughter Terry, moved to Florida.

In 1964 while working and going to school, Merrill and Dick went to the drag races in there spare time. Dick was trying to figure out a way to time the cars better from start to finish, by having a large display screen at the finish line so the crowd could see instantly exactly how fast the car ran and how many seconds it took.

While working on the Minute Man Missile in 1964, he found a flaw in the schematic drawings and halted the project. A colonel from U.S.A.F. intervened and told him he didn't know what he was doing and ordered him to change his mind. This sparked Dick's intensity and neither one would back down. In the end, Dick was correct and was promoted in his job status. But, with the birth of his second child in June 1964, and an offer to start a drag strip back in Salt Lake City, Utah, the Godfreys and the Thompsons returned to Utah; Dick only had one semester to go before completing his engineering degree.

Dick, along with Bob Gee, Jim Campbell and Gordy Jensen started Bonneville Raceway Park at 3500 West 2100 South. At the same time, Richard M. Godfrey Trucking was formed hauling Vista Liner Campers, to supplement the short drag racing season that ran from May to September. On July 23, 1968 the first race took place at their new location at 6500 West 2100 South, which included drag racing, sprint car and motorcycle racing.

In 1969 Dick built the Husky Truck Stop at 6380 West 2100 South on two-and-a-half acres. This served as both a fueling station and yard for his trucking business. In 1974 he sold that facility to Dave Rock and built another truck stop and repair shop. In 1975 he sold all of his stock in Bonneville Raceway Park.

Diane would do the books, accounts payable, accounts receivable and payroll at home. Dick and Diane's philosophy is "A family that plays together, stays together." Diane would have the camper and truck loaded to go camping with the three kids: Traci, Scott and Gregg. She would tell Dick, " I'm going camping, whether you are going or not." He often worked

Dick and his toys at the Great Salt Lake Truck Show.

One of the Godfrey's show trucks.

18-hour days during the summer, but he always made it camping.

Now Dick could fully concentrate on trucking. He had good friends like Gordy Jensen, Paul Vanderlinden and Jack Kartchner who, together, had a few trucks. They would help each other haul freight. In 1980, deregulation changed the way trucking companies did business. This was a new day, and a new era. Now the shippers had people bidding for their freight. It was a great time for growth. Starla Mortensen came on board, ran the operation of dispatching and doing payroll for eight trucks. In 1984 Scott Godfrey joined the company full time. Dick, whose philosophy was that there wasn't any job too big or too small, would train his people by his example of hard work. Godfrey Trucking, Inc. was formed in 1985. By 1991 Ric Mortensen and Jim Jensen joined as a salesman and Derek Roberts as controller, and Godfrey Trucking, Inc. grew overnight. By 1996 there were 69 tractors leased or owned by Godfrey.

Godfrey Trucking, Inc. is a niche carrier; they have been hauling and setting up the Browning Arm's trade shows since 1975.

Godfrey set high standards for maintenance appearance and professionalism. In the mid-1980s they were the first in the intermountain west to convert their fleet to Air Ride tractor's and Air Ride trailers, to accommodate special hauling like trade shows, blanket wrap products, and electronics.

Erma Thompson came on board as safety director in 1991. Since then, she has set a mark that safety pays in the long run.

Scott Godfrey , Ric and Starla Mortensen purchased the company in 1998 from Dick and Diane Godfrey. Scott is president, Starla is vice president, Dick still drives 3 months out of the year. He still visits customers.

Godfrey moved into their 41,000 square foot office/ warehouse in West Valley City, Utah in December 1999, with an emphasis on being a "one-stop shop" for their customers. Godfrey has 51 owner-operators, 30 company trucks and 150 trailers, and their motto is, "Large Enough to Serve You—Small Enough to Care."

Godfrey's trucks en route to customers.

GOSSNER FOODS, INC.

Edwin Gossner, Sr. was born in 1909. He came from the eastern region of Edliswiel Waldkirch, Switzerland, where five generations of his family had lived as farmers. Today, the seventh generation of Gossners carry on the family tradition and continue to maintain the same homestead that has been a part of the family heritage for all these years.

Due to a declining European economy and limited prospects for the future, Edwin Gossner decided to seek a new life in America. He immigrated to the United States in 1930, scarcely speaking a word of English, and immediately went to work for his older brother Ernest, in Wisconsin. Ernest had preceded Edwin to the U.S. seven years earlier, after graduating from the Swiss cheese making School of Switzerland, and now owned his own cheese factory. For the next three years Edwin Gossner served his own apprenticeship and learned the art of making fine Swiss cheese following the traditional methods of the old country.

In 1933 Edwin married Josephine Oechslin of Darlington, Wisconsin; who was to be a major influence on him for all their married life. Two children, Edwin, Jr. and Dolores, soon followed. It was also in 1933 that his brother received an offer elsewhere and Edwin was asked to take over as cheese maker at the Burke factory. He held this position until 1937, when the factory burned down. Edwin then moved on to California, where he accepted a position as cheese maker with the Rumiano family. While there he converted the plant from a Monterey Jack to a Swiss cheese facility. This was to be an invaluable experience, as he was able to improve upon his knowledge of making Swiss cheese utilizing milk from cows fed on fermented feeds (silage) instead of fresh feed. The traditional method of making Swiss cheese did not allow for the use of milk from cows fed on silage, but he proved that it could be done. This was an important new concept that Gossner would later successfully employ in Cache Valley.

Edwin Gossner, Sr., circa late 1930s.

Gossner today.

Ed kept an eye open for a place of his own where he could make Swiss cheese. In 1941 he located such a place in Northern Utah (Cache Valley) while on vacation to Yellowstone National Park with his family. Cache Valley proved to be an ideal location, with its climate and elevation closely resembling that of Switzerland. There was also an abundant supply of milk with hundreds of dairymen producing milk locally. By the end of the year Gossner had moved to Utah and was set-up for business. Within five years he had built what was at the time the largest Swiss cheese making factory in the world, producing 120, two-hundred pound wheels of cheese a day.

In the ensuing years Gossner was the guiding force in upgrading Cache Valley milk production to Grade A market status. He brought sustained benefits to the dairymen by opening new markets for them and increasing their overall profits. Gossner also made important innovations such as introducing the means of making processed cheese and a more efficient recovery method of whey by-products.

In 1966 Edwin Gossner and his family began anew by starting Gossner Foods. Again the focus was placed on making Swiss cheese. They started with a half vat of milk (12,500 pounds) every other day, and Ed was quoted as saying that he would be happy if he could make up to two vats (50,000 pounds) every other day. Today, 25 years later, Gossner Foods uses over one-half million pounds of milk a day for cheese production.

Founders Edwin Gossner, Sr. and Josephine Gossner in the late 1970s.

In 1967 Gossner began packaging a line of cheeses, starting with Swiss, Cheddar and Monterey Jack. Eventually Muenster and others were added, so that in time over 30 varieties carried the Gossner name.

Edwin Gossner had his eye on the future and in 1982 he introduced a new fluid milk product that utilized ultra high temperature packaging technology. Rather than compete with the existing Grade A milk market, this new technology allowed Gossner to open up new marketing avenues. Gossner milk can be kept unrefrigerated at room temperature for months, and as such has proved to be highly desirable to the military community and others. Today, Gossner milk travels all over the world with U.S. troops, and is sold in places as diverse as Puerto Rico and Panama, where milk supplies and refrigeration are limited.

The mainstay of Gossner Foods continues to be Swiss cheese. It is made using the same formula that Edwin Gossner developed years ago. The Gossner Swiss cheese is a specialty cheese that has a milder flavor and softer body than other Swiss cheeses, yet it remains distinctly Swiss. Gossner Foods now utilizes state-of-the-art equipment for aseptic packaging and cheesemaking and is currently exploring new ideas to expand its product line.

When Edwin Gossner died in 1987, part of his legacy was a well-oiled machine that consisted of a corps of caring, knowledgeable, and well-trained employees. It is duly noted that were it not for these dedicated people Gossner Foods would not be what it is today, a successful family business.

In 1984 Dolores Gossner Wheeler, Ed's only daughter, was named president/CEO of Gossner Foods, Inc., and remains so today. Dolores has continued her father's pioneer spirit by overseeing Gossner's growth from a small, labor-intensive company to a streamlined operation with substantial examples of current technology. Under Dolores Wheeler's leadership, the company has undergone many positive changes. Gossner's plant footage, product line, and sales have tripled over the last 16 years. Most recently Dolores and the Gossner management have also combined forces with Kuhn Dairy of El Centro, California, to open a second cheese plant in California. This plant, Imperial Valley Cheese of California, will be the third Swiss cheese plant west of the Mississippi; all three plants were originated by a Gossner.

Today, only one of the original four members of the Gossner family that came to the Valley in 1941 is still alive. During their lifetimes, Edwin, Josephine, and Edwin, Jr. were greatly respected in the community and received numerous civic awards in recognition of their involvement and contributions. That tradition of service to the community continues to this day, with the fourth generation Gossners employed in the family business.

Early picture of Gossner Foods, circa 1967.

KERRY HOLT HAY CUBES, INC.

In 1969, Enterprise, Utah-native Kerry Holt returned home after a tour of duty in Vietnam. His war injury robbed him of the use of his right hand; but Kerry was convinced that the wound took him off the front lines just in time to save his life. And, at 25, he set out to make the most of the time he'd been given. At that point, Kerry had a wife, an infant son, an intense work ethic and very little else. But, in the 30 years that followed, he steadily built the company that would become one of the state's most successful farming operations.

Born in Enterprise in 1944, Holt was the second of five children. He remembers having little money as a child, but he credits his father, Jay Overton Holt, with introducing him to farming and teaching him the importance of hard, honest work. Kerry worked on the family farm throughout his school years, and after high school took odd jobs—fencing, paving and trucking—to save for his own first farm.

In the early 1970s, Kerry bought a 160-acre grain farm in the nearby Escalante Valley. Over the next decade he modernized the operation, improving the land's irrigation system and working with state agriculture officials to explore various forms of fertilization and pest control. Kerry reinvested his profits into the operation, buying additional acreage and equipment.

In 1980, Kerry took a professional gamble and mortgaged his farming operation to buy a cubing plant in Beryl, Utah. The facility compresses alfalfa into small cubes the size and shape of a candy bar. Cubes are made of "chopped" alfalfa compacted with heat and water. They're denser than traditional bales of hay, and they dry more quickly, which prevents spoilage. Their size and shape make them ideal for shipping long distances. Kerry capitalized on this portability, and soon after purchasing the cubing operation was selling hay cubes to, not only California dairies, but to large dairy operations overseas, as well.

Kerry Holt, circa 1967.

Kerry Holt directing swather crew.

Kerry has always professed that success depends on hiring the right people. He staffed his organization with friends and family whom he could trust to share his commitment and vision. His father-in-law, Voi Sorensen, ran the cubing operation for its first decade. His wife, DeeAnn, managed the operation's billings and finances. His two sons, Lynn and Ryan, each worked at the operation from youth to adulthood. Ryan continues to work with his father, while Lynn calls in from nearby Las Vegas to trade stock tips.

In the early 1990s Kerry partnered with another family member, his brother Robert, to buy the expansive Geyser Ranch in Central Nevada. The tract, which Kerry now owns independently, consists of 15,000 acres of ranch land, 5,000 acres of farmland and grazing rights to more than 1.5 million acres. Kerry leases those grazing rights to other operators so that he can focus on his area of expertise—growing, cubing and selling hay.

In its first year, Kerry Holt Hay Cubes, Inc. processed 200 tons of alfalfa. Today the operation processes 150 times that amount: 30,000 tons in two states. "On a good day, we can do 1,000 tons of hay and still be home for supper," Kerry has said. "We push hard." The operation employs about 40 workers during the busy summer months and about half a dozen year round. The company's equipment holdings include 12 tractors, 12 swathers which cut the hay, 12 choppers which grind the hay into fine particles and 32 wagons to haul the hay from the field to one of two stationery cubing plants. The operation runs 24-hours-a-day, seven-days-a-week during each of three hay crops.

Kerry has said that farming is 30 percent planting and harvesting and 70 percent big business. He has operated his cubing company accordingly, working with brokers and exporters to make inroads into the Japanese market, where land for growing feed is scarce and buyers will pay a premium for top quality alfalfa. Although he dislikes travel, he has taken an active role in the marketing of his product, visiting Japan for all-important face-to-face time with overseas buyers. He invites Japanese executives to tour his Southern Utah and Southern Nevada farms. As his guests roam the fields in business suits and leather-soled shoes, Kerry remains clad in his signature denim pants, blue workshirt and workboots. When he appeared in the pages of *Forbes* magazine, Holt wasn't photographed in a studio or lavish office. Instead, he was shown standing in the fields he knows so well, clad, of course, in blue jeans.

Kerry Holt checking pivot and alfalfa hay.

Kerry Holt in front of Utah Cuber with Japanese buyers.

KIRTON & MCCONKIE

From a three-attorney practice heavily involved in real estate, to one of the largest and most diversified legal firms in Utah. That's the story of Kirton & McConkie's first half century.

The firm's goal is to provide quality legal services ethically, efficiently, at a reasonable cost, and to its clients' satisfaction. It uses the most modern of tools, and encourages its attorneys to improve society through involvement in community, bar and service organizations.

With more than 60 attorneys, the internal capability of communicating in 13 languages in addition to English, and a network of outside legal professionals, Kirton & McConkie works throughout the world. Its practice areas include Commercial Litigation; Constitutional, Religious and Appellate; Construction and Land Development; Corporate and Taxation; Education Law; Employment Law; Healthcare and Risk Management; Immigration; Insurance Defense; Intellectual Property; International Law; Real Estate and Land Use Planning; Surety; and Workers' Compensation. It also has lawyers who devote substantial time to bankruptcy and creditor rights, and to advising financial institutions.

The firm's story begins with Wilford W. Kirton. Bill, as he was known, graduated from the University of Utah College of Law in 1948 and clerked for the Utah Supreme Court before setting out to establish his own practice in Salt Lake City.

He first joined with Merrill Faux, later a district judge, and Lothair Rich to form Faux, Rich and Kirton. He worked mainly with Rich on real estate, though he would quickly tell anyone who asked what he specialized in, "Clients!"

Developing a reputation as a lawyer who could be trusted both for his professional integrity and his legal skills, Kirton established a clientele of his own. He formed a new partnership with Dee Lowry and Verden Bettilyon in 1951. Over the next six years it flourished and the partners decided to buy their own building. Lowry, however, chose to go to work for the Church of Jesus Christ of the Latter-day Saints, leaving Kirton, Bettilyon and a new partner, Richard Harris, to make the purchase in 1957. They razed an old structure and built a two-story professional building at 336 South 300 East.

Oscar W. McConkie and Wilford W. Kirton.

Kirton & McConkie headquarters in Salt Lake City.

The site, closer to the district courts and county offices as well as to many of the firm's clients, would be home to the Kirton practice of law for the next three decades. Initially, it occupied the upper level of the building and rented the lower level to other businesses. It grew into the rest of the building in the years that followed, mostly by hiring promising young lawyers just out of law school.

Along the way, the names on the door changed, from Kirton, Bettilyon and Harris to Kirton, Bettilyon and Strong, and then to Kirton & Bettilyon when Strong left the firm.

During this time, Kirton took on a variety of civic and religious responsibilities in the Salt Lake City community. This activity would set a new course for his firm.

In 1964, President Hugh B. Brown of LDS Church First Presidency asked Kirton to his office. Expecting to be called to serve a mission for the Church, Bill was surprised when Brown asked him to leave his private practice and take charge of the

Oscar W. McConkie.

Church's Office of General Counsel. Vernon Snyder, who headed the Church's attorneys, was about to retire. At that time, the Church hired outside firms for large-scale legal projects and litigation.

Kirton asked for time to consider. On one hand, he had a thriving practice with more than enough work for all his attorneys. On the other, he knew that David O. McKay, president of the Church, was in his later years and that his successor would have the prerogative to appoint new counsel. If Kirton was the incumbent general counsel and was not re-appointed, he knew he would have to restart his own practice from the beginning.

A few days later, while he was in Atlanta at a meeting of the American Bar Association, Kirton's wife called to tell him he had been invited to meet with the entire First Presidency of the Church the next morning. He headed home.

The members of the First Presidency said he could accept the position within the framework of his private law firm. There was one condition: he had to assimilate the lawyers already in the Office of the General Counsel, including Richard R. Boyle, Robert M. Dyer, and Lowry, his former partner.

Kirton became general counsel of the Church that October, though not without misgivings. He later admitted, "At the time, I wondered if there was enough legal work for the Church to keep me busy. That is probably the best example of poor judgment in my entire life."

The leadership of the firm continued to change. S. Burton Howard joined the firm, and it became Kirton, Bettilyon and Howard. In 1966, Bettilyon and Howard withdrew and Oscar W. McConkie, Jr., a long-time friend and associate of Kirton's, joined. The practice became Kirton and McConkie for the first time.

McConkie, a former president of the Utah State Senate, brought the firm a political expertise that would help achieve recognition for the Church in countries around the world. Bolstered by this work, the firm grew to 30 attorneys, and it established a presence throughout the United States and in Canada, Eastern and Western Europe, Latin America and the Far East.

In 1972, Harold R. Boyer, who joined the firm, and Boyle, by then managing partner, became named partners in Kirton, McConkie, Boyer and Boyle. A year later, Dan S. Bushnell, General Counsel of Silver King Mines and Little America Corporation joined, bringing in a significant trial practice. At the same time, the firm became heavily involved in providing legal services to the Church's hospital system in Utah, Idaho and Wyoming, a role it retained when the hospitals were divested as Intermountain Health Care, a non-denominational, non-profit hospital system.

In the late 1970s, the office building at 336 became too small. Kirton leased temporary offices so it could be renovated with an additional story. With Boyle retiring and its name again Kirton and McConkie, the firm returned home in 1979.

In 1981, the practice reorganized to a professional corporation. Over the next 13 years its name changed several more times, reflecting participation and retirement of additional partners, until it was again, and since, Kirton and McConkie. Kirton's death in July 2000 didn't change this, as his inspiration remains an active presence. McConkie was chairman of the firm's board.

Through the '80s, the firm hired several individuals who had established practices in Utah and elsewhere, as part of a policy of growth to benefit its corporate, Church and individual clientele. This approach added a breadth of expertise, as well as expanding its numbers beyond the capacity of 336 South 300 East.

In 1990, the practice moved into the new Eagle Gate Tower in the heart of Salt Lake City, returning its long-time home to the rental market. A decade later, with 65 attorneys and some 50 legal assistants and staff, it occupies three floors of the tower.

Oscar W. McConkie III.

LARSON DAVIS, INC.

Larson Davis, Inc. of Provo has a very clear business philosophy –"Empowering our Customers Success". As innovators in the field of noise and vibration measurements, Larson Davis designs and builds instruments used to analyze noise and vibration generated by automobiles, aircraft and machinery—helping to make the world a quieter place. Its customers are major government and industrial companies in domestic and international markets.

Founded in September 1981 and incorporated in February 1982 by former company president Brian Larson and co-founder Larry Davis, Larson Davis and its five employees soon outgrew its first home, Larson's Pleasant Grove basement. The first office was fondly called a "Better Basement Business" (BBB) and featured such perks as late night "brain food" in the form of malts or shakes made in the upstairs kitchen. Work duties also occasionally called for employees to provide childcare for the Larson children.

The company's first product, a sound level meter, was the first of its kind to use a computer interface on noise monitoring instrumentation. This product opened the door to many new applications in noise monitoring. In another first, Larson Davis also developed specialized spectrum analyzers for the U.S. Navy for its submarine noise testing. Larson Davis' noise monitoring systems are also used at Salt Lake International Airport and other locations throughout the world to monitor noise emission in jet aircraft.

By 1984, "BBB" had outgrown the basement, and the company moved to 280 South Main in Pleasant Grove. Once again, Larson Davis needed more space, and moved in 1988 to the larger facility at 1681 West 820 North in Provo. In 1989, the company purchased that building and the adjacent building to accomodate their 70 employees. The company went public in 1994 and was subsequently traded on the NASDAQ stock exchange under the symbol "LDII" until April 1999.

In 1999, Larson Davis was sold to the PCB Group, Inc., of Depew, New York. PCB, founded in 1967 by Robert and Jim Lally, specializes in the development and marketing of piezoelectric quartz, tourmaline and ceramic sensors for measuring dynamic pressure, force, shock and vibration.

Larson Davis head office - Provo.

Larson Davis Product Group.

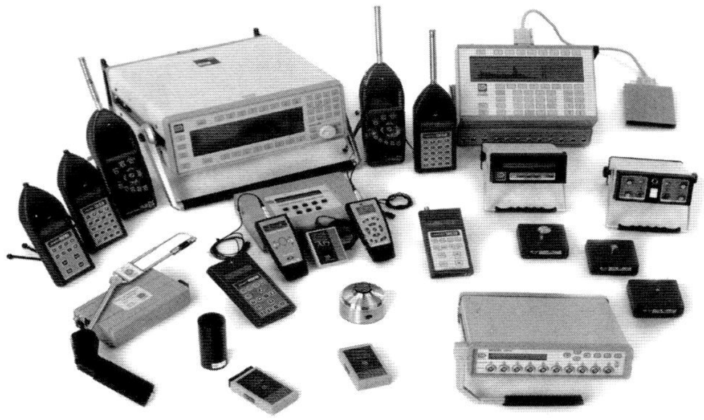

Larson Davis now consists of two product groups that are designed to take advantage of unique market opportunities in the solution of noise and vibration applications. Larson Davis Laboratories (LDL) provides solutions for Laboratory, Research and Development and Environmental Noise applications. Larson Davis Industrial (LDI) provides solutions for Industrial Hygiene and Worker Safety applications.

Laboratory products include sound level meters and real-time analyzers for vehicle noise, building acoustics and sound power applications. Environmental noise products include short, medium and long term systems for community noise based applications. LDI products include noise dosimeters, which evaluate sound exposure within the workplace and help to protect employees from noise induced hearing loss.

In January 2000 Larson Davis welcomed a new President, Dr. Thomas Lagö, who brings a driving force and stimulus to the organization that will enable the company to step up to the next level of growth. Dr. Lagö has extensive experience in the acoustic and vibration market as well as business administration. With his arrival in Provo, a new Larson Davis is born and a successful future is already emerging through a renewed team spirit.

Larson Davis and the PCB Group recently announced the formation of the "Acoustic Alliance," consisting of Larson Davis, The Modal Shop, GRAS, Brüel Acoustics and Brüel, Bertrand & Johnson Inc. This conglomerate of companies serves as an integrated network of resources including acoustic measurement product, acoustics experts, consultancy and applications support resources.

Larson Davis is proud of its high performance to cost ratio, and its creativity as a problem solver. For instance, a recent German law called for a "stepped" approach to the measurement of annoyance noises. Larson Davis responded with a specifically created product, which included a user-friendly sound level meter, a real-time spectrum analyzer, and a German-specific tonality analyzer to allow the user to quickly determine the severity of the noise problem under investigation. By building instruments that are defined by their programming, Larson Davis is able to continue to adapt to the ever-changing demands of a global market.

To the benefit of its loyal customers, Larson Davis uses the latest electronic devices and technologies to provide more advanced features for a great value. By staying current with the latest development in microprocessors, communication interfaces and Digital Signal Processors (DSP), Larson Davis continues to lead its market and maintain a reputation for technical progress and innovation.

Other services that Larson Davis provides to its customers include a product rental program, comprehensive product training at locations around the globe, and a product repair and calibration service that is dedicated to servicing equipment.

Larson Davis has just as strong a commitment to its team members as it does to its customers, and offers continued education, career development and a stimulating enjoyable work environment. The company's strong link to the community is evidenced by its close relationship with local universities and schools and team members regularly contribute their time to social service and local charities.

As Larson Davis team members can relate, sometimes the intent of those measuring sound pollution is not fully understood. One disgruntled and misinformed neighborhood resident stole a noise monitor that was being used to test area traffic noise, dismantled it and mailed the individual parts back to the Department of Transportation. The Larson Davis repair and calibration team effectively reassembled the instrument and returned it, fully functional and certified. As a result, the neighborhood eventually received a sound barrier to reduce the impact of highway noise. This type of response is typical of the repair and calibration team's ability to act quickly and effectively to provide the best service in the industry, and also serves as testimony to the durability of Larson Davis products.

Recent Larson Davis innovations include the first digital sensing array for vibration monitoring. By using the latest in communication technologies, Larson Davis will continue to provide advanced tools to allow its customers to solve their noise or vibration measurement problems, and help to make the world a better place. In short, Larson Davis lives the vision "Empowering Our Customers Success".

Larson Davis permanent outdoor noise monitoring system.

NORBEST, INC.

In 1930, a group of independent turkey growers had the foresight to found a small Utah-based cooperative—an organization that today has expanded into Norbest, Inc., the world's oldest and largest turkey marketing cooperative, as well as one of the world's largest turkey processors. Seventy years of experience in turkey breeding, growing, processing, and marketing make Norbest unsurpassed in product quality and customer service. The Norbest®-brand name commands the respect and confidence of consumers and trade buyers around the world.

Norbest actually had its early roots in the early 1920s as a producer-owned marketing cooperative called Utah Poultry. In 1930 Utah Poultry, along with other related businesses from Utah, Washington, Oregon, Idaho, Montana, Colorado, and Nevada combined to form the first regional turkey marketing co-op in the United States. Its headquarters was established in Salt Lake City, Utah, on October 9, 1930. The new cooperative was known as Northwestern Turkey Growers Association.

The objectives of the new association were to "...produce and pack a higher grade of birds, to establish a known quality...to eliminate as much speculation as possible...and pack a product, using federal grades, of uniform standard quality that will command both respect and the confidence of buyers." In its first year of operations, the co-op had revenues of $1 million on 3.5 million pounds of product; a far cry from the 140 million pounds annually produced by Norbest today.

In 1931 the Northwestern Turkey Growers Association was among the first to adopt federal grading standards. Throughout its second year of operation, Northwestern produced a "Number One" grade, which proved to be a significant marketing advantage. Ever since, the co-op has adhered to the highest government and industry standards of quality. Today all Norbest®-branded whole birds are USDA Grade A—the highest grade possible.

Open range bronze turkeys in the 1930s.

A familiar trademark was needed to help consumers recognize the new co-op's products. In 1934 someone suggested "Norwest," short for Northwestern Turkey Growers Association. This was soon changed to "Norbest." The new brand proved so popular that after a few years the cooperative changed its name to Norbest Turkey Growers Association, and later to Norbest, Inc.

Despite the Great Depression, Norbest stepped up its promotional efforts. In 1936 Norbest hit a publicity jackpot with the presentation of a large turkey to President Franklin D. Roosevelt just before Thanksgiving. This holiday tradition continues today through annual presentations by the National Turkey Federation.

"New York-dressed" turkeys, with feet, head, and eviscera intact were the standard until the 1950s.

During World War II turkey became a mainstay of U.S. troops serving both at home and abroad. Norbest earned the Armed Forces Meritorious Services Award for Outstanding Performance in supplying the Quartermaster Corps.

After the war, domestic demand for turkey lagged behind the production capacity built to cover wartime needs. Norbest researchers set about to improve the appeal of turkey as an everyday menu item. Norbest became an industry leader in improvements in the breeding, growing, processing, and marketing of turkeys. It was the first marketing group to sell fully-eviscerated, ready-to-cook turkeys. Prior to this time turkeys were sold as "New York Dressed," with the head, feet, and viscera still intact.

The following years saw an expansion of the whole bird business, as well as strong strides in marketing bone-in breasts and parts. Based on successful wartime experience, these years also heralded an international expansion, leading to Norbest's receipt in 1964 of the President's "E" award for excellence in exporting. Today, Norbest® products are distributed to many countries in the Pacific Rim, Latin America, the Caribbean, and the Middle East.

Recognizing the homemaker's need for more convenient products, Norbest again became the leader in new product development in the 1960s and 1970s. Norbest was first with the TenderTimer® pop-up cooking gauge that pops its stem at precisely the time when the turkey is done. Norbest also led the way with prebasted turkeys, bone-in breasts, boneless roasts, and other successful new products.

Other product line extensions have followed over the years. Norbest now offers not only whole turkeys, but a full line of raw and cooked further processed products including bone-in breasts and boneless roasts for both retail and foodservice; ground turkey; turkey steaks; smoked turkeys; cooked, roasted, and smoked deli breasts; turkey ham; turkey pastrami; and a host of other fine products.

All this growth has been built on traditions of high quality and the strength of a popular brand name. Norbest® whole birds are still rated #1 west of the Continental Divide and number three nationally. In heavy turkeys for foodservice use, Norbest holds the #1 U.S. national market share position.

A corporate vision focused on the future has been a hallmark of the leadership of Norbest, beginning with early presidents Clyde C. Edmonds (1930–1933), Herbert Byres (1933–1969), and J. Ray Garrett (1969–1972), all the way to the current president and CEO, Steven R. Jensen (1992–present).

Modern turkey growout facilities provide for state-of-the-art management of the comfort, health, safety, and biosecurity of the turkey flock.

Norbest was one of the first companies to provide completely ready-to-cook turkeys.

Membership in the Norbest cooperative has changed a few times over its 70 years of existence, as local farmer co-ops have merged, dissolved, or changed focus. Today, the members of the Norbest, Inc. cooperative are: Moroni Feed Company in central Utah, including about 80 growers raising five million turkeys annually; and Nebraska Turkey Growers Cooperative in Nebraska, which processes three million turkeys raised by 20 independent turkey growers. These local cooperatives operate three Norbest processing plants in Moroni and Salina, Utah, and in Gibbon, Nebraska.

Norbest's continuing progress is still in keeping with the founders' original objectives in 1930, of providing unique marketing opportunities for independent turkey growers. This is reflected in the modern cooperative mission statement of Norbest, Inc.: "The purpose of Norbest, Inc. is to deliver maximum long-term return to our producer members by strategically marketing high-quality turkey products worldwide. This requires total commitment to provide both our trade customers and our ultimate consumers consistently high-quality product and service."

The consumer's standard of high quality food is evolving. In the future, food must be easier and faster to prepare, and highly nutritious. With 70 years of proven success in product innovation, quality assured production and processing, combined with a proactive management philosophy, Norbest, Inc. has a unique balance of "'old fashioned" and "new" that gives the company an unequaled potential for continued success in the 21st century.

NOVELL, INC.

Novell has been a leader in computer networking since the birth of the networking industry. In 1982, Novell created network operating system software that became the basis for deploying local area networks (LANs). LAN solutions enabled files and peripheral devices such as printers to be shared between the various personal computers (PCs) on the network. Today, Novell envisions a world in which all types of networks—intranets, extranets, and the Internet, corporate and public, wired to wireless—work together as one Net to simplify the complexities of eBusiness and provide the power and flexibility organizations need to succeed in the Net economy. Novell is the leading supplier of Net services software used to simplify and secure the emerging one Net, and accelerate companies' transition to eBusiness.

Novell Data Systems began in 1979 as a computer manufacturer and maker of disk operating systems. In January 1983, Safeguard Scientific and Raymond J. Noorda reincorporated NDSI as Novell, Inc. to design and market software and hardware used for local area networks. Noorda became president, chief executive officer, and ultimately chairman of the board of the new company.

In 1983, Novell introduced NetWare, the first LAN software based on file server technology. NetWare is a personal computer networking system that designates one computer (the server) to manage the network and control access to shared devices, such as disk drives and printers. This marked an important step in the network revolution that has culminated today in the one Net economy.

Novell became a public company in March 1985, and began acquiring other networking companies to expand its product line, including Santa Clara Systems, a storage subsystems manufacturer; CXI, a developer of LAN to IBM host computer communications software; and Excelan, at the time the world's largest supplier of TCP/IP communications protocols.

The early market for Novell products grew as a result of smaller companies using computers for the first time, with PCs connected together on a LAN. Over time, large organizations began deploying departmental networks of PCs. By the early 1990s, corporate requirements for networks had grown significantly. Departmental LANs were interconnected over wide area networks, or WANs, which unified large corporations with offices around the world. Novell's NetWare operating system was the foundation of most of these networks, with nearly a 70 percent market share. Beginning in 1992, Noorda made a series of acquisitions intended to increase the company's competitiveness in a rapidly changing market. The objective was for Novell to become a supplier of client/server computing solutions. The company acquired Digital Research Corp., developer of DR DOS; AT&T's UNIX System Laboratory and its operating system technology, and word processing and personal productivity software maker WordPerfect, in 1994.

Novell Netware was the first LAN software based on file server technology.

Noorda retired from Novell in 1994 as the company was in the midst of efforts to expand as a client/server solution provider. Hewlett-Packard executive Robert Frankenberg succeeded him. Seeking to better leverage Novell's historical strengths in networking, Frankenberg chose to refocus Novell on its core networking software business. The company sold the UnixWare operating system to The Santa Cruz Operation in Fall 1995. In 1996, Novell sold the WordPerfect business productive suite to Corel Corporation. Novell was back full-time on its core strength—networking software.

Frankenberg resigned from the company in 1996, just as the Internet was beginning to revolutionize the traditional network market. Interim CEO John Young initiated a program to make the company's products Internet ready.

Dr. Eric Schmidt, formerly Sun Microsystems' chief technology officer, took over the reins at Novell in March 1997. Schmidt accelerated Novell's efforts to leverage its core networking strengths in the Internet arena. He quickly announced a product roadmap to base the communications for all of Novell's products on IP, the Internet communications protocol. The following year, NetWare 5 and Novell Directory Services (NDS), which had become the basis for new Net services software products from Novell, began shipping with native IP support.

Novell first brought NDS to market in 1994. By early 1996, deployments of NDS on very large corporate and government networks began to rapidly increase. Novell quickly became the market leader for new directory-based network solutions. In 1997, the company began shipping the first of its new Net services software products that use information stored in the directory to simplify the management of networks and better secure access based on the identities of users. Novell began to promote its NDS and Net services software as a means to manage how different operating systems, applications, and other resources are deployed across highly-distributed networks. The company also announced its commitment to develop Net services software to support Internet solutions.

In 2000, Novell announced an expansion of its Net services software model to lead the industry in delivering software as services over the Net, rather than packaged, boxed products.

Novell maintains its corporate headquarters in Provo, Utah. The company continues a strong commitment not only to technology innovation, but also to the state of Utah, through an extensive program of corporate philanthropy, software donations, and employee volunteer efforts in the areas of education, critical community needs, and cultural development.

From its earliest days as a maker of disk operating systems, Novell is now the world's leading provider of Net services software, with annual revenue of more than $1 billion.

The one Net world envisioned by Novell—where intranets, extranets, and the Internet, corporate and public, and wired to wireless work together—presents challenges and opportunities for business. In a one Net world, individuals must be able to access their own information, as they want it, any time, anywhere, from any device. Businesses will electronically manage their relationships with customers, partners, and even their own employees, using networking technology to determine who has access to what, when, and how. With its one Net vision and Net services software strategy, Novell remains at the forefront of this networking technology, continuing to leverage the core network skills it has built over the past 20 years.

Ray Noorda (left), president, chief executive officer, and chairman of the board, with Senator Orrin Hatch.

ORBIT IRRIGATION PRODUCTS, INC.

It makes sense that Max Ericksen, who founded Orbit Irrigation Products in 1971, made the company's home in Utah. His ancestors, who were early pioneer emigrants to Utah, were the first to realize the importance of irrigation. They depended on it for survival. Crops couldn't live without water being distributed to them on a regular basis. Orbit took that concept and combined it with technology.

Portraying the honesty and work ethic exemplified by his ancestors, Max began manufacturing products because he was determined to make great products that targeted a value customer. "Our goals haven't changed, we're still determined to manufacture high quality, innovative products at a good value," explains executive vice president, Mike Ericksen.

Orbit Irrigation Products has been marked by a constant, intense focus on one concept: the customer. Orbit designs, produces, tests, and markets WaterMaster, DripMaster, SunMate and Arizona Mist lines to home improvement centers around the world. Ericksen states, "Rather than a pinnacle style of management, we listen to our customers." The success of the company is attributed to this "customer first" type attitude.

The company's innovative, driven state of mind, keeps them on the forefront of technology. "We want to be the first ones to introduce something new into market," states Ericksen, "and even as products become more technologically advanced, we want to be sure that they remain very easy to use. We're the pioneers of constantly creating something that's new and advanced—we'll always try to use less water to do more. The company slogan, 'Conservation through Innovation,' signifies our commitment to developing innovative products that manage water." With the ongoing creation and testing of new products, Orbit will continue to respond to the needs of its customers. "Innovation is vital," Ericksen states, "innovation and new products are driving every single company that I know."

Founder, Max Ericksen.

Orbit manufactures a full line of irrigation products.

Orbit's dedicated customer approach to product development is exemplified by numerous Orbit products that have become industry standard. Orbit's WaterMaster timers use one programming method; they are simple to program and easy to use. The company was the first to introduce a WaterMaster sprinkler timer with remote control to the retail market. The WaterMaster timer is the first ever that allows the convenience of controlling your sprinkler system from as far as 200 feet. It saves time and prevents the need of running back and forth to the timer when making adjustments or repairs. Most recently, Orbit has introduced a pre-assembled manifold system. The pre-assembled manifold is expandable and is the easiest way to install a manifold, add a sprinkler line or replace a valve. Also, part of the WaterMaster line are the superior Voyager II and Saturn III pop-up gear driven heads. They are professional quality sprinklers that are incredibly quite and easy to adjust.

Corporate headquarters, located in North Salt Lake City, Utah.

The company was also the first to introduce retrofit micro-watering, often referred to as "drip" irrigation (derived from Orbit's micro-watering line DripMaster). This type of watering system conserves water by taking it right where it needs to go, to the root of the plant. It is most often used for watering individual plants, flower pots, hanging baskets, and small hard-to-water areas.

Orbit's SunMate hose-end line recently introduced an Ultralight line of watering nozzles. "Ultralight" because of it's lightweight aluminum construction. The heavy-duty aluminum withstands extreme conditions while maintaining the light weight of aluminum products. SunMate offers a wide variety of hose-end products including hand held nozzles, hose end timers, oscillators, and impact heads.

Orbit manufactures a timer that combines a battery-powered electronic timer and valve. The timer connects directly to a hose faucet and a wire remote accessory can be added to move the timer to a more convenient location. For the ultimate in convenience, the WaterMaster hose faucet timer enables underground sprinklers, micro-watering, hose end sprinklers, or patio mist cooling systems to be operated from a hose faucet.

Over the Internet customers can log on to www.orbitonline.com and download a sprinkler design software to assist in designing a sprinkler system. By answering a limited number of questions and inputting the landscape measurements, the customer receives a completed sprinkler layout, parts list, and assembly instructions, in 24 hours. Customers can then find a location near them to purchase the products and get answers to product questions.

Under the guidance of a solid management team, the company has widened it dominance of the irrigation industry, while also creating the best value for customers. Orbit provides state-of-the-art, reliable products that are affordable. Orbit's ability to oversee the entire production process allows it to offer superior products at an affordable price. Consistency is maintained by strictly controlling all phases of development including design, molding, production, and packaging. In addition, Orbit's advanced computer system ensures that orders are shipped accurately, quickly, and complete.

Being located in Utah has given Orbit the ability to test products under real conditions—everything from the Wasatch Mountains to the blazing deserts down south, and from the freezing cold winter nights to blistering summer days.

The conservation green earth approach in manufacturing and marketing make Orbit one of the broadest, most innovative, and most reliable lines of irrigation products available, driven by the company's desire to lead its customers into the future of irrigation.

PEAK ALARM COMPANY

Jerry D. Howe and his wife Gayle started their business on April Fool's Day, but they do take it completely seriously. They always have, and always will.

"Protecting people's lives and security is an interesting business," says Jerry Howe, president and CEO of Peak Alarm Company. "When we reduce our clients' risk, it's quite an accomplishment."

Back in 1969, Jerry was a Navy veteran who had spent the previous five years working for alarm companies in the Oakland, California area. A native of Albuquerque, he had married Gayle, who was from Salt Lake City, in 1964. They both wanted to move to a smaller city and decided to start their own business in Gayle's hometown. Jerry prepared to start from scratch.

As luck would have it, their plans were boosted when they received a call from the owner of Day and Night Alarm Company in Salt Lake City. He wanted to sell his business and its 134 commercial accounts. Jerry said, "Yes!" and the Howes headed for their new life with a small, growing business on which to build.

Jerry and Gayle arrived at their new home on April 1. They hit the ground running; they had to. Even as they were unloading their belongings from a U-Haul truck, the phone began to ring.

"I had no experience with the area," Jerry recalls, "but it's a '24-7' business. Our clients needed service. We parked the U-Haul and I started making service calls. I'd ask Gayle where something was, she drew me maps, and off I went. We were working before we'd unpacked."

In those early days, Jerry worked from the basement of their home. Gayle did the billing on her grandmother's Underwood typewriter, a model from the 1930s. ("I wish I still had it," Jerry confides.)

One of the first things they did was change the name of the business.

A service technician checking out the alarm system.

The front entryway to the office building.

"Gayle's mother Amy Bruerton, came up with Peak," Jerry says. "And, while it goes with the mountains that are all around us, she suggested it to represent our performance. It gave us something to work toward."

At first, Jerry had one employee, who had stayed on from Day and Night. Peak had about $50,000 in revenues that first year. Now their gross sales will reach $7 million this year.

In 1972, Peak Alarm incorporated. Its commercial security business "...grew through knocking on doors and a substantial number of referrals," Jerry says. He handled every aspect of the business.

"Often I worked all night."

To get family time, he and Gayle would load a mattress in the back of their car and take their five-year-old son and two-year-old daughter with them on calls.

"Gayle, Rick and Julie would play in the back while I was inside, and the kids could go to sleep there. When I was driving we were all together."

Alarm calls were taken and help dispatched by an answering service. Jerry helped out there, too.

In 1975, Peak was accepted into the Western Burglar & Fire Alarm Association, now part of the National Burglar & Fire Alarm Association (NBFAA), and in May 1977, it added its own central station, with nine dispatchers. By that time, it had established its headquarters at 2182 South West Temple, a site they have since enlarged and remodeled several times over the years, and in 2000 planned to replace with a new 15,000-square-foot building on two-and-a-half acres. Its new Salt Lake City location, expected to be ready during the second quarter of 2001, combines the facilities from three buildings into one.

The central station monitoring center.

In 1985, Peak Alarm started serving residential, as well as commercial, clients. It also bought out General Alarm Corporation, and turned to computers to support its services. It was the first company in the region to develop and install a fully-computerized central monitoring center.

In 1997, Peak added a guard and patrol company.

By 2000, Peak had about 9,000 accounts, half residential and half commercial. It is one of the largest and fastest growing alarm companies in Utah and Idaho, with several corporate subsidiaries: Peak Alarm Guard and Patrol Company, Peak Alarm of Idaho, Peak Alarm of Wyoming, and Peak Alarm of Utah. It was ranked 71st-largest alarm company in the U.S. In addition to Salt Lake City, it has offices in Park City, Utah, and in the Idaho cities of Idaho Falls, Meridian, Burley, and Pocatello.

With 150 employees, Peak is a full-service security company. Installations include burglar and fire alarms, card access systems, and closed circuit television.

To provide the 24-hour monitoring that is an essential part of any security system, Peak's Central Station has 16 trained dispatchers who immediately notify the police or fire departments in case of an alarm. The station is built to Grade A Underwriters Laboratory specifications, enhanced by the latest technology, including direct connections to local emergency jurisdictions and backup electricity from its own generator and batteries.

Seventy patrol officers are on client premises or patrol government, residential and commercial sites. Though unarmed, these guards are trained in emergency procedures, electronic security monitoring, and protection of public and employee areas, including first aid and fire prevention. All are licensed and certified by the state.

Peak Alarm Security offers key holding and alarm response services so that its officers can act on behalf of clients in case of alarm activation.

Peak sells equipment from a full range of manufacturers. It carries the region's largest stocked inventory of systems and parts and its fleet of more than 30 installation and service trucks, including a patrol division with 11 cars, is radio dispatched 24-hours-a-day. It can quickly fix almost any type of system on the market.

Installers are factory trained and certified, and state licensed, bonded and insured. Installations are UL certified. Protection can be enhanced with airlink technology, which protects premises even if phone lines are damaged.

Installations are engineered to fit the clients needs. "You can't use a bank alarm in a bakery shop," says Jerry Howe.

But the main asset of Peak Alarm is its people. Jerry says, "We seek better quality people, and we have a good staff. We've been around for 31 years and have a couple of people who have been with us for 25 years or more. We have 20 people with us more than 10 years."

This includes three of Jerry and Gayle's children, who eventually numbered six. Rick, now 35, graduated from the mattress in the back seat of the car to operations, where he worked for 20 years. Son Jeff, at 24, is central station manager, secretary and treasurer, and Tyler, 20, is a graveyard shift supervisor. Julie is married to a captain in the Army. Son Tim, 28, is not in the family business, nor is daughter Renee, age 14—at least not yet.

Still gratifying, the alarm business has changed dramatically over the last 36 years, Jerry reflects. "Computers really made a difference.

"But the neat thing for me has been being able to work with my wife. She has been the best partner. She may have been at home, behind the scenes, but her energy and knowledge were invaluable."

One of Peak Alarm Company's service van.

S & S POWER, INC.

Stan Checketts is the founder and CEO of S&S Power, Inc., the world's leading manufacturer of vertical thrill rides. S&S Power, Inc. is based in Logan, a scenic valley in the northern Wasatch mountains in the great state of Utah. Throughout his life Stan, who has been called an "adrenaline junkie," has always loved to build and create things. Even when he was a kid he was building huts, swings and thrill rides on ropes hanging from barns for his friends to enjoy. Stan and his wife Sandy thoroughly enjoy their "yours, mine and ours" family of nine children, four daughters-in-law, two sons-in-law, 10 grandchildren, and two more grandchildren on the way.

Stan is unique in his ability not only to manage and operate his company, but to create and design the rides. He has produced some of the most exciting, unique and innovative ride prototypes from a scribble on a restaurant napkin or from a sketch on a piece of scratch paper. These are not rides that have been done before by someone else. In fact, the tower ride designs involve a patented technology that utilizes compressed air. If a ride has ever been done before, he has no interest in copying someone else's idea. This too, seems to be a phenomenon unto itself in the amusement ride industry.

Several high-thrill tower rides are currently offered by S&S Power, Inc., including the Space Shot™, the Turbo Drop™, a Combination Space Shot/Turbo Drop, the Double Shot, children's rides, the Frog Hopper™ and Rodeo Rider™, and the world's first air powered coaster, the Thrust Air 2000. Stan is still very instrumental in the sales of his rides. Whenever possible, Stan travels to the amusement parks to attend their grand opening ceremonies for any of the new S&S Power, Inc. rides. He has thrilled park owners and park patrons by climbing to the top of the ride, which can be anywhere from 185–315 feet tall, and having his photograph taken. Stan has climbed to the top of many of these rides and waved at the camera crews-making front page news around the world.

On a visit to the S&S Power, Inc. offices, you will be more likely to find Stan outside working on the latest prototype or showing the guys in the shop how to make a particular fixture than sitting behind a desk. No one cares more about his employees than Stan; he knows each of them personally and is interested in their happiness and well-being. He literally glows with excitement and passion for his products. According to his wife Sandy (the other "S" in S&S), he can hardly wait to get to work each morning.

Stan Checketts, founder and CEO of S&S Power, Inc.

S & S Power, Inc headquarters in Logan, Utah.

Stan and Sandy made their debut in the amusement industry in 1989, with the formation of Sports Tower, Inc. This company developed a very safe and subsequently very popular system built for bungee jumping. Sports Tower was sold in 1995, but continues to be the world's largest and most successful bungee jumping company.

S&S Sports, Inc. was founded in January 1993 and manufactured The Trampoline Thing™, a combination bungee jump and trampoline. Since that time, hundreds of these units have been shipped throughout the world. The company was sold in 1996.

In early 1994, S&S Sports Power, Inc. was founded and soon began manufacturing and distributing the Space Shot® vertical amusement ride. The Space Shot® air launches passengers up a standard 185-foot tower and gently bounces back to the starting position. Stan Checketts holds the U.S. Patent on the Space Shot® technology.

Stan Checketts on top of the Big Shot (Space Shot), Stratosphere Tower, Las Vegas, NV (approximately 1,200 feet above the Las Vegas Strip).

Knott's Berry Farm, Buena Park, CA, "Supreme Scream," 312 feet tall.

S&S Original Amusements, Inc. was founded in September 1995. This S&S division manufactured the first thrill rides for children, the Frog Hopper® and Rodeo Rider™ and a vertical drop ride, the Turbo Drop™.

Aerial view of the S&S Factory & Thrust Air 2000 prototype.

S&S Sports Power and S&S Original Amusements made up the S&S Group, and in 1998, S&S Sports Power and S&S Original Amusements merged into one company, S&S Power, Inc. The first product introduced from the new company was the Double Shot™, an 85-foot tall tower ride. S&S employees are continually working on ways to improve the current rides.

Stan introduced the newest ride sensation in November 1999, the world's first air-launched coaster, Thrust Air 2000™. This coaster really pushes the thrill ride envelope, accelerating from 0 to 80 miles per hour in under two seconds. The new coaster and other tower rides can be checked out at the S&S web site at www.s-spower.com, for the most up-to-date information.

Entertaining business associates who visit the S&S offices is one of Stan's favorite pleasures. Stan's snowmobiling adventures are legendary among park owners and managers who have been fortunate enough to accompany him. Stan appreciates the hard work and dedication of the S&S employees. He attributes a large part of the S&S success to these extended "family members." Stan and Sandy often show their gratitude through thoughtfulness and great parties. Through a lot of hard work, long hours, and lots of fun and excitement, S&S Power has 91 tower rides operating in 24 countries and 134 Frog Hopper rides operating in 22 countries around the world, as of July 2000. The rides are so popular because Stan built his reputation on selling safe, dependable, low maintenance, thrilling rides. Millions of people have ridden S&S Power's rides and absolutely love them. The only thing that is almost as exciting as riding one of Stan's rides is anticipating what new ride the "thrill master" will unveil next. Thanks for the thrills, Stan.

Six Flags Fiesta Texas, San Antonio, TX, USA.

STATE BANK OF SOUTHERN UTAH

On November 21, 1956 local business leaders, spearheaded by Warren H. Bulloch and Lorin Whetten, met in Cedar City, Utah to organize a new community bank. This meeting was the beginning of State Bank of Southern Utah, organized to have a "hometown" bank to offer financial services to people in southern Utah. The bank opened on November 25, 1957 in a rented building located at 99 North Main Street, without FDIC Insurance and with $180,000 of capital raised by community-spirited investors. The founders chose Warren Bulloch as chairman, and elected L.V. Broadbent, Stanley Bradshaw, Maeser Dalley, Arthur Joseph, Clarence E. Miller, William R. Thorley, Elwood J. Corry, Lehi M. Jones, Loren A. Whetten and Alex B. Williams as members of the Board of Directors. The directors hired Robert B. White as the first cashier and lending officer and Eldon Schmutz as an officer.

From the beginning the bank grew steadily because it met the needs of local businessmen, ranchers and consumers. By 1959 the Bank was able to secure FDIC Insurance to protect their depositors. The 1960s were a decade of building customer relationships and community support in Cedar City and Iron County. The bank and its employees were contributors to many local events and charitable efforts such as the Southwest Junior Livestock Show. By 1969 the Bank had $7,682,769 in deposits and $5,336,071 in loans, and had built a solid reputation of friendly, hometown banking. With this experience the Board approved the construction of a new 12,000 square foot building at 26 North Main Street. This modern building was the springboard for growth and served the bank for 30 years. With the expanded space the bank entered the computer age, began branching and enlarged its lending area over southwestern Utah.

Original Board of Directors and Officers of State Bank of Southern Utah. Back Row: Arthur Joseph, Loren A. Whetten, William R. Thorley, Alex B. Williams, Leroy V. Broadbent, M.D., Stanley Bradshaw, Warren H. Bulloch, Clarence E. Miller. Front Row: Eldon W. Schmutz, Robert B. White, Elwood J. Corry, Maeser Dalley, Lehi M. Jones.

New Corporate Office: 377 North Main Street, Cedar City

The 1970s marked the approval of the first branches for State Bank. Led by Eldon Schmutz and Warren H. Bulloch, State Bank opened its first branch in Orderville, Utah in November 1975. Shortly after, in 1978, a branch was approved in Kanab. Thus began the bank strategy of serving rural communities anchored by the trade center of Cedar City.

The 80s were marked by growth in the first half and retrenching during the later part to weather the effects of a nationwide banking crisis. State Bank grew to $50 million in assets by the mid '80s, adding a new branch in Circleville in 1984. In the second half of the 1980s the bank worked out of an economic recession and credit quality problems under the leadership of President Kerry Jones and the management team of Ronald Heaton and John Westwood.

By 1990 the bank was firmly established on a track for unprecedented expansion. In 1991 State Bank opened its Cedar South Main office for mortgage loans and during the balance of the '90s added offices in St. George, Parowan, Santa Clara and Tropic. As the bank neared the new millennium it had progressed to the point where the main office in Cedar City was inadequate to handle increased operations. As a result, the Board sold the old Main Street office to Cedar City Corporation and built a beautiful corporate office building with modern processing and banking facilities at 377 North Main Street. The building was occupied on November 11, 1999. In February 2000 State Bank purchased the Richfield branch of Community First Bank. By June 30, 2000 State Bank of Southern Utah had $245 million in assets, $206 million in deposits and $161 million in loans. Over 47 years, State Bank has become a leader in financial services in southwestern Utah.

SOUTHERN UTAH UNIVERSITY

In the late 19th century, local Southern Utah residents longed for an institution of higher education. The nearest universities were 220-250 miles away, and there was a great need for trained teachers in Southern Utah public schools. In March of 1897, the state legislature approved a bill sponsored and pushed-through by Southern Utah legislators to establish a State Normal School in the area as a branch of the University of Utah. A prestigous three-person commission was appointed to visit the several communities vying for the school and to choose its location.

In May 1897, the commission announced its unanimous choice as Cedar City. Although the community had pledged six acres of land on Academy Hill for the school campus, a minimum of 15 acres was required, so several Cedar City citizens quickly mortgaged their homes to raise money for additional land. This was just the first of three times that residents mortgaged property to save the Normal School.

The first classes, consisting of 46 girls and 72 boys, were held in the Ward Hall, and were completed by a flurry of activity in August 1897. Residents were shocked to learn that the enabling bill stipulated that a $15,000 appropriation for the first academic year's operation, but would not be available until a permanent building was completed and deeded to the state with at least 15 acres of land. Residents again mortgaged property to pay operating costs and the salaries of four teachers—Principal Milton Bennion, $1,100 per year; George W. Decker and Howard R. Driggs, $800 each per year; and Annie Spencer, $500 per year. Later, when the first building, Old Main, was completed it proved unacceptable to the State Building Board because it lacked a heating plant. So, for a third time dedicated citizens mortgaged personal property to secure a bank loan.

The permanent building that the community promised to provide was estimated to cost $35,000. To reduce cash outlays, residents agreed to donate labor to cut and haul 15,000 board feet of lumber from the mountains over 30 miles east of Cedar City. The building had to be completed by September, 1898 or Cedar City would lose its school. The first crew left Cedar City on January 5, 1898. Before it reached the sawmill, it began to snow, adding to already deep drifts. When the morning of January 9 found snow continuing to fall, the men decided to load what lumber they could and return to Cedar City, rather than await additional work crews.

They soon encountered drifts 10-15 feet deep. A 1,600 pound percheron grandshire horse named Old Sorrel came to the party's rescue by plunging against the snow, rearing and pawing with his front feet to break down drifts, some as long as 100 yards; his efforts saved the party and also the school. Despite the winter conditions, lumber was soon being relayed to town. Only enormous sacrifice and effort on the part of Cedar City citizens got the lumber out, built Old Main, and brought Branch Normal School into existence.

In 1913 the school was changed to a branch of Utah State Agricultural College at Logan and its name changed to Branch Agricultural College (BAC). In 1953 the name was changed again, to College of Southern Utah (CSU). The state legislature, in 1965, approved changing the status from junior college to a four-year college and also making it an independent college. The name was again changed in 1969 to Southern Utah State College (SUSC), and then on January 1, 1991, with university status granted, the name was changed to Southern Utah University (SUU).

Since 1983 SUU's growth and development have been dramatic. The student body has grown from 1,800 students to 6,100, and eight new buildings have been added and others

The Southern Utah University campus from the west with sports playing fields and the Centrum Arena of the Sharwan Smith Center in the foreground.

October 28, 1898 dedication ceremonies for Old Main, the first campus building, which was barely completed in time to satisfy a State of Utah mandate threatening the Cedar City location of what is now Southern Utah University.

Entry to the modern Gerald R. Sherratt Library. The second floor of the sky-lit rotunda portion of the library houses the Jon and Karen Huntsman Reading Room.

extensively renovated. The campus now sits on 133 acres of well-manicured grounds with 73 buildings, 26 computer laboratories, and a radio and television station. The institution also has 1,032 acres at its valley farm and 2,502 acres of mountain property, which includes the beautiful Mountain Center used for campus and continuing education programs.

The University's successful Division I men's and women's basketball and gymnastics teams call the 5,300 seat Centrum arena their home. Men's and women's track and cross-country teams have home facilities, along with the Division I AA football team, at Eccles Coliseum. The men's golf, women's softball, women's tennis and men's baseball teams, along with the basketball teams compete very successfully in the Mid-Continental Conference. The football and gymnastics teams compete as independents.

More than 600 employees, including over 230 faculty, work to serve the needs of students and to conduct specialized programs such as the Tony Award-winning Utah Shakespearean Festival, the Braithwaite Fine Arts Gallery, the American Folk Ballet, the Ashcroft Observatory, and the Utah Summer Games. The University is divided into five colleges with 16 departments offering 42 major programs as well as a School of Continuing and Professional Studies and two centers—the Utah Center for Rural Life and the Center for Politics and Public Service.

The philosophy of the institution holds that the central role of the University is to foster academic excellence, to instill ethics and values, and to honor thought in all its finest forms.

Southern Utah University is first and foremost a superior teaching institution, with academic programs in business, teacher education, applied technology, science, humanities, social science, forensics, and the performing and visual arts receiving recognition for their excellence. The University is also noted for its commitment to scholarly endeavors by its faculty and students, as well as to public service.

As a fully-accredited, state-supported, comprehensive, regional university, SUU attracts students from all of Utah's 29 counties, most states, and many foreign countries. The majority are undergraduate students, but master's degrees in accounting, education, business administration, arts administration and a cooperative master's degree in social work are offered.

A 10-member Board of Trustees implements policy as assigned by the 15-member State Board of Regents. Administration is carried out by the President, the President's Council, the Dean's Council, the Faculty Senate, and the faculty staff.

Southern Utah University is proud of the commitment that brought the institution into existence in 1897 and the continuing commitment of students, faculty, staff, administration, and the citizens of Southern Utah to meet the University's changing role and to promote excellence. Southern Utah University graduates have gone forth to serve and lead their communities, their states and their employers well. The institution boasts among its graduates and faculty several corporate chief executive officers, professional athletes, doctors, lawyers, prominent educators, coaches, city mayors, county commissioners, state legislators, a United States senator, and two governors. The University has grown to more than match the vision the residents had when they originally sacrificed so greatly to establish a little normal school at Cedar City in 1897.

The Harris Center houses athletic administration offices and a gymnastics training facility. The center is located on the south end of Eccles Coliseum, home for SUU Thunderbird football, track and field, and special events.

TELEPERFORMANCE USA

Teleperformance USA opened its doors in autumn of 1993, after CEO and President Dominic Dato joined forces with Teleperformance International, headquartered in Paris, France. Teleperformance International has been a leader in the global direct response industry for many years and was interested in partnering with a well-experienced telemarketing industry leader in the United States. Through a mutual acquaintance, Mr. Dato was introduced to the senior executive team at Teleperformance International. Because a partnership looked promising, Dato began pursuit of a U.S. startup project. Teaming with three long-time industry peers, Dato took his venture to Salt Lake City, Utah.

Dato's team diligently set to work, using folding tables as desks throughout months of construction. In fact, the company's first payroll included fewer than 25 employees. Seven years later, Dato's original start-up team is still intact at Teleperformance USA, which now boasts more than 3,000 employees on payroll, at 18 locations throughout Utah, Montana, Idaho, Washington, Nevada, Colorado, Wyoming, Kansas and Tennessee.

While Teleperformance USA could have settled anywhere in the U.S., several key elements attracted Dato and his team to Salt Lake City. A favorable climate with year-round recreation opportunities and ample business resources, complemented by fond memories of his formative years spent in the area, pointed Dato toward the Wasatch Front. Salt Lake's abundant business resources, including an easily-accessible, international airport and an eager workforce, has proven the decision to be a sound one. Several members of Dato's team have relocated to Salt Lake City and find Utah to be a great place to raise their families and flourish in the culture and outdoors.

Telemarketing is a difficult industry by its very nature. However, Teleperformance USA's dedication to employees, reinvestment in state-of-the-art technology, and pursuit of top personnel has given them an edge in the industry. While other firms might have closed their doors or conducted lay-offs when market conditions were difficult, Teleperformance USA has occasionally operated at cost—or even at a loss—in the hope of maintaining its large team of teleservices representatives (TSRs) while pursuing increasingly larger projects.

Dato's style, and commitment to making Teleperformance USA an industry leader, has earned him great respect among his partners, employees, peers and clients—all of whom Dato affectionately calls friends.

Today, Teleperformance USA maintains a stable client base with services including: memberships, publications, catalogs, financial services, telecommunications and consumer clubs. These applications include inbound customer service, order-taking, outbound services, database management and e-commerce production. Today, and perhaps most proudly, Teleperformance USA can state that their efforts have made them the largest, most profitable telemarketing segment for Teleperformance International. It is fair to say that the risk-taking of the early days has paid off.

Teleperformance USA has certainly experienced phenomenal growth in a short period of time. In fact, Teleperformance USA was recently recognized as #11 of the Top 50 U.S. Service Agencies, as ranked by size. (*Telemarketing & Call Center Solutions* magazine, March 2000.) In August 2000, Teleperformance USA received, for the seventh year in a row,

Teleperformance USA has a great deal to be proud of: a strong reputation in its industry, a versatile staff with dedication and talent, and a commitment to give back to its employees. Says Dato, "We made the right decision to start up in Utah, and we hope that Utah feels the same!"

TP USA corporate headquarters, Salt Lake City, UT.

Staff photo. Top row: Nathan Chenney, Lyle Hardy, David Weaver and Lee Gills. Second row: Kelly Dworak, Julie Loppe-Peyrin, Dominic Dato, Lori Sell and Joe Meehan.

Telemarketing & Call Center Solutions magazine's highly-acclaimed "Rising Star" award, placing fourth as ranked by percentage of growth.

When asked about his remarkable leadership and success, Mr. Dato is modest. This reserve, according to his associates, is parallel to Mr. Dato's personality. Dato proudly praises Teleperformance USA's senior team members, whom he describes as talented, dedicated individuals who each average 15 plus years' industry experience, and who have continually proven to go the distance—often working round-the-clock for days on end to reach their goals. "Our clients' success is our success," says Dato. "This philosophy has made us who we are."

SOUTH CENTRAL UTAH TELEPHONE ASSOCIATION

South Central Utah Telephone Association, Inc., traces its roots back to 1908, when Forest Service crews completed the first open wire line from Teasdale to Escalante, stringing the line on poles and trees as they went. In 1910 they strung a galvanized wire from the switchboard in Escalante across the Antone Flats and over the Death Hollow Trail to the ranger station in Boulder. Telephones in Escalante were located at Forest Service Supervisor Henry Barney's residence, the Forest Service office, and Riddle's store.

Over the next few years several individuals bought telephones and ran their own lines to the switchboard. In 1919 Leander Shurtz borrowed $1,000 from the bank and, with the help of his father and three brothers, built the Escalante Telephone System. Leander, who was blind, continued to operate the system with marvelous efficiency for the next 26 years. There were no numbers—callers simply asked Leander to connect them to Aunt Mandy or Uncle Don, for example.

In 1945 the system was sold to Randal and Gwen Lyman, who continued to operate it as Leander had. Gwen handled the duties at the switchboard and Randal maintained the system, including the 65-mile line to Panguitch. Service was good, and rates were $1.25 a month. But the people in Boulder, with 35 phones on the old galvanized wire line, were dissatisfied. When Rural Electrification Administration (REA) telephone systems became available, the people in Boulder wanted one.

Leland Haws, a Boulder resident who was president of the Garkane Power Association, and several other influential gentlemen in what would become South Contrail's original service area, made application for creation of the South Central Utah Telephone Association with themselves as members. One condition for granting of the application was that the Escalante Telephone Company would have to become part of the new cooperative.

Randal & Gwen Lyman in front of their home, which served as the office for the Escalante Telephone Company from 1945 until 1953. Gwen operated the switchboard and Randal maintained the system.

In June 1951, Mr. Haws asked Mr. Lyman if he would be interested in selling his business. In his response Mr. Lyman stated, in part, "We have 110 subscribers, including Boulder, Utah. This business is grossing between $800-900 a month at the present time. If you are interested in this property, we will be glad to have you make an offer to what you think it is worth."

Gwen Lyman at the switchboard of the Escalante Telephone Company in 1950. Callers simply told her who they wanted to talk to—there was no published directory.

On March 9, 1953, Articles of Incorporation and Oaths of Office were filed in the Office of the Secretary of State, and South Central Utah Telephone Association was granted the authority to operate as a telephone company and was officially incorporated by the State of Utah. The officers of the cooperative were Victor Magleby, president; Leland Haws, vice president; Jasper Henderson, Heber Covington, and Herbert Gleaves, directors; and Birt Gardner, secretary/treasurer. On March 16 the proposed bylaws were adopted, with the Board of Directors stating, "It shall be the aim of the South Central Utah Telephone Association, Inc. to provide dependable area-wide telephone service on the cooperative plan and at the lowest cost consistent with sound economy and good management." The Escalante Telephone Company, including franchises, licenses, and permits, was subsequently purchased in July 1953 for $10,000.

In 1955 South Central actually began providing telephone service in Escalante, Boulder, Grass Valley, Bryce Valley, Long Valley, and the Escalante Desert. The business office was established in Tropic and Bruce Burr was hired as an office worker and secretary to the Board of Directors for a monthly salary of $300. He also installed phones and maintained the system. At the end of the year there were 249 lines in service and operating revenues totaled $20,530.

South Central's digital microwave backbone consists of several remote mountaintop sites, including this 195' tower at Long Valley.

In 1957 the office was moved to a rented space on Main Street in Escalante. In 1963 the construction of a new building to house the business office and Escalante exchange was approved by the Board of Directors, and in March 1964 the facility was opened. After undergoing two substantial building additions and numerous remodels, that building still houses the business office today.

In 1973 the Board of Directors negotiated a $1.8 million loan from REA to enable South Central to provide one-party service to all of its subscribers, replacing the existing two and four party service. In 1975 one-party service became a reality for most of South Central's exchanges, and Direct Distance Dialing began in Escalante, eliminating the need for an operator to place long distance calls.

The acquisition of a number of U.S. West exchanges, complete with their old aerial distribution cable, required the training of several employees in the fine art of climbing poles.

The decade of the '70s witnessed a dramatic change in South Central's appearance, as the aerial cable and wire throughout the system were replaced with buried cable. Not only was there tremendous aesthetic appeal with the removal of poles and wires, but an equally dramatic increase in efficiency of the system was realized with reduced exposure to lightning and other natural hazards.

Also during the second half of the '70s the interexchange plant and toll facilities were converted from open wire to microwave radio transmission. The conversion to microwave greatly enhanced not only efficiency and capacity, but the quality of the voice signal as well. By the end of 1985 nearly all of the analog microwave had been changed to digital transmission, further enhancing the quality of service. And in 1987 the remaining step and electromechanical switches on the system were replaced with digital Nortel DMS-10 switches, which meant that every South Central subscriber had digital dial tone. This made it possible to provide calling features like call waiting and call forwarding.

South Central's construction crews do all of the cable installation, from customer service drops to interexchange fiber optic cable.

During its entire history South Central has maintained consistent growth in access lines and revenues. By the end of 1985, 30 years after its incorporation, the company was providing service to more than 2,000 customers and was generating more than $1.5 million in annual revenues. At the end of 1990, just five years later, subscribers numbered 2,673 and annual revenues were nearly $3.4 million.

As the decade of the '90s dawned the Board of Directors felt that it was time to establish a mission statement to provide direction for future decisions. In May 1990 the Board adopted the following: "South Central Utah Telephone Association, Inc. is a full-service, consumer-owned telephone cooperative. We are dedicated to providing the highest quality telecommunications service for the lowest possible cost to all within our service area who desire it. We are committed to provide the highest quality service available and increase our technology and capabilities as new advancements develop in an ever-increasing telecommunications field."

In 1992 U.S.West announced that it would be divesting itself of some its rural exchanges in Utah, among them Panguitch, Hatch, Loa, Bicknell, and Bryce Canyon. U.S.West was under order by the Utah Public Service Commission to upgrade facilities in those exchanges and decided it would be in their best interests to sell them instead. After lengthy negotiations with U.S.West and the Utah PSC, the final hurdles were overcome and on December 29, 1993, South Central began providing service to those areas. South Central suddenly jumped to more than 5,500 subscribers and took over the responsibility of upgrading facilities in "the new exchanges."

That upgrading was accomplished by installation of a new Nortel DMS-100 at Panguitch and all of the other exchanges were "homed" off of it by means of either fiber optic cable or microwave radio. The benefits of the new technology contained in the DMS-100 became available to all of South Central's subscribers, including a wide array of custom calling features.

In February 1995, South Central opened a new chapter in its history with the purchase of Southwest Cablevision, an operating cable TV company providing service in Panguitch and Circleville. The purchase represented South Central's first true venture into the world of deregulated telecommunications activities. Deregulated activities must pay their own way, without benefit of revenues from regulated ratepayers.

On September 13, 1996, South Central acquired the Kanab, Milford, Minersville, Enterprise, Marysvale, and Circleville exchanges from U.S.West and immediately became the largest independent telephone company in the state, serving more than 12,000 customers. During the same period South Central also bid successfully on an "F" block wireless license from the FCC. This gave South Central the authority to provide wireless PCS service along Interstate 15 north from the Arizona State line to the junction of Interstate 70. The license also includes South Central's entire existing service area within the state of Utah.

South Central employees assist in the hanging of Christmas decorations in Panguitch, affirming their commitment to be more than just "the phone company" in the communities they serve.

The signing of the first acquisiton of U.S. West exchanges on December 29, 1993. Seated: Board President Robert Hampton, Board member Dee Porter. Standing. left to right: Board members Norm Christensen, Joe Thompson, Howard Meldrum, General Manager Dan Spencer, and Board Secretary Geraldine Liston.

After many lengthy discussions, the Board of Directors elected to proceed with borrowing $8 million from CoBank and begin building wireless facilities along the I-15 corridor. Business offices for South Central Wireless were opened in Cedar City and St. George, and officially began offering digital wireless telephone service on April 1, 1999. Within one year service was being provided to more than 3,000 customers. Considering the fact that it required more than 35 years to reach that milestone for the wireline company, the future for wireless looks bright, indeed. New customers are being added at the rate of 200 to 250 each month, and digital wireless service will be offered in Kanab and Milford by the end of 2000.

The telecommunications industry has been constantly changing since its infancy, with new technologies emerging virtually every day. And throughout its history South Central Utah Telephone Association has taken on the future at every opportunity, offering practically every telecommunications service possible. South Central Communications, its non-regulated subsidiary, offers Internet service, digital wireless service, long distance service, and cable TV (in some areas) with the same high quality of service and attention to customer care that have characterized South Central since its inception. Although South Central now provides service to more than 18,000 total customers and posts revenues in excess of $1 million each month, it still prides itself on being large enough to serve, yet small enough to care.

UBTA COMMUNICATIONS

The Uintah Basin, located beneath the rustic Uintah Mountain range in northeastern Utah, has long been a hub for communications, as evident by the many ancient petroglyph writings still visible in remote parts of the area. Today, this area continues to be a center for telecommunications as UBTA Communications and its subsidiaries provide communications for the 21st century.

Its beginnings were humble, but they can look back at a proud history of accomplishment. To farmers and ranchers in 1948, telephone service was merely a dream. One determined man by the name of E. Floyd Ross, organized a board of directors consisting of seven other ranchers and farmers, each representing a locality in the basin. The objective of the Board was to create a cooperative that would supply telephone service to the Uintah Basin.

The Board of Directors spent their time convincing the people of the Uintah Basin that by becoming a cooperative, they could supply modern telephone service themselves. By the time Congress passed the Telephone Act in 1949, Uintah Basin Telephone Association was already incorporated and ready to provide service. On June 1, 1953, Uintah Basin Telephone turned up service to their first customers. At that time, Uintah Basin Telephone's serving area extended over 100 miles from end-to-end and boasted over 750 customers.

UBTA has invested in the communities it serves. They have a stake in the future of their subscribers and in the communities where they live and raise their families. UBTA's Board and management feel that one of the greatest responsibilities and challenges facing the nation is the education of its youth. This is especially true in the rural communities that UBTA serves. In 1987, the Board of Directors of UBTA Communications established a scholarship fund. UBTA annually awards scholarships to local area high school youth. These scholarships allow for those with a deep commitment to the rural communities to continue their higher education. UBTA looks for high school graduates that will exemplify the fine citizens and enormous talent that comes from the schools located throughout the Uintah Basin.

Early in 1990, Uintah Basin Telephone formed a subsidiary, Uintah Basin Electronic Telecommunications (UBET Cellular), and began to offer service to those outside their traditional boundaries. UBET was able to obtain a wireless spectrum in Duchesne and Uintah counties. UBET was the tenth Rural Service Area to go online in the nation, investing in telecommunication advancement for the convenience and safety of local residents.

UBET was a successful bidder for PCS licenses in Duchesne, Uintah, Daggett and parts of Wasatch, Summit and Morgan counties in Utah, along with Uinta and Sweetwater counties in

UBTA Lineman Rod Bell tests aerial lines.

Wyoming and Rio Blanco, Routt, Moffat and Grande Counties in Colorado.

Wireless use has dramatically increased as costs have dropped, allowing for use as a tool for emergencies and in general applications, and offering telephone service in extremely remote locations, as well as adding convenience to every day life. At UBET's start-up, it had two employees and zero customers. UBET's 2,000th wireless customer was connected in April 1994. Since that time, UBET's customer base has increased to over 6,000, and the company now has nearly 20 employees. UBET has built its customer base by giving the best customer service at the best price possible.

UBET, while small in comparison to other wireless carriers, is committed to ensuring that their operations and services represent the very latest in wireless technology. UBET's Board feels UBET Wireless has had a positive impact on the quality of life in the communities they serve, not only in terms of

Current UBTA General Manager, Bruce H. Todd.

service, but also because of the jobs, income and taxes generated.

In 1992, UBTA's Board of Directors made a decision that would have positive impact on the area youth. With the objective to establish an interactive education program for the rural schools in Duchesne County, the Dutel system was born, linking Altamont, Tabiona, Duchesne and Roosevelt schools through distance learning. Distance learning was not a new concept. Schools and colleges had used television since the 1950s, to air the image and voices of teachers in more than one classroom at a time. This process is now interactive; instructors and students can communicate instantly although miles apart, asking and answering questions and participating as if in the same room.

UBTA's Board of Directors was so dedicated to this project, that they provided total funding until the Duchesne County School District obtained a state grant to finance their portion of the project. Governor Mike Leavitt made the first broadcast over this Dutel system in February 1993, speaking of his vision for the future of Utah.

In 1994, Bruce H. Todd, a native to the Uintah Basin, took the helm at UBTA Communications, as General Manager/CEO. Mr. Todd has been instrumental in the development of many of the subsidiary ventures.

In response to subscriber requests, UBTV was formed in 1994, to provide direct broadcast satellite service to residents in a tri-county area. Using an 18-inch digital satellite system and dish, residents may opt to give up one to three television channels with poor reception, for 150 channels with clear reception.

Since 1994, UBTV has been providing affordable, quality digital satellite service to Duchesne, Uintah and Daggett counties. With broadcast satellite service, residents of these three counties have been able to enjoy the same variety of programming as the people in larger, more populated areas of our state. UBTV has been awarded NRTC's Market Performance Award, as well as a National DBS sales award from STARZ, making UBTV the leader in digital satellite television. With UBTV and the other members of the UBTA Communications family, customers work directly with in-house customer service departments, resulting in faster activation and the security of knowing there will be someone to handle their problems and requests.

Rural life in the Uintah Basin.

UBTA has worked for a number of years to build a fiber optic route linking residents of the Uintah Basin to the Wasatch Front. As well, they have opened educational opportunities for Basin youth and have also made available the sophisticated technology of modern medicine from around the world, to their physicians, without them having to leave the hospital.

Transmission through fiber optics will allow eCommerce to become a way of life for people in the Uintah Basin. As a neighborhood communications company, UBTA has a vested interest in providing reliable Internet service with a local focus in the communities it serves. UBTA, through its subsidiary company UBTAnet, has been providing Internet access since 1996. By setting up storefronts in cyberspace and marketing to the world, UBTA will help to eliminate the distance penalty the community has struggled with in the Basin. The industrial age lured people to the big cities in droves, to work in the factories. Now people are moving back. And, why not? The quality of life here is excellent, and now people can work from anywhere there's a modem and a phone line.

Seeing the need to provide UBTA's members with their own long distance service, Uintah Basin Long Distance began operations in October 1997. Customers are now able to use their locally-owned long distance carrier for all long distance calls. UBLD offers competitive rates and has a calling plan to fit everyone's needs. Calling cards, along with prepaid calling cards and toll free numbers are available through UBLD.

UBTA is one of almost 1,200 small rural telecommunication providers nation wide, which serve about 5 percent of the United States population. Even though in terms of size they are small, they are proud to be able to offer better service at better rates than the larger, corporate giants. Beyond affordable phone service, UBTA is committed to keeping abreast of new technology and delivering that technology to its members.

Because UBTA is based locally, its members have direct access to the companies employees, directors and management. UBTA employees are members of the communities they serve and UBTA is proud to say that many are heavily involved in local charities and volunteer organizations. As a partner in the communities they serve, UBTA is able to make contributions to many worthwhile projects throughout the Uintah Basin. Member involvement has brought about their present viable position in these communities. In a telephone cooperative, the members dictate policy through their elected representatives. Through decision of the Board of Directors, new communication technology has been embraced, in order to keep pace with the growing demands of the subscribers. It's an ongoing process. As technology changes, so does the cooperative. Only through the involvement of its members, can UBTA be sure of meeting the needs of the Uintah Basin.

UBTA-UBET Communications currently services 3,200 landline subscribers in northeastern Utah. By first quarter of 2001, the company will add an additional 15,000 subscribers with the purchase of three US West exchanges, which are adjacent to current company exchanges.

UBTA fully understands that in a service economy, the success of many ventures depends on the quick and efficient transfer of information over telecommunication highways, rather than on interstates and railways. UBTA believes that with their proud history of accomplishments, their wide variety of services and their dedication and commitment to improvement, they will look ahead to a promising future of growth, adaptation and continued service to their subscribers and their communities.

Cellular and PCS towers providing coverage throughout the Basin.

A TIMELINE OF UTAH'S HISTORY

11,000 B.C. Paleo-Indians, Utah's earliest people arrived on the scene.

6,500 B.C. A second cultural adaptation, the Archaic peoples arrived.

200 B.C. The Basket Maker I phase of the Anasazi culture is first apparent. The Fremont Culture is also discernable.

1050 to 1300 High point of Anasazi Culture attainment.

1100 Shoshonean or Numic peoples who practiced a hunting and gathering lifestyle arrived on the scene in Utah.

1300 Anasazi and Fremont cultures disappear from Utah.

1620 The Navajo an Athabascan-speaking Native American peoples arrived having come from Canada.

1765 Juan Maria Antonio Rivera led the first documented Spanish exploring expedition in the vicinity of Monticello and Moab.

1776 Francisco Fathers Atanasio Dominguez and Fray Silvestre Velez de Escalante led 12 explorers from Santa Fe into Utah. They explored southward to the Colorado River before returning to Santa Fe in January of 1777.

Kit Carson, trapper, explorer, guide, and trading post operator who built one of the first trading posts in Utah and later served as a guide to John Charles Fremont's 1843-1844 and 1845 expeditions through Utah. Courtesy, Brigham Young University Archives

1819 Michael Bourdeau led a North West Company fur trapping party to Utah's Bear River.

1820 Joseph Smith, Jr., who established the Church of Jesus Christ of Latter-day Saints (the Mormon Church), had his first religious experience in New York State.

1822 William H. Ashley and Andrew Henry sought to enlist adventurers for a fur gathering expedition into the Rocky Mountains.

1824 John H. Weber led trappers of the Ashley-Henry Company into Cache Valley Utah. That fall Jim Bridger became the first Euro-American to see the Great Salt Lake from the north end. Etienne Provost may be the first Euro-American to have seen the Great Salt Lake from the south end.

1825 Peter Skene Ogden of the British Hudson Bay Company entered Utah. Johnson Gardner challenged Ogden's men at Deserter Point and 23 men left Ogden's crew before he abandoned Utah to the American fur trappers. William H. Ashley began the first of sixteen annual fur trapper rendezvous.

1826 Jim Clyman and three other fur trappers paddled around the Great Salt Lake in a skin boat and found no outlets. Jedediah Smith left the 1826 rendezvous for an expedition that took him through Utah to California and back across the Sierra Nevada.

1827 Jedediah Smith left the rendezvous on the shores of Bear Lake and traversed the length of Utah, to California and Oregon in one of the great expeditions of the American West.

1828-29 Peter Skene Ogden led an expedition into Cache Valley and north of the Great Salt Lake on his way to Nevada and the eventual discovery of the Humboldt River.

1830 The *Book of Mormon*, upon which the Mormon Church was based was published and the Mormon Church was

Samuel Brannan lead 238 Mormons on the ship Brooklyn *around Cape Horn to California in 1846. He attempted to persuade Brigham Young to bring the Mormon pioneer company to California to join his colony there. Unable to persuade Brigham Young, Brannan returned to California to become that state's first millionaire and to later part company with the Mormons. Courtesy, LDS Church Archives*

established at Fayette, New York.

1831 Mormons began settling at Kirtland, Ohio and Joseph Smith visited Jackson County, Missouri and proclaimed the principle of the Mormon gathering.

1833 Mormons were forced to leave Jackson County by other residents who found the Mormons uncomfortable neighbors.

1836 The Mormons dedicated their first temple at Kirtland, Ohio.

1837 Philip Thompson and William Craig established Fort Davy Crockett on the north bank of the Green River. Antoine Robidoux established a fort at the Whiterocks Fork of the Uinta River. Mormons began to have trouble at Kirtland, Ohio largely due to the founding of the Kirtland Anti-bank which went broke.

1838 Mormons from Far West in Caldwell County began to experience persecutions. Governor Boggs issued an

On May 10, 1869 the last spike was driven to mark the completion of the Transcontinental Railroad. It turned out to be a momentous event for Utah. The Territory was never the same again as the non-Mormon population and influence increased significantly. Courtesy, Utah State Historical Society

order that Mormons were to leave Missouri or be exterminated.

1839 Joseph Smith began the purchase of land along a big bend of the Mississippi River and founded Nauvoo, Illinois as a Mormon gathering location.

1841 The Bartleson-Bidwell Company brought the first wagons, the first white woman and first white child through Utah.

1843 John C. Fremont made the first scientific observations of the Great Salt Lake. At Nauvoo, Illinois Joseph Smith began teaching plural marriage to a select few.

1844 John C. Fremont on his return trip from California entered Utah by way of the Old Spanish Trail and left by way of the Dominguez-Escalante route of 1776. Joseph Smith and his brother Hyrum were both murdered at Carthage, Illinois on June 27, 1844. In August the vast majority of Mormons voted to follow the leadership of Brigham Young and the Quorum of Twelve Apostles.

1845 Mountain Man Miles Goodyear established what is regarded as the first site continuously occupied by Euro-Americans in Utah at Fort Buenaventura. On his third Western expedition of 1845-46 Fremont explored Utah Lake and crossed the Salt Flats to Pilot Peak. Lansford W. Hastings published his *Emigrant's Guide to Oregon and California* proposing a shortcut to California by way of the south end of the Great Salt Lake and across the Salt Flats.

1846 Four companies: the Bryant-Russell Party, the Harlan-Young Party, the Heinrich-Lienhard Party, and the ill-fated Donner Party took Hastings Cutoff by way of the south end of the Great Salt Lake. Mormons began the evacuation of Nauvoo and the winter trek across Iowa. The Mormon battalion was organized to assist in the Mexican War.

1847 The pioneer Mormon company left Winter Quarters and arrived in July in the Valley of the Great Salt Lake.

1848 The Mexican War came to an end and the Mexican Cession Territory,

In 1869 Brigham Young began the co-op system known as Zion's Cooperative Mercantile Institution of ZCMI throughout the Utah Territory to keep Mormon money in the Territory and to promote trade with Mormon merchants. ZCMI businesses were identified by the "all seeing eye" and the inscription "Holiness to the Lord." Courtesy, LDS Church Archives

which included Utah, became an American property. Mormons in the Salt Lake Valley experienced a poor harvest and a starving time.

1849 The Mormons sent a petition to Washington, D.C. asking for territorial status and later a petition asking for statehood. Discovery in California began bringing many travelers across Utah. Their trade and abandoned goods proved beneficial to the Utah pioneers.

1850 Congress passed the Compromise of 1850 giving Utah territorial status. Brigham Young was appointed as the first territorial governor. The publication of the *Deseret News*, the official newspaper of the Mormon church was begun.

1851 The Mormons established the Iron Mission in southern Utah to provide iron for Mormon self-sufficiency.

1852 The Mormon Church-owned *Deseret News* announced the practice of polygamy among the Mormons.

1853 Captain John W. Gunnison and seven others of the Topographical Engineers were killed near the Sevier River by a band of Pahvant Paiutes. The Walker War between Utes and Mormons began. The Mormons began the construction of the Salt Lake Temple.

1854 The Indian War known as the Walker War came to an end.

1855 President Franklin Pierce appointed Judges George P. Stiles and Willis W. Drummond as federal judges in the Utah territory. Soon a running conflict developed between these judges and Utah Mormons.

1856 Utah submitted a second petition for statehood which was rejected. Brigham Young announced the handcart plan to bring European immigrants to Utah. Five companies made the trip in 1856 but the last two, the Willie and Martin Companies, were trapped by early snow in Wyoming and before a rescue could be effected over 200 lost their lives.

1857 In response to Judge Drummond's resignation and request for new territorial officials and an army to support them, President James Buchanan sent Johnston's army to Utah. The Mountain Meadows Massacre carried out by Mormons and Indians in southern Utah resulted in the death of 120 members of the Francher Party from Arkansas.

1858 A peaceful solution to the Utah War was negotiated and Alfred E. Cumming took over as Governor of the Utah Territory.

1860 The Handcart experiment ended.

1861 Camp Floyd, renamed Camp Crittenden, was abandoned with the onset of the Civil War.

1862 Col. Patrick E. Conner and the California Volunteers were sent to Utah to protect the mail and the overland trail from Confederate raiders and Indians and to keep an eye on the Mormons of Utah. Fort Douglas was established on the foothills east of Salt Lake City. Utah's Third petition for statehood was submitted and rejected. The United States Congress passed the Morrill Act outlawing polygamy in the territories.

The Brigham City Cooperative was established under the leadership of Lorenzo Snow in 1864. It operated so well that it became the model for the church-wide communal venture that Brigham Young began in 1874 known as the "United Order." The various shops of the Brigham City Cooperatively produced nearly all of the community necessities, provided useful employment and security for the citizens of the town. Photo Credit: LDS Church Historical Archives

1863 During an Indian campaign by Connor against Northern Shoshones, about 250 Indians were killed in what became known as the Bear River Massacre.

1866 Mormons began a boycott of non-Mormon merchants.

1867 Daniel S. Tuttle became the Bishop of the Utah Episcopal Church and established St. Marks Day School, the first non-Mormon school in Utah.

1869 The first transcontinental railroad line was completed at Promontory Summit, Utah. The Godbeite heresy led by prominent Mormon businessmen who opposed the Mormon Church's economic program began. The cooperative merchandising system known as Zion's Cooperative Mercantile Institution was begun in many Mormon towns.

1870 The Liberal party, made up mostly of non-Mormons was organized at Corrine, Utah to challenge the Mormon theodemocracy system of government. Mormons responded by organizing the Peoples Party. Utah women were given the right to vote and they exercised that right in February, 1870 in city elections.

1872 Utah's fourth petition for statehood was submitted and rejected. Daniel S. Tuttle and the Episcopal Church established St. Mark's Hospital as the first hospital in Utah.

1873 Lawrence Scanlan arrived and became an influential religious leader as a Catholic Priest. He remained in Utah until his death in 1915.

1874 The United States Congress passed the Poland Act canceling civil and criminal jurisdiction for Utah's probate courts. Brigham Young announced the cooperative program known as the United Order of Enoch.

1877 John D. Lee was executed for his role in the Mountain Meadows Massacre. Brigham Young died at the age of 76 in Salt Lake City.

1878 John Taylor who succeeded Brigham Young organized Zion's Central board of Trade to oversee the Utah economy.

1879 The United State Supreme Court ruled in the case of *Reynolds v. the United States* that the Morrill Act was constitutional.

1880 The Utah Southern Extension Railroad was completed to Frisco.

1882 Congress passed the Edmunds Act making polygamy a felony and cohabitation a misdemeanor and establishing the Utah Commission to oversee elections in Utah. Utah's fifth petition for statehood was submitted and rejected.

1884 Judge Charles S. Zane launched a judicial crusade to arrest and imprison Mormon polygamists. Rudger Clawson became the first conviction under the provisions of the Edmunds Act. Many Mormon polygamists went on the underground to escape capture and imprisonment.

1885 A federal court decision, *Murphy v. Ramsey*, generally upheld the Edmunds Act but it declared the test oath being required by the Utah Commission of Mormons "null and void."

1887 Congress passed the Edmunds-Tucker Act, designed to destroy the Mormon Church economically and politically if it did not give up the practice of polygamy. Mormon Church President John Taylor died and the government began confiscation of Mormon Church property. A sixth petition for statehood was submitted and rejected.

1889 The Mormon Church First Presidency and Quorum of the Twelve counseled men to live with but one wife under the same roof.

1890 Wilford Woodruff announced the Manifesto advising Mormons to refrain from contracting any marriage contrary to the laws of the land. A Mormon Church general conference unanimously accepted the Manifesto.

Salt Lake City's Temple Square in Salt Lake City was completed after about 40 years of labor. It was begun in 1853 and completed in 1893. Today it is a major tourist attraction. Courtesy, LDS Church Archives

1891 The Mormon Church Peoples party was disbanded and the National Republican party was organized in Utah.

1893 The Liberal party was disbanded. The Salt Lake Temple was completed after 40 years of construction. The Saltair Resort was built on the south shore of the Great Salt Lake.

1894 Congress passed an enabling act for Utah to call a constitutional convention, to draw up a constitution, and apply for statehood. All Mormon Church property seized under the Edmunds-Tucker Act was restored to the Church.

1895 A constitution was written and approved by the Utah voters and submitted to the United States Congress. In a special election, Heber M. Wells was elected as the first and youngest governor.

1896 Utah was granted statehood and became the 45th state in the Union with a constitution that outlawed polygamy and enfranchised women.

1897 Lucien Nunn set up the world's

largest alternating-current transmission system in Provo Canyon to provide power for the ore-processing plants at Mercur.

1898 Italian immigrants began to arrive in Utah to work in mines and for the railroads as Utah's first new immigrants. They were soon followed by Serbs, Croats and Bosnians from the Austrian-Hungarian Empire.

1899 Brigham H. Roberts was denied a seat in the U.S. Congress that he had been elected to in 1898 because he continued to practice plural marriage. Samuel Newhouse and Thomas Weir with William Rockefeller's financial backing organized the Utah Consolidated Mining Company.

1900 Over 200 men were killed in the Winter Quarters coal mine explosion near Scofield, Utah. It still ranks as one of America's worst mine disasters.

1903-04 Reed Smoot began a 30-year career in the United States Senate. He organized Utah's most effective political machine ever, which was known as the Federal Bunch. Daniel C. Jacklin incorporated Utah Copper Company.

1904 As a result of Senate hearings regarding the seating of Reed Smoot, the Mormon Church made the performing of plural marriage an excommunicable offense.

1905 The Uintah-Ouray Reservation was opened under provisions of the 1887 Dawes Severalty Act to white settlers. After his defeat for reelection to the U.S. Senate, former senator Thomas Kearns organized the American Party and bought the Salt Lake *Tribune* to carry out a campaign against the Mormon Church.

1906 Some Utes began to flee to the Plains to seek alliances with Plains Indians to resist the loss of reservation lands in Utah. The Ogden Stock Yards were built and became one of the largest meat-processing plants west of Omaha, Nebraska.

1908 The Ute trek to the Plains that began in 1906 ended in failure.

1910 Utah Copper and Boston Consolidated were merged into Utah Copper Company, the largest copper producer in the country at the time.

1911 The American Party came to an end and its members generally returned to the Republican party.

1912 Reed Smoot's Federal Bunch was so effective as to deliver Utah as only one of two states to give electoral votes to Republican presidential candidate William Howard Taft.

1913 The Utah Power and Light Company was formed by the merger of eighteen competing power companies.

1914 John G. and Arling Morrison were murdered by robbers in Salt Lake City. Joe Hill an I.W.W. union organizer was arrested after seeking medical aid for a gun shot wound. He was tried and convicted on what many felt was circumstantial evidence.

1915 After appeals to commute the sentence, Joe Hill was executed by a firing squad at the Sugar House Prison.

1916 Simon Bamberger was elected Utah's first Democratic governor and the second Jewish governor elected in the United States.

1917 The United States entered World War I. The war brought prosperity to Utah's farms and to its mining industry.

1919 A post war depression began as Utah's production of metals fell by more than 50 percent.

1920 The post war depression began to negatively impact Utah farmers.

1921 Utah Copper Company ceased copper production entirely. Many Utah mine and mill towns lost over half their population.

Street scene of Salt Lake City with horse and carriage near the time of statehood in the 1890s. The street is Sixth East at 400 South. Courtesy, Edward B. Rogers, Utah Title and Abstract 629 East 400 South SLC

1922 Utah's first radio station, KZN, began broadcasting.
1923 The Union Pacific Railroad completed a spur line 33 miles from Lund to Cedar City giving better access to southern Utah's scenic beauty and its mountain resources.
1925 A black man, Robert Marshall, was lynched by a mob at Price, Utah.
1926 Air mail traffic began through Utah. Before the year was out, the first passenger flights were flying through Salt Lake City.
1929 The Mormon Tabernacle Choir broadcast began on CBS radio.
1931 A severe drought struck the state of Utah.
1932 Utah's unemployment was at 35.8 percent and per capita income had dropped by nearly half. In a major political surprise, University of Utah professor, Elbert D. Thomas, upset five-term senator and Mormon Church Apostle, Reed Smoot.
1933 Former Governor George Dern was appointed Franklin D. Roosevelt's secretary of defense.
1934 Marriner S. Eccles joined the Treasury Department.

New immigrants attempted to maintain their traditional ways. At first few women immigrated to Utah. At this Yugoslavian baptismal dinner, circa 1900 immigrant miners at Bingham Canyon celebrate in traditional ways despite the visible presence of but two women for this occasion. Courtesy, Utah State Historical Society

1935 Marriner S. Eccles left the Treasury Department and became the chairman of the Federal Reserve Board where he exerted great influence to have President Roosevelt adopt a federal compensatory fiscal policy.
1936 The Mormon Church introduced the Church Security Program which was later renamed the Church Welfare program to help members who needed food assistance. The *Deseret News* editorially opposed the reelection of Franklin D. Roosevelt, but the outcome of the election was a Democratic landslide at all levels in Utah. President Roosevelt received 69 percent of the Utah vote. The Utah Symphony Orchestra was launched under a Works Progress Administration (WPA) music grant.
1937 The Springville Art Gallery was begun as a WPA project. Today it is one of the finest collections of western art in the country.
1939 World War II broke out in Europe and it brought a return of economic prosperity to Utah.
1940 Hill Field, now Hill Air Force Base, was constructed in Weber County to become a major air defense, supply and training base.
1942 The Federal Government began construction of the Geneva Steel Plant on the eastern shores of Utah Lake. The Central Utah Relocation Center (Topaz) a Japanese Relocation center was opened west of Delta, Utah with over 8,000 Japanese internees.
1943 The Geneva Steel Plant was completed at a cost of $214 million.
1945 The crew of the Enola Gay, the B-29 bomber that dropped the atomic bomb on Hiroshima trained in Utah at the Wendover Air Base. The Topaz Japanese relocation center was closed.
1948 Reva Beck Bosone was elected as Utah's first woman representative in the United States Congress.
1951 Open air atomic testing began in Nevada, which later caused major concern in Utah.

1952 Charles Steen discovered the Mi Vida uranium mine in the Lisbon Valley near Moab and began Uranium rush days in Utah.

1953 A large number of sheep in southern Utah sickened and died following an atomic test.

1954 The bizarre political fraud of Representative Douglas R. Stringfellow unraveled. When these claims were laid bare, he resigned from the race just sixteen days before the election.

1956 The Atomic Energy Commission won a lawsuit against the sheep owners whose sheep had died following the 1953 open air test.

1957 Utah Senator Arthur V. Watkins chaired the Senate hearings that ended in censure of red hunting Senator Joseph R. McCarthy.

1959 The Mormon Tabernacle Choir won a Grammy for the recording of "The Battle Hymn of the Republic."

1962 The Utah Shakespearean Festival in Cedar City was inaugurated by founding director Fred C. Adams. It has become one of the cultural gems in the state of Utah.

1963 Defense was Utah's largest industry.

1964 Democrat Calvin L. Rampton was elected governor. With his re-elections in 1968 and 1972 he became Utah's only three-term governor to date.

1965 Agreements were signed that began the Central Utah Water Conservancy District allowing the Central Utah Project to go forward. The state legislature began passing civil rights legislation that demanded equal treatment of all people regardless of race, color, religion or ethnic origin.

1976 This election represented a major decline in the fortunes of the Utah Democratic party and the beginning of domination of state politics by the Republican party.

1977 Utah's International Women's Year conference was taken over by conservative groups who passed a conservative agenda. The Kennecott Copper Company fell on hard times causing cutbacks and thousands of layoffs in Utah's mining industry.

In 1916 the Republican monopoly on the office of governor of Utah was broken by the election of Democrat Simon Bamberger as governor. He was the first non-Mormon governor of Utah and the second Jewish governor in the United States. Courtesy, Utah State Historical Society

1978 The Church of Jesus Christ of Latter-day Saints (Mormons) announced a new policy allowing all faithful, worthy men in the church to receive the priesthood.

1979 Residents of southern Utah, calling themselves Downwinders and maintaining their health was negatively impacted by the atomic tests, filed suit in Salt Lake City for damages from the Atomic Energy Commission. The Sagebrush Rebellion, to transfer ownership of public lands from the federal government to the states, got nowhere. The Utah Jazz of the National Basketball Association moved to Utah to use the Salt Palace for its home games.

1980 Fundamentalist, polygamist Ervil LeBaron went to prison for planning the murder of a rival polygamist leader. Utah gained a third Congressional seat.

1981 Robert Redford and his Sundance Institute began hosting the Sundance Film Festival, which offered promising artists an opportunity to exhibit their films. It now stands only second to Cannes as the preferred premiere for new films.

1982 Doctors at the University of Utah hospital performed the first artificial heart transplant in a human subject when Barney Clark was equipped with an artificial heart developed in Utah.

1983 Floods, diverted by sandbags, ran down State Street in Salt Lake. For over two weeks tourists observed this State Street River. Other flooding also caused a slide at Thistle Junction that blocked the road, the railroad and created a lake that caused 22 families to abandon the town.

1984 Congress passed Utah's National Forest Wilderness Act. This was the first statewide national forest wilderness act passed in the nation. The Brigham Young University football team won the national college championship and ended the season as the nation's only unbeaten major college team.

1985 Mark Hoffman killed two people, Steven F. Christensen and Kathy Webb Sheets in one of the most bizarre forgery and bombing murder cases in history. Police investigations determined that the bombings were an attempt to cover up a convoluted maze of forgeries of historic documents.

1986 Western Air Lines which had Salt Lake City as its hub city sold out to Delta Airlines. Delta has retained Salt Lake as its western hub.

1987 Geneva Steel, formerly owned by USX, was purchased by Utahns headed by Joseph Cannon.

1988 Utah made its first bid to host the winter Olympics hoping to get the 1998 games.

1990 Congress passed the Radiation Exposure Composition Act to apologize to the victims of atomic test fallout and to set up a trust fund to compensate for some injuries. Ty Detmer, Brigham Young University's quarterback, became the state's first winner of college football's Heisman Trophy awarded to the outstanding player of the year.

1991 The State Legislature passed one of the strictest pro-life laws in the United States. It resulted in considerable litigation and an eventual federal district court defeat for the state.

1992 A referendum for pari-mutuel betting that was strongly opposed by the LDS Church leadership was defeated. Karen Shepherd was elected as the second woman ever to serve Utah in Congress, Olene S. Walker was elected as the state Lieutenant Governor and Jan Graham was chosen as the state attorney general in what could be termed as Utah's year of the women. The Utah Jazz opened their new home in the Delta Center, which seats over 20,000 fans.

1993 Salt Lake City determined to build a new baseball park at the site of old Derks Field. The Utah Jazz hosted the National Basketball Association All Star game and the two Jazz starters, Karl Malone and John Stockton, shared the most valuable player trophy.

1994 Enid Greene Waldholtz defeated Karen Shepherd in a campaign that was later discovered to contain many irregularities. The Salt Lake Buzz, a triple A baseball team, began to play at the new Franklin Quest Field built where the old Derks Field had been.

1995 Utah was awarded the 2002 winter Olympics on the first ballot. The announcement sparked a wild celebration in Utah. The University of Utah gymnastic team won its tenth national NCAA championship, its second in a row, and the fourth of the 1990s.

1996 Enid Greene Waldholtz, incumbent Republican Congresswoman, was forced off the ticket by what many felt were illegal tricks. President Clinton used the Antiquities Act of 1906 to proclaim the largest national monument in the lower 48 states, Southern Utah's Grand Staircase-Escalante National Monument containing 1.7 million acres.

1997 The Olympic bobsled and luge track was dedicated and named Albert's Alley for Prince Albert of Monaco. Utah began reconstruction of I-15 creating a ten-lane freeway at a cost of $1.59 billion. The Utah Transit Authority also began a $294 million project to build a 16-mile light rail commuter line from Sandy in the south end of the Salt Lake Valley into downtown Salt Lake City. The Utah Jazz won the Western Conference Championship of the National Basketball Association, but lost the world championship to the Chicago Bulls in six games.

1998 The University of Utah basketball team lost to Kentucky in the finals of the NCAA tournament. The Utah Jazz repeated as Western Conference Champions of the N.B.A. but again lost the world championship to the Chicago Bulls. It was first revealed that Utah Olympic organizers paid money and gave gifts to influence the International Olympic Committee members.

1999 Utah experienced a rare tornado that killed one and injured at least 81 others. Over 300 homes suffered damage and 40 of them suffered extensive damage. A mentally deranged man entered the L.D.S. Genealogical Library and in a hail of bullets killed two people and wounded five. Senator Orrin Hatch became the first Utahn to officially announce his candidacy for the presidential nomination on either of the major national tickets.

2000 Senator Hatch withdrew his bid for the Republican presidential nomination after a poor showing in the New Hampshire Primary and the Iowa caucus. At Zion National Park a shuttle operation was put into effect to help preserve the ecology of the park. The Mormon Church opened its 21,000 seat Conference Center at its April Conference.

Following the Japanese bombing of Pearl Harbor on December 7, 1941 about 120,000 individuals of Japanese ancestry were removed from the coastal areas of California, Oregon and Washington to inland relocation centers. Over 8,000 were uprooted and relocated at this government built camp, known as Topaz, about fifteen miles west of Delta. This picture of Topaz was taken from the compound's water tower and shows the buildings of the camp. Courtesy, Utah State Historical Society

Suggestions for Further Reading

Those interested in Utah history have a wealth of reading material available. Several general histories of Utah are of value. The oldest is Hubert Howe Bancroft's *History of Utah* (1889, reprinted 1964). Then came Orson F. Whitney's *History of Utah*—4 volumes—(1892-1904) and Levi Edgar Young's *The Founding of Utah* (1923). More recently there have been Gustive O. Larson, *Outline History of Utah and the Mormons* (1958 and revisions), S. George Ellsworth's comprehensive junior-high-school textbook, *Utah's Heritage* (1972, rev. 1985), and Charles S. Peterson, *Utah: a Bicentennial History* (1977). Finally, there is the principal college text on the market, *Utah's History* (1978), with the writings of 28 contributing authors, edited by Richard D. Poll.

For specific areas of interest in Chapter I the reader might consult Wallace W. Atwood, *The Physiographic Provinces of North America* (1940), Lehi F. Hintze, *Geologic History of Utah* (1973), and William Lee Stokes, "Subdivisions of the Major Physiographic Provinces of Utah," found in *Utah Geology,* Vol. 4, No. 1. John Wesley Powell, *Report on the Lands of the Arid Region of the United States* (1879), is good and can be read in conjunction with Wallace Stegner's *Beyond the Hundredth Meridian: The Exploration of the Grand Canyon and the Second Opening of the West* (1953). C. Gregory Crampton, *Standing Up Country* (1965), is well researched and richly illustrated, and Angus M. Woodbury, "A History of Southern Utah and Its National Parks," *Utah Historical Quarterly,* July to October 1944, provides much useful information about the Colorado Plateau. It would be well to also consult David E. Miller's *Utah History Atlas* (1968).

A recommended reading list for Chapter II begins with Jesse D. Jennings, ed., *Ancient Native Americans* (1978) as well as Jennings' *Danger Cave,* University of Utah Anthropological Papers, No. 27 (1957). Edward Norbeck and Jennings collaborated to produce *Prehistoric Man in the New World* (1964) which is useful. Works of more specific interest would include Richard A. Thompson, et al., *Class I Cultural Resources Inventory for the Cedar City District of the Bureau of Land Management, Part I, Cultural Resource Overview* (1983); S. Lyman Tyler, "The Spaniard and the Ute," *Utah Historical Quarterly,* October 1954; and Helen Z. Papanikolas (ed.), *The Peoples of Utah* (1976), which includes some important material on the Gosiute, Navajo, Southern Paiute, and Ute tribes.

Selected reading in Chapter III probably should begin with the best translation of the Dominguez-Escalante Journal, by Fray Angelico Chaves (trans.) and Ted. J. Warner (ed.), *The Dominguez-Escalante Journal: Their Expedition Through Colorado, Utah, Arizona and New Mexico in 1776* (1976). One might also consult Herbert Eugene Bolton's *Pageant in the Wilderness: The Story of the Escalante Expedition to the Interior Basin, 1776* (1950). Donald Cutter's "Prelude to a Pageant in the Wilderness," *Western Historical Quarterly,* January 1977, tells of Juan Maria de Rivera's 1765 trek to southeastern Utah. Leland H. Creer, *The Founding of an Empire 1847-1869* (1947) discusses Spanish-American slave trade.

For information about the fur traders, Dale L. Morgan's *Jedediah Smith and the Opening of the West* (1953) is recommended. Maurice S. Sullivan has two Jedediah Smith volumes, *The Travels of Jedediah Smith* (1934) and *Jedediah Smith, Trader and Trail Breaker* (1936). David E. Miller, "Peter Skene Ogden's Journal of His Expedition to Utah, 1825," *Utah Historical Quarterly,* April 1952, along with Miller's "William Kittson's Journal Covering Peter Skene Ogden's 1824-25 Snake River Expedition," *Utah Historical Quarterly,* April 1954, are good treatments of Odgen's experiences in Utah in 1825. LeRoy R. Hafen has contributed "Mountain Men," *Utah Historical Quarterly,* October 1958, and "Etienne Provost," *Utah Historical Quarterly,* Spring 1968, as well as editing the ten-volume *The Mountain Men and the Fur Trade of the Far West* (1965-1972). Hafen also coauthored with W.J. Ghent *Broken Hand* (rev. ed. 1973), a biography of Thomas Fitzpatrick. J. Cecil Alter, *James Bridger* (rev. ed. 1962) deals with Bridger, the celebrated and important mountain man of Utah history. Fred R. Gowan's *Rocky Mountain Rendezvous* (1976) deals with that important mountain institution.

Wagon trains and early explorers also have their histories well documented in such works as David E. Miller's "First Wagon Train to Cross Utah," *Utah Historical Quarterly,* Winter 1962, and the 1846 migrations are examined in J. Roderic Korn, ed., *West from Fort Bridger* (1951) and Dale L. Morgan, ed., *Overland in 1864: Diaries and Letters of the California-Oregon Trail* (1963). Thomas F. Andrews, "Lansford W. Hastings and the Promotion of the Salt Lake Desert Cutoff: A Reappraisal," *Western Historical Quarterly,* April 1973, is very sympathetic to Hastings, and George R. Stewart's *Ordeal by Hunger* (rev. ed. 1960), is the best treatment of the Donner Party.

John C. Fremont is dealt with by David E. Miller, "John C. Fremont in the Great Salt Lake Region," *The Historian,* Autumn 1948. Mary Lee Spence and Donald Jackson, *The Expeditions of John Charles Fremont,* 2 volumes (1970-1973), is good.

The amount of material relative to Chapter IV, "The Mormon Kingdom," is unusually large. Reading on this subject could well begin with James B. Allen and Glen M. Leonard, *The Story of the Latter-day Saints* (1976). Brigham H. Roberts, *A Comprehensive History of the Church of Jesus Christ of Latter-day Saints: Century I,* 6 volumes (1930), would involve a major commitment to read them in their entirety, but it contains much valuable information. Leonard J. Arrington, Feramorz Y. Fox, and Dean L. May, *Building the City of God* (1976), and Klaus J. Hansen, *Quest for Empire: the Political Kingdom of God and the Council of Fifty in Mormon History* (1967) are both worthy of consideration. Robert B. Flanders, *Nauvoo: Kingdom on the Mississippi* (1965) deals with the move out of Nauvoo. Frank Golder, *March of the Mormon Battalion* (1928) deals with the battalion aspect of the Mormon migration. LeRoy R. and Ann W. Hafen, *Handcarts to Zion: The Story of a Unique Western Migration, 1856-1860* (1960) is a readable history of the handcart experiment. Other studies dealing with various aspects of the Mormon migration and settlement include Andrew Love Neff, *History of Utah, 1847-1869* (1940), Nels Anderson, *Desert Saints: The Mormon Frontier in Utah* (1942), Ray B. West, Jr., *Kingdom of the Saints: The Story of Brigham Young and the Mormons* (1957), Andrew Karl Larson, *I Was Called to Dixie* (1961), David E. Miller, *Hole in the Rock: an Epic in the Colonization of the Great American West* (1959, reprinted in 1966) and Milton R. Hunter, *Brigham Young, the Colonizer* (1940). One should also see Lowry Nelson, *The Mormon Village: A Pattern and Technique of Land Settlement* (1952) and Fred R. Gowans and Eugene E. Campbell, *Fort Bridger: Island in the Wilderness* (1975) and their equally good *Fort Supply: Brigham Young's Green River Experiment* (1976). Finally, there are two extremely objective, detailed, and readable accounts of Utah colonizing that one must read: Wallace Stegner's *The Gathering of Zion: The Story of the Mormon Trail* (1964) and the classic that pertains to so many of the chapters on Utah history, Leonard J. Arrington's *Great Basin Kingdom, An Economic History of the Latter-day Saints, 1830-1900* (1958). If there is one book to read to gain an understanding of nineteenth-century Utah, it is *Great Basin Kingdom.*

The general histories listed at the outset of this bibliography and most of the suggestions for Chapter IV are also applicable to Chapter V. In addition, one should see Dale L. Morgan, "The State of Deseret," *Utah Historical Quarterly,* January 1940, Norman F. Furniss, *The Mormon Conflict, 1850-59* (1960), Juanita Brooks, *Mountain Meadows Massacre* (1950, rev. ed. 1962), and Brooks, *John D. Lee* (1962).

For Chapter VI, additional reading should include the summer issue of the *Utah Historical Quarterly,* 1963, which is devoted to mining, and the winter issue of 1969, featuring the railroads in Utah. It would also be well to read Gustive O. Larson, *Prelude to the Kingdom* (1947), El Roy Nelson's *Utah's Economic Patterns* (1956), and Brigham D. Madsen's *Corinne: The Gentile Capitol of Utah* (1980). Again Helen Z. Papanikolas, *The Peoples of Utah,* and Arrington's *Great Basin Kingdom,* are very useful. Howard R. Lamar, "Political Patterns in New Mexico and Utah Territories," *Utah Historical Quarterly,* October 1960, has value for chapters V through VII. Robert J. Dwyer, *The Gentile Came to Utah* (1941, reissued 1971) is of interest, as is William Mulder and A. Russell Mortensen, eds., *Among the Mormons: Historical Accounts by Contemporary Observers* (1958). The fall issue of the *Utah Historical Quarterly* for 1975 contains useful articles on Utah educational beginnings. Stanley S. Ivins, "Free Schools Come to Utah," *Utah Historical Quarterly,* October 1954, and C. Merrill Hough, "Two School Systems in Conflict, 1867-1890," *Utah Historical Quarterly,* April 1960, are also good on the subject of education. T. Edgar Lyon, "Religious Activities and Development in Utah, 1847-1910," *Utah Historical Quarterly,* Fall 1967, and Ronald W. Walker, "The Commencement of the Godbeite Protest: Another View," *Utah Historical Quarterly,* Summer 1974, are instructive. O.N. Malmquist, *The Salt Lake Tribune: The First 100 Years* (1971) and Monte B. McLaws, *Spokesman for the Kingdom* (1977) focus on the two major journalistic voices in Utah and their perceptions of that turbulent era.

For Chapter VII one should see Orson F. Whitney, *Popular History of Utah* (1916) and more especially Gustive O. Larson, *The "Americanization" of Utah for Statehood* (1971). There are also some good articles on special episodes of the statehood controversies, including Thomas G. Alexander, "Charles S. Zane, Apostle of the New Era," *Utah Historical Quarterly,* Fall 1966, Kenneth Godfrey, "The Coming of the Manifesto," *Dialogue,* Fall 1970, and Henry J. Wolfinger, "A Reexamination of the Woodruff Manifesto in Light of Utah Constitutional History," *Utah Historical Quarterly,* Fall 1971. See also Howard R. Lamar, "Statehood for Utah: A Different Path," *Utah Historical Quarterly,* Fall 1971, S. George Ellsworth, "Utah's Struggle for Statehood," *Utah Historical Quarterly,* Winter 1963, and Richard D. Poll, "A State is Born," *Utah Historical Quarterly,* Winter 1964.

For the new-immigrant aspects of Chapter VIII one must begin with Papanikolas, ed., *The Peoples of Utah* (1976) and then go to Papanikolas, *Toil and Rage in a New Land: The Greek Immigrants in Utah* (second ed. rev. 1970). Allen Kent Powell's "Tragedy at

Scofield," *Utah Historical Quarterly,* Spring 1973, should be read if one desires greater detail on this tragedy. For labor developments see Sheelwant B. Pawar, "The Structure and Nature of Labor Unions in Utah: An Historical Perspective, 1890-1920," *Utah Historical Quarterly,* Summer 1967, and J. Kenneth Davies' works on labor including "The Utah Labor Movement Before Statehood," *Utah Historical Quarterly,* Summer 1966, "The Secularization of the Utah Labor Movement," *Utah Historical Quarterly,* Spring 1977, and *Deseret's Son of Toil: A History of the Worker Movements of Territorial Utah, 1852-1896* (1977). For economic and political developments of the Progressive Era, consult Jan Shipps, "Utah Comes of Age Politically: A Study of the State's Politics in the Early Years of the Twentieth Century," *Utah Historical Quarterly,* Spring 1967. Some additional material is also found in Frank H. Jonas, ed., *Politics in the American West* (1969). A good study of economic developments is Leonard J. Arrington and Thomas G. Alexander, *A Dependent Commonwealth: Utah's Economy from Statehood to the Great Depression,* ed. by Dean L. May (1974). One might also want to consult El Roy Nelson's *Utah's Economic Patterns* (1956) and Wain Sutton, ed., *Utah Centennial History,* three volumes (1949).

Chapter IX supplemental reading suggestions again are many and varied. Wayne K. Hinton, "Some Historical Perspective on Mormon Responses to the Great Depression," *Journal of the West,* October 1985, and Hinton's "The Economics of Ambivalence: Utah's Depression Experience," *Utah Historical Quarterly,* Summer 1986, are a starting point. Leonard J. Arrington and Wayne K. Hinton coauthored "Origin of the Welfare Plan of the Church of Jesus Christ of Latter-day Saints," *B.Y.U. Studies,* Winter 1964. Arrington and George Jensen coauthored the important study on the impact of World War II on Utah, *Impact of Defense Spending on the Economy of Utah* (1967) and Arrington and Anthony T. Cluff's *Federally-financed Industrial Plants Constructed in Utah During World War II* (1969) is a worthy discussion of major industrial facilities built during the war. The *Utah Historical Quarterly* issues from the winter of 1963 through the fall of 1965 contain several articles on Utah's defense industry. Malmquist's *The First 100 Years: A History of the Salt Lake Tribune* (1971) gives some insights into religious and political controversies of the twentieth century. Thomas F. O'Dea, *The Mormons* (1957) is the best sociological study of the Mormons and stresses within the faith in the modern era. On minorities in the twentieth century there are several worthwhile studies, including Richard O. Ulibarri's "Utah's Ethnic Minorities: A Survey," *Utah Historical Quarterly,* Summer 1972, and, most important, there is Helen Z. Papanikolas, ed., *The Peoples of Utah* (1976). Thomas G. Alexander and Leonard J. Arrington, "The Utah Military Frontier, 1872-1912: Forts Cameron, Thornburgh and Duchesne," *Utah Historical Quarterly,* Fall 1964, details the military experiences of blacks in Utah. Finally, there is the cooperatively produced Utah Writer's Project, *Utah, A Guide to the State* (1941), a useful reference in many areas of Utah history.

Happy reading to the enthusiast.

Index